Harley-Davidson
Design and Development

Harley-Davidson
Design and Development

John Tipler

amber
BOOKS

This Amber edition first published in 2019

Published by Amber Books Ltd
United House
North Road
London N7 9DP
United Kingdom
www.amberbooks.co.uk
Instagram: amberbooksltd
Facebook: www.facebook.com/amberbooks
Twitter: @amberbooks

First published in 2002 as *Harley-Davidson: Design and Development 1903 to the Present*

ISBN: 978-1-78274-924-0

Project Editor: Conor Kilgallon
Designer: Graham Curd
Picture research: Lisa Wren

Printed in China

Contents

Introduction

No other motorcycle has the same
following as the Harley-Davidson. It has
developed such an aura that it has become
an icon. There are people who own
these motorcycles not to ride, but rather
to polish as art objects in their homes.

Love it or hate it, the Harley provokes an emotional
response to which no other bike can compare. There is
nothing in the two-wheeled world like the mystique of
the Harley-Davidson. It has developed into an entire
genre of motorcycling that draws on a depth of heritage
unmatched by any other make.

Part of this heritage is down to the fact that Harley-
Davidson has been in business for almost as long as the
motorcycle itself. The company had its origins in 1903,
when four young men built an engine and fitted it into
a simple bicycle frame. Other like-minded engineering
talents were getting started at around the same time, but
none of them endured as motorcycle manufacturers – to
the present day in fact – without a break in production.
There were hard times at Milwaukee, to be sure, but, more
than almost any other facet of its existence, the fact that
production has never been halted for any reason indicates
that the Harley-Davidson ethos was always pretty much
spot on.

**Left: Every August, the town of Sturgis, South Dakota, comes alive
to the guttural sound made by thousands of throbbing V-twins, as
hordes of Harley-Davidson fans from all over the world move in to
see and be seen.**

The Harley family had emigrated to the United States from Manchester, England, while the Davidsons had similarly migrated from Scotland in the nineteenth century. William S. Harley and Arthur Davidson found themselves working at the same Milwaukee engineering plant and that's where the story of the Harley-Davidson begins. Back in 1903, Bill Harley and the Davidson brothers, Arthur, William and Walter, opted for the hard way. Operating in a confined 10 x 15ft (3 x 4.5m) shed at the Davidsons' family home, they created their own engine and strengthened the cycle frame to suit its new role. At this stage, the motorcycle project was only a hobby – that is, until they moved to a new 28 x 50ft (8 x 15.5m) workshop erected in 1906. The following year, the Harley-Davidson Motor Company was established.

Road conditions in the United States in the early twentieth century were not good, and there were vast distances between towns. As a result, for a motorcycle to be considered viable transport, it needed to be reliable

Above: Bravery indeed. The partnership of Red Parkhurst and Fred Ludlow – the one in the bullet-like sidecar – set four new world records aboard their eight-valve Model-J Harley-Davidson, topping 84 mph (134 km/h), at Daytona Beach, Florida, on 17 February 1920.

and sturdy, as well as practical and powerful. Harley-Davidson's machines embraced all these virtues from the outset and output rapidly rose from just three motorcycles in 1903 to 50 in 1906. By 1909, the figure had risen to more than 1100 units, and double that the following year. The prototype of 1903 spawned the bike that would remain in production until 1918, known as the Silent Gray Fellow.

By 1914, the tiny Juneau Avenue workshop had expanded to cover 225,234 square metres (2,424,479 square feet), while the number of employees had risen from the original four to more than 1500. By 1920, the firm was producing more than 23,000 bikes a year, making it the second-biggest US manufacturer after the rival Indian concern, which had turned out 32,000 bikes back in 1913. It was not Indian, however, that threatened Harley-Davidson particularly, as ownership of the Indian company had passed from the two enthusiasts that set it up to a regime that was interested only in profit, rather than the product. Rather, Harley-Davidson's main opposition came from the car, in particular, Ford's Model T, which became much more widely affordable as Henry Ford's production line methods were incorporated and refined, to the point where the car was less expensive than the majority of motorcycles.

It reached the point where motorcycles were only being bought by hard-bitten enthusiasts or police departments. The latter recognized that high-performance motorcycles were the best option for apprehending motorists in low-performance automobiles. This performance factor was demonstrated on the country's wooden arenas and, later, cinder tracks, as Harley-Davidson set up a factory racing team known as The Wrecking Crew in 1914, with immediate success. During this period, the company was contracted to supply machines to the US military as transport for dispatch riders active in World War I. However, unlike Indian, which turned its entire production over to the war effort, Harley retained half its output for the civilian

market. When peace returned in 1918, this decision stood the company in good stead.

The factory competition department was abruptly disbanded in 1921, at a point where Harley-Davidsons were sold from agencies in 67 countries worldwide. This number of concessionaires has never been exceeded as, during the 1920s, production volumes slipped back as the domestic market dwindled. Harley-Davidson went on an export drive. In addition to Europe and the countries of the old British Empire such as Australia – where distances were of similar vastness to those found in the United States – machines were also exported to Japan. Ironically, these very machines would be used in combat against Allied forces in the Far East during World War II. Meanwhile, to make up sales deficits, US dealers received increased support as advertising programmes escalated and credit schemes were instituted. Even though the Milwaukee plant was not running at its former capacity, it was in better

Below: Harley-Davidsons have always been rugged machines, which is just as well since in the early days, a bit of manhandling was required, as demonstrated here with this belt-drive 494cc (30cu. in.) Model-7C, from around 1911.

shape than other manufacturers, outstripping its rival Indian in the mid-1920s to become the biggest motorcycle manufacturer in the United States and, briefly, the biggest producer in the world.

Inevitably, the Wall Street Crash of 1929 which presaged the Great Depression, had a profound and severe impact not only on the US economy, but also on Harley-Davidson and its competitors. Hardest hit of the four major US producers was Cleveland, which ceased trading in 1929. Then Ignatz Schwinn's Excelsior-Henderson Company was forced to stop motorcycle production in 1931. Two years later, Harley-Davidson production had plummeted to fewer than 4000 units, its lowest figure since 1910. The only reason that the company survived the Depression at all

Below: The factory-backed Harley Owners' Group – HOG – was set up in 1983 as an owners' club, and has attracted 400,000 members world-wide. Along with other clubs, they flock to annual rallies at Daytona in March and Sturgis in August.

was because it remained in family ownership. This meant that, although there were redundancies, there was also no responsibility towards shareholders.

In spite of the prevailing economic gloom, the Harley-Davidson paint shop was in fine form and the predominantly brown and khaki colour schemes of the 1920s gave way in the early 1930s to smart black frames and red tanks with gold coachlines, some of which featured contemporary art deco motifs. A contemporary upgrading of image was taking place at Ariel and Triumph in the United Kingdom. The most important new Harley-Davidson to come out at this time was the 61E Knucklehead, which served as the vehicle to introduce the all-new Knucklehead engine, so named because of the knobs on the ends of its alloy rocker boxes. Introduced in 1936, the 61E's livery manifested a certain amount of art deco influence as well, decorating a more elegant teardrop-shaped fuel tank. Even so, the release of such a model in an uncertain economic climate was still hazardous and certainly a bold move on the part of Harley-Davidson. The 61E's Knucklehead engine specification was technically advanced, with its overhead-valves with hemispherical combustion chambers, four-speed gearbox and recirculating lubrication system. In fact, this engine was to prove the ancestor of Harley-Davidson's big-twins right up to the 1990s.

World War II

By the outbreak of World War II, Harley-Davidson was secure once more, with a sound model range, a broad-based dealer network and a good reputation among its customer base. Prior to the Japanese assault on Pearl Harbor in December 1941, Harley-Davidson's civilian motorcycle production had been suspended and output shifted to a war footing. In the four years up to 1945, more than 90,000 motorcycles were supplied to the Allied forces. Although actual battlefield use was limited, the proliferation of WLAs helped broaden the general awareness of Harley-Davidson as a brand. Ironically, the abundance of army surplus WLAs after the war's end had an adverse affect on sales and production of civilian stock did not return to full capacity until 1947.

There was another knock-on effect from these wartime machines. There were also now large numbers of de-mobbed military personnel with adrenaline to spare and, to these guys, the availability of cheap motorcycles was manna from heaven. What better way to spend their spare time than customizing motorbikes. All extraneous and superfluous components were chopped from standard machines for lightness and easier handling, and their

engines were tuned for greater performance. Known as 'bobbers', these creations were the forerunners of the 1960s choppers and featured in the notorious Hollister incident of July 1947 which sparked the whole concept of the outlaw bike rider as exemplified by the Hell's Angels. Largely overblown and exaggerated into almost mythic status, the incident involved the so-called Booze Fighters, who were alleged to have caused mayhem at a motorcycle rally being held in the sleepy California town of Hollister.

Nothing of the episode was filmed and the only photographic evidence was a shot of a single rider sprawled on his Harley-Davidson. He was surrounded by empty beer bottles, probably placed there for effect by the San Francisco Chronicle photographer who got there too late to record any of the real brawling. The photograph was subsequently featured in Life magazine. Thus, the damage was done and, in the years that followed, Harley-Davidsons became inextricably associated with the mean-looking, leather-clad, hard-riding tough guys exemplified by outlaw gangs, with the Hell's Angels top of the list.

The movie industry was not slow to get in on the act, with *The Wild One*, starring Marlon Brando and Lee Marvin, an early example of this biker stereotype. In the film, Brando rode a Triumph Thunderbird, but Marvin rode the Harley. By no means were all Harleys ridden by hooligans, of course. Touring clubs began to take off in a big way during the 1950s, with conventional Harley-Davidsons very much to the fore. Other stars who rode or owned Harleys at that time were Clark Gable, Tyrone

Above: The patrolman's favourite. A line up of Model-GE ServiCar three-wheelers, displaying the luggage box and weather shields that characterized these side-valve machines. Introduced in 1932, they remained in production until 1973.

Power, Roy Rogers and Elvis Presley, who appeared on the cover of Harley-Davidson's magazine, *The Enthusiast*, in 1956, astride his KH.

Another side effect of the presence of US soldiers in Europe was that they acquired a taste for British motorcycles and sports cars. These machines had the advantage of lightness, good handling and performance, and many of them found their way back to the United States; in their wake came imported new models. For the first time since the Indian domination, Harley-Davidson's market leader position was under threat. Indeed, the last motorcycles rolled off the Indian assembly lines in 1953, leaving Harley-Davidson – then celebrating its 50th anniversary – as the only major manufacturer in the United States.

Meanwhile, the next phase of engine development was unveiled in 1948. It was an updated version of the Knucklehead big-twin, known as the Panhead engine because that is exactly what the rocker covers looked like. The Panhead was built to retain engine oil better than the Knucklehead and there were new hydraulic valve lifters as well. Following on from the new engine came Harley-Davidson's first hydraulically damped telescopic forks, fitted on the debutante 74F Hydra Glide. This was a

radical departure from the springer leading-link forks that had been in service since 1907, and the name Hydra Glide was intended to reflect the improvement in ride quality. A high-compression version was dubbed the 74FL and the foot-shift, hand-lever clutch version built from 1952 was the FLF model.

New Machines

In 1952, Harley-Davidson responded to the wave of British imports with the new 740 cc (45 cu. in.) side-valve K Sport. Unfortunately, low compression ratios and poor cylinder breathing, combined with poor performance, made for limited sales success. What the K-series did have, however, was swinging-arm rear suspension that complemented telescopic forks. Cubic capacity was raised to 883 cc (54 cu. in.) in 1955 and a unit-construction powertrain with overhead-valves was adopted in 1957, when the K Sport was renamed the Sportster. Here at last was a worthy challenger to the European bikes and the Sportster went on to become the longest-running model in the world.

Until 1958, Harley-Davidson riders had to rely on the sprung seat post, which dated back to 1912, for a comfor-

Above: Riders who were keen on the traditional look of a Harley-Davidson could specify period features like the leather saddlebags and chrome trim on this 1990s Electra Glide. The look is retro, but comfort is ensured by its Softail rear suspension.

table ride. All that changed with the introduction of the F-series Duo Glide, which made long-distance work more pleasurable than ever before. Around this time, the fad for customizing and adding to the original factory specification was also growing. The makers introduced ranges of accessories and colour schemes to cater for this trend, with bikes thus festooned soon to become defined as 'dressers'.

It was not just the British 500 cc and 650 cc bikes that posed a threat to Harley-Davidson. From 1959, the arrival on the US scene of Honda and its other Japanese counterparts brought a new attitude to motorcycling. It was only logical that customers who got started on small bikes might upgrade and, again, Harley-Davidson responded in 1960 with another small machine of its own. Alongside the Topper scooter, the air-cooled two-stroke 165 cc Model-BT Super 10 was brought in to replace the Model-ST single. The same year, Harley-Davidson bought a 50 percent stake in the Italian company Aeronautica

Macchi and gained access to its 175 cc and 250 cc Aermacchi machines. These bikes were re-badged as Harley-Davidsons to augment the Harley range, providing an instant line-up of small-capacity machines. In a similar manner to the way it had reluctantly handled the scooter business, however, the Harley dealer network was ill prepared for the Italian-made machines. Despite this, they sold reasonably well against the Japanese competition, helped by successes on the race a branch of youthful subculture to which the chopper was a lifestyle object. But the company was still short of money, and Harley-Davidson went public with a share issue in 1965 in a bid to generate some revenue.

From 1965, Harley-Davidson equipped its FL models with an electric start, largely in response to the high-spec Japanese imports, ushering in the Electra Glide model. Having a cult film named after it – *Electra Glide in Blue* (1973) – not only made it one of the most famous motorcycles in the world but it also provided the chassis for the incoming engine design, the Shovelhead.

More funds were needed, and the best means of gaining these, plus a degree of protection in the market place, was to go in with a heavyweight partner. Thus, in January 1969, the AMF (American Metal Foundries) took a controlling stake in Harley-Davidson, promptly investing heavily in

new plant with a view to recouping its funds quickly by upping production volumes. It had a detrimental effect on quality and reliability, which in turn reflected on the bikes' reputation.

The fashion for customizing anything on wheels was at its height in 1969 when the movie *Easy Rider* hit the screens. Starring Peter Fonda and Dennis Hopper as a pair of free spirits pursuing the American Dream and experiencing a raft-load of psychedelia on the way, it accurately reflected the sentiment of the time. The Harleys they rode in the film were crucial: no other make would have done. The bikes had been chopped in the most extreme way, with raked frames and ridiculously extended forks, ape-hanger bars and peanut tanks sporting wild paint schemes, all served up with lashings of chrome. The look was everything, as there was no way could these machines have handled or performed at high speed. For years, Harley-Davidson had studiously ignored the outlaw movement and its choppers, enraged at what its owners saw as the butchery carried

Below: The 1312 cc (80 cu. in.) FLSTF Fat Boy is so-called because of its wide girth. Metal shrouds on its telescopic fork legs, and the use of 16-in (406-mm) alloy disc wheels on both front and rear are used to create this 'Fat' effect.

Above: The FLHR Road King was a comprehensively-equipped middleweight tourer that first appeared in 1995. It was powered by the 1312 cc (80 cu. in.) fuel-injected Evolution V-twin, allied to five-speed transmission and belt-drive.

it enjoys today. The FX1200 Super Glide appealed directly to riders that admired the outlaw image from a safe distance, and they could now emulate it legitimately. There is much commercial merit in producing modular ranges, where a number of different styles and subtly different images can be created around the same chassis and powertrain. The renaissance of Triumph motorcycles in 1990 followed exactly the same formula.

From Gloom to Boom

Back in the 1970s, however, Harley-Davidson was becoming increasingly marginalized on the international scene. It was the era of the big Japanese sports bikes that were well specified, lightweight, powerful, cheap to buy and backed up by servicing networks. One bright spot was the introduction of the XR750, which used the Sportster-based cast-iron engine and, with aluminium cylinders and heads, was good enough to became the most successful dirt-track racer for 20 years. But Harley-Davidson was embroiled in production problems to do with tooling, a direct result of the American Machine and Foundry (AMF) takeover, and the AMF board was itself reconsidering its position as custodian of the two-wheeled icon. In 1978, Harley-Davidson sold off its interest in Aermacchi, bringing to an end its brief dalliance with small-capacity lightweight machines. Its overall US market share was also hardly enviable, accounting for a paltry four per cent of all motorbikes sold. It was the company's darkest hour.

The first hint of a turnaround was in 1980, when the FLT Tour Glide came out. It was 1981, however, that was vastly more significant in the grand scheme of things as far as company history was concerned. A management buy-out led by Willie G. Davidson and Vaughan Beals and a dozen Harley-Davidson executives reclaimed the company from AMF, who by then were glad to be relieved of it. Independent once more, Harley-Davidson began a new chapter in its story.

out on their fine machines. Yet still the torch was borne by popular culture, with hit records such as Steppenwolf's 'Born to be Wild' and Bruce Springsteen's 'Born to Run' essentially biking anthems.

At the time of the *Easy Rider* release, the company's director of styling was William ('Willy') G. Davidson. As the grandson of founder William A. Davidson, his view carried considerable weight and it was Willy's vision that enabled the creation in 1971 of the FX1200 Super Glide. This was in effect a hybrid created from the front end of a Sportster combined with the big-twin Shovelhead engine and the frame of the Electra Glide – just what any right-thinking customizer might have attempted. Here was the factory's own ready-made custom bike, and one which paved the way for the company's recovery and the stability

The new management was as hard-nosed as the company's founders, taking the fight to the competition by adopting Japanese manufacturing techniques of 'just-in-time' (kan-ban), whereby components are made or procured only when they are needed and placed in bins at points on the assembly line prior to assembly. A degree of robotic automation crept in and quality control became an important factor. It was now no longer necessary to stockpile components that tied up large amounts of capital resources.

The price of such efficiency, however, was staff redundancies in the plant and more than a third of the workforce was laid off. The next step was to check the flow of imports and the US International Trade Commission was petitioned to bring in tariff restrictions on Japanese motorcycles. Such a move would give Harley-Davidson enough breathing space to effect a turnaround. That grand old cowboy, Ronald Reagan, was only too aware of the all-American soul that ran deep inside Harley-Davidson and, in 1982, as President of the United States, authorized the imposition of import tariffs on all Japanese bikes of more than 700 cc.

Traditional Values

Patriotism ruled and, as US icons began to be revered once again, a new sense of self-assurance pervaded Milwaukee, as Harley-Davidson took steps to protect its brand identity and patents. It was an emotional rather than rational appeal. All of a sudden there was virtue in traditional products – and that was certainly true of Harley-Davidson, the only serious manufacturer of motorcycles in the United States, with a heritage as long as any car maker. There is simply nothing to beat the patina of history. Equally, the environmental issues that were becoming more prominent meant that, in some quarters, high-performance machines were considered somehow repugnant and once again there was integrity in unhurried robustness. Too late, the Japanese manufacturers cottoned on to the Harley renaissance, hastily coming out with clones that, despite adequate production and competence, fell short of the mark because they lacked that elusive Harley essence – the engine noise of the classic V-twin, the idiosyncratic build quality and the authentic American character. The pretenders were shunned and, by 1986, Harley-Davidson was the best-selling manufacturer of big tourers and cruisers in the United States, and the company's recovery and stabilization was well under way.

One of the new ingredients came on the scene in 1984 when the company introduced its Evolution overhead-valve big-twin engine. It was similar in appearance to the Shovelhead that it was replacing, but contained aluminium barrels and heads for optimum heat dissipation, proving more reliable, more powerful and less expensive to produce. Significantly, it did not drink oil and it did not leak the way previous machines did. At first it was known as the Blockhead, but the term Evo proved to be longer-lasting. Members of the workforce who had lost their jobs were reinstated and Harley Davidson was back in profit. The Sportster range got the Evolution engine in 1986, rated at 883 cc (54 cu. in.).

Another major model launch was the Softail chassis in 1984, in which the rear suspension was concealed beneath the engine, so the bike came over as a hardtail suspension-free motorcycle from a previous era. A variation on this theme was the Softail Springer which used anachronistic vintage springer forks. Other introductions were the Dyna Glide of 1991, which came with rubber engine mounts, the FXDB Sturgis that was named in homage to one of the world's biggest motorbike festivals (held in Sturgis, South Dakota), and the Bad Boy, which came even closer to the chopper image.

In 1983, a former Harley-Davidson employee called Eric Buell built a prototype RR1100 as a commission from the Vetter fairing company and patented his Uniplanar frame, which suppressed engine vibrations. Enter the Harley-engined sports-roadster. In 1993, Harley-Davidson took a 49 per cent interest in Buell and the S2 Thunderbolt was the result of the new partnership. The subsequent Lightning X1 of 1998 carried on Buell's big-twin sports-roadster theme, with Harley-Davidson now owning 98 per cent of the company. Also in 1998, Harley-Davidson introduced its new Twin Cam engine, which did not feature overhead camshafts, but relied on the tried and tested 45-degree overhead-valve configuration. Innovations on this engine were electronic ignition and fuel injection.

In 1983, when the revival was getting under way, the factory-sanctioned Harley Owners' Group (HOG) was set up for the benefit of owners and new riders. It subsequently attracted some 400,000 members worldwide. Along with other clubs, members flock to annual rallies at Daytona and Sturgis in their leather-clad hordes. In addition to the introduction of a Harley-Davidson credit card, products totally unconnected with motorcycling such as aftershave (something that would make a Hell's Angel do more than cringe) and beer (more like it) were endorsed by Harley-Davidson, as were the trendy Harley-Davidson cafés in Manhattan and Los Angeles. The yuppie generation had embraced the Harley-Davidson in its bid for the final frontier, and there was no going back.

Chapter 1

The Birth of an Icon 1903–1945

Like most of the motorbikes made by pioneering motorcycle manufacturers a century ago, the machine that spawned the revered Harley-Davidson icon that we know today started life as little more than a bicycle with an engine attached to the frame. From those humble beginnings a world movement was born.

At the beginning of the 20th century, the transition from horses to bicycles and motor vehicles as a means of private transport was well under way, and in towns and cities in Europe and the United States, engineering firms were applying internal combustion engines to bicycle frames. In 1903, two of the Davidson brothers, Arthur and Walter, together with William S. Harley, built a 10 cu. in. (160 cc) single-cylinder motorcycle in their leisure time. Although it worked well enough, it lacked hill-climbing ability, so they built two better ones in 1904. Since the intention was to sell them, the Davidson brothers' Aunt Janet coach-lined the finished machines. It was the start of the business,

Left: From the outset, Harley-Davidson motorcycles meant business. In stripped-down form, they were ideal for off-road competition work, as shown by this eight-valve J-frame special from the 1930s. The rear tyre wears a chain for better traction in mud and hill-climbing.

and production grew exponentially. Their first workshop was little more than a shed built by the Davidsons' father, however. In 1905 the group made eight motorcycles, in 1906 they produced 50, then 150 during 1907 and over 400 in 1908. It was at this time that the third Davidson brother, William A., joined the organization. Harley-Davidson filed its incorporation papers in 1907 and the company was formed. It would stay under the control of the Harley and Davidson families until 1969, when American Machine and Foundry took over.

The first successful Harley-Davidson V-twin was produced in 1911, known as the Silent Gray Fellow on account of its colour scheme and the effectiveness of its silencer. It was followed a year later by the SE, a 45-degrees 61 cu. in. (1000 cc) V-twin. In 1913, sales of Harley-Davidsons reached a record 12,904 units and the company began to consider exporting their products. They engaged an Englishman, Duncan Watson, to arrange imports and sales in the UK and Europe, but the outbreak of the First World War less than a year later meant that exports to European dealers were halted and did not resume again until 1919. The war provided Harley-Davidson with the opportunity to supply the US Army with motorcycles, although, unlike Indian Motorcycles which diverted its

Below: Named after its colour scheme and efficient silencer, the Silent Gray Fellow of 1911 brought mobility to increasing numbers of adventurous souls. By 1913, sales had topped the 12,000 mark.

entire output to the military, the company prudently maintained its civilian lines, which would stand it in good stead when peace returned.

In 1921, Douglas Davidson became the first person to exceed 100mph (161km/h) on a motorcycle in Britain, accomplished on a Harley-Davidson on the Brooklands speedway at Byfleet, England. He recorded a speed of 100.76 mph (162.12km/h). However, a minor recession held sway and, as a result, Harley-Davidson made its first end-of-year loss. Another reason for the drop in sales was the widespread availability of Ford's mass-produced car, the Model T, which was selling for almost the same price as a motorbike and sidecar. The company embarked on an extensive programme to bolster sales around the globe.

The First 74

After the 1921 slump, sales began to increase again, aided by the introduction of the first 74 cu. in. (1200 cc) models. The engine's large capacity made it more suitable for pulling a sidecar and was a match for the engines made by Harley-Davidson's major rivals Indian Motorcycles who were based at Springfield, Massachusetts. This first 74 was known as an F-head, a term that indicated the position of the inlet and exhaust valves, in contrast to earlier models that were designated IOE for inlet-over-exhaust.

In 1928, a new chapter opened for Harley-Davidson. Not only did they start fitting front brakes to their products for the first time, but they released a new engine. It was a side-valve V-twin that displaced 45 cu. in. (740 cc). The new model was tagged the Model-D, but an unreliable gearbox and clutch and a maximum speed of only 55mph (88km/h) got it off to a bad start. The model was discontinued for 1929 and returned in 1930 in three guises, the D, DL, and DLD. In the midst of this came the Wall Street Crash of 1929 and, along with thousands of other businesses, Harley-Davidson was in trouble. Another leading American motorcycle manufacturer, Henderson-Excelsior, was unable to withstand the financial pressures, and closed in 1931, leaving Indian as Harley-Davidson's only domestic competitor. Harley-Davidson was able to keep going because it was not beholden to shareholders, but drastic measures were necessary, and it began to offer a wider choice of colours, extra chromed parts, and optional accessories in a bid to attract customers. There was even a tricycle variant. In 1932, the Milwaukee company unveiled the ServiCar, a three-wheeled machine powered by the 45 cu. in. (740 cc) side-valve engine. With a luggage boot, tool box or cargo deck at the rear, it was the ideal utility vehicle for small businesses, garages and police departments. The

Above: In many respects, the mighty 61EL Knucklehead set the standard for all future Harley-Davidsons. The imagery is all there – big twin power, broad mudguards and lashings of chrome.

first ServiCars featured the Model-D engine, although the vehicles were later upgraded in line with the solo 45 cu. in. (740 cc) models. The upgrades included new designations, R and RL models and subsequently WL models. The 80 cu. in. (1310 cc) Flatheads were also introduced in 1936 and designated U models.

Parallel to the development of the side-valve engine, Harley was developing an overhead-valve engine, and this went into production in 1936. Designated the Model-61E (the 61 referred to its displacement in cubic inches, the equivalent of 1000 cc), the engine soon became referred to as the 'Knucklehead' and was the first Harley to have dry sump lubrication instead of a total loss system. The horseshoe-shaped oil tank was located under the seat, the engine was fitted into a double loop frame and a new style of fuel tank appeared. It was made in two halves, with hidden frame tubes, and the speedometer was set into a

dash panel that fitted between the two halves of the tank. The innovative design of the 1936 61EL Knucklehead prevails in Harley-Davidsons today.

As the decade rolled on, apprehension grew with the increasing likelihood of war in Europe, and the United States making preparations for intervention. Harley-Davidson tendered to supply motorcycles to the US Army and shipped some WL models to Fort Knox for evaluation by the Mechanized Cavalry Board. Both Indian and Harley-Davidson were successful, and received contracts to supply motorcycles. Harley-Davidson's brief was to supply the WLA machine, an army version of the WE. The Canadian military also ordered a number of motorcycles, and a machine designated the WLC was built specifically for them, differing only slightly from the WLA. The WLA and WLC changed a little from year to year as refinements were made. Harley-Davidson made approximately 88,000 motorcycles during the war years and a large percentage of these were subsequently supplied to other allied nations. The factory received a number of accolades in the form of Army/Navy 'E for Excellence' awards for their efforts.

Silent Gray Fellow

The Silent Gray Fellow was the first Harley-Davidson to look like a motorcycle rather than a bicycle, with a sloping top tube allowing a lower seat height.

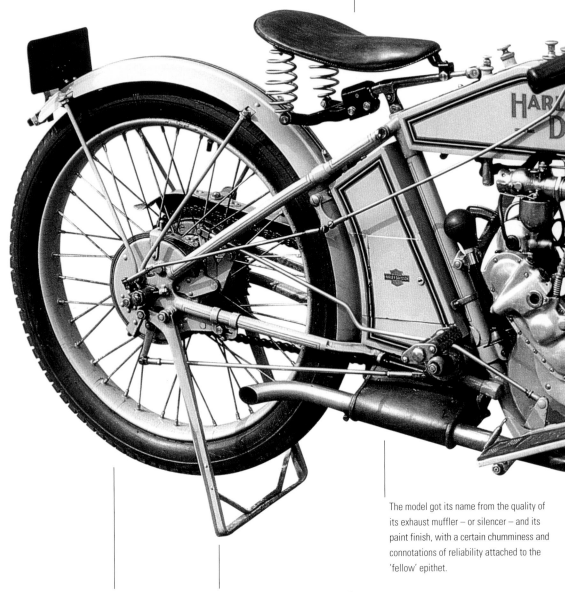

The model got its name from the quality of its exhaust muffler – or silencer – and its paint finish, with a certain chumminess and connotations of reliability attached to the 'fellow' epithet.

From 1912, a lever-operated rear hub clutch enabled the bike to be brought to a halt without having to stall the engine, although this was an optional extra.

After 1913, another option on the Silent Gray Fellow was the chain-driven final-drive, which was a replacement for the earlier belt-drive system.

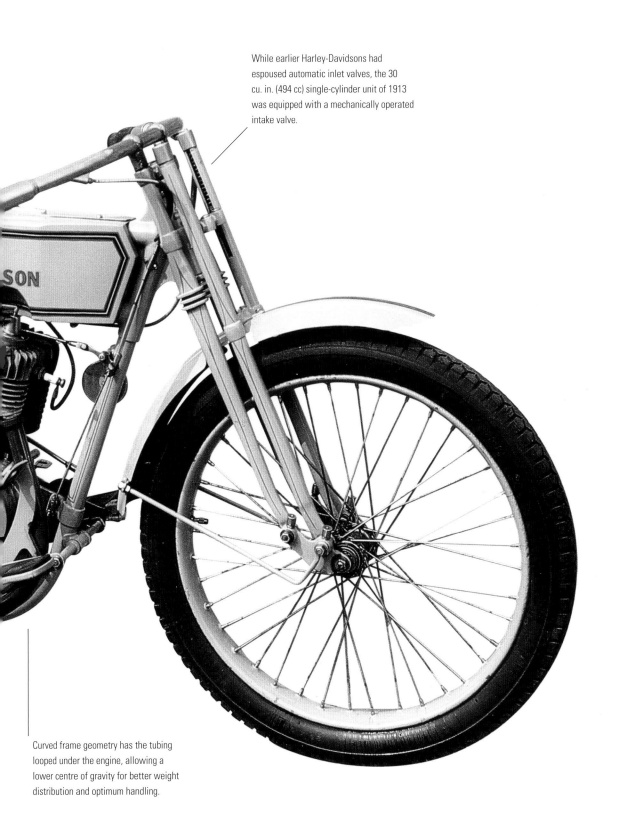

While earlier Harley-Davidsons had espoused automatic inlet valves, the 30 cu. in. (494 cc) single-cylinder unit of 1913 was equipped with a mechanically operated intake valve.

Curved frame geometry has the tubing looped under the engine, allowing a lower centre of gravity for better weight distribution and optimum handling.

Above: The original Harley-Davidson singles were finished in black, but in 1906 a Renault grey, with carmine pin-striping, was offered as an option. The name Silent Gray Fellow reflected both the paint job and the unusually effective silencer (muffler).

carburettor and throttle linkage, and rear hub coaster brake – which was operated by back-pedalling – meant that these machines were hardly viable as reliable everyday transport.

Leading Player

From 1903 until 1909, the company built only one model line, the 24.74 cu. in. (405.41 cc) inlet-over-exhaust single, which was improved upon with each successive year. Then came the X-8, better known as the Silent Gray Fellow because of its colour scheme and its effective silencer – this model looked much more like a proper motorbike. The Silent Gray Fellow can be seen as a direct development of the original 1903 machine and it remained in production until 1918.

By the time the Silent Gray Fellow appeared in 1912, Harley-Davidson was already recognized as a leading player in motorcycle manufacturing, not only in the United States. Indeed, motorcycles in general had become more refined through engineering developments that included the introduction of sprung forks, magneto ignition, cables instead of rod linkages, an optional hub-clutch, float carburettor, revised frame geometry and the inclusion of a full-length fuel tank in the traditional position. It still had no gearbox and the belt final-drive and pedal-start system were retained, together with the atmospheric inlet valve; however, developments that would render these systems obsolete were imminent. One evolution that took place out of aesthetic rather than technical considerations was the shift to black rubber tyres, as they showed the dirt less obviously than the white ones used originally. By the time of the Silent Gray Fellow, valanced mudguards had appeared in a bid to keep the rider slightly cleaner.

Harley-Davidson has always had a reputation for employing more cubic inches than most other motorcycle manufacturers. Even at the beginning, in 1903, the company founders used a larger engine than most of their contemporaries. Muscle power was an essential adjunct to the engine in order to pedal the machine up hills, however, so the bicycle layout with its bottom bracket and crank survived for almost a decade in Harley-Davidson's earliest motorcycles. In order to accommodate the engine as low as possible in the frame, the bottom tube was bent under the crankcases and the bike's handling was improved as a consequence. Although the company's first offerings were above average in the motorcycle market place, aspects such as the belt drive, battery ignition system, relatively crude

Early single-cylinder engines were relatively inefficient and therefore underpowered; although Harley-Davidson's were among the best available at that time, it sought to remedy the deficit by lifting the capacity of the engine.

It was raised by degrees to 26.8 cu. in. (440 cc) in 1906, then to 30 cu. in. (494 cc) in 1909, and had risen to 35 cu. in. (576 cc) by 1913.

The cylinder head and barrel were a single cast-iron item, while the crankcase was aluminium alloy. The single-cylinder engine's atmospheric inlet valve was a simple system, but it only worked at low engine speeds. The valve was forced open by the atmospheric pressure created by the vacuum caused by the falling piston. The fuel-air mix was supplied by the float-feed carburettor, which was sourced from the Schleber company from 1909, and the inlet valve was closed off by an exposed spring at the top of the cylinder. From 1909, a Bosch high-tension magneto was fitted and within the timing gear case were four gears that drove the magneto, although bikes with battery ignition lacked this facility. To assist cooling, the cylinder head featured vertical fins from 1911.

The quantum leap that was eventually manifest in the Model-F of 1915 actually took shape as early as 1907, when Harley-Davidson built its prototype V-twin. The simplest way to double engine capacity is to add an extra cylinder

Below: Pedal-power starts the engine and helps on hills, while control cables replaced rod linkages by 1909. Footboards and air horn are prominent.

1914 Silent Gray Fellow	
Engine model:	Inlet-over-exhaust single-cylinder
Engine capacity:	30 cu. in. (494cc)
Cases:	Harley-Davidson
Carburation:	Harley-Davidson
Air filter:	n/a
Ignition:	Magneto
Pipes:	Single
Transmission:	Single-speed, belt drive
Frame:	Tubular loop
Suspension:	Front: leading-link forks Rear: hardtail
Brakes:	Front: none Rear: back-pedal hub
Wheels:	Wire-spoke front and rear
Mudguards (fenders):	Bicycle-type
Handlebars:	Pull-back
Risers:	Integral with bars
Headlight:	None
Tail-light:	None

and that is just what it did. Four years later, the first V-twin models rolled off the production line. The V-twin engine consisted of two single-cylinder units running one crankshaft and crankcase. In order to continue using the same bike frame, a narrow angle V was chosen – 45 degrees – which became the classic configuration. Engine capacity was lifted to 61 cu. in. (1000 cc). Interlocking male and female connecting rods ringed the crankshaft, and the barrels and cylinder heads were in cast-iron as single units, while the crankcase was in alloy. The timing gear case on the side of the crankcase housed the magneto drive and the mechanical oil pump. When the mechanical inlet valve was introduced, the engine could attain higher speeds with consequent increase in performance. A two-branch inlet manifold linked the carburettor to inlet ports, and inlet valves were operated by rocker arms. These early V-twins gained the nickname 'F-Head', as their inlet valves were located on top of the cylinder heads and the exhaust valves were at the side of the cylinders, notionally taking the shape of a letter 'F'. The spark plugs were housed in the valve pockets at the sides of the cylinder heads.

Model-W5 'Sport'

Regular factory-fitted extras included mudguard-mounted luggage carriers and rear stands hinged off the rear drop-outs, although electric lighting was less frequently specified.

The smooth-running Model-W5 'Sport' had gear-driven primary-drive and an enclosed chain for final-drive, making for an efficient, if slightly odd-looking machine.

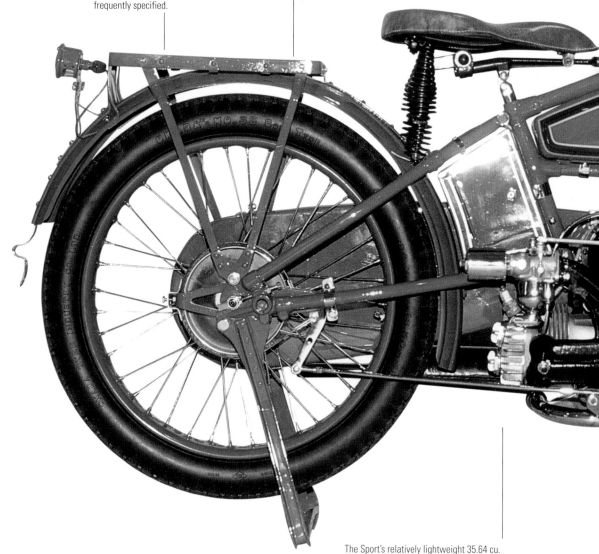

The Sport's relatively lightweight 35.64 cu. in. (584 cc) horizontally opposed twin was 100lb (45kg) lighter than the contemporary Harley V-twin, while lower centre of gravity made for good handling.

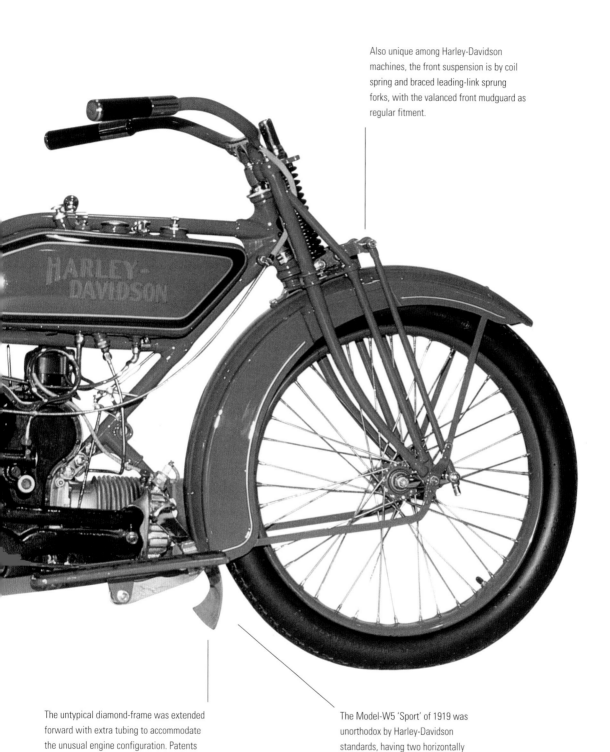

Also unique among Harley-Davidson machines, the front suspension is by coil spring and braced leading-link sprung forks, with the valanced front mudguard as regular fitment.

The untypical diamond-frame was extended forward with extra tubing to accommodate the unusual engine configuration. Patents granted to Harley-Davidson indicate they had big plans for it as an entry-level model.

The Model-W5 'Sport' of 1919 was unorthodox by Harley-Davidson standards, having two horizontally opposed cylinders and an external flywheel on the left-hand side.

Above: High-class paint jobs with coachlines characterize Harley-Davidson motorcycles, especially from the 1920s. For many years, rear suspension was non-existent, relying on the 'Ful-Floteing' sprung saddle post and regular springs.

It is common knowledge that Harley-Davidson motorcycles have relied on V-twin power plants almost since the company's inception. There were singles in the early days and they were offered as economy machines in the 1920s. Faced with declining sales in the face of the burgeoning market for cars and the Model T Ford in particular, however, the company came out with a horizontally opposed, flathead-twin Sport Model in 1919, which it officially designated the Model-W. Desperate measures were necessary to combat the onslaught of the automobile and the Harley-Davidson management imagined that they could attract the car buyer with little money at his disposal with an efficient entry-level model. Shortly after the Model-W came out, they launched the Model-CD, a 37 cu. in. (600 cc) F-head single-cylinder machine aimed at commercial users, but that lasted only a year.

Entry-level Model

Capacity of the Model-W's flat-twin side-valve engine was 35.64 cu. in. (584 cc) and from 1920 it was available in W, WF and WJ specifications. At the time, Harley-Davidson saw it as the two-wheeled equivalent of the ubiquitous Model T Ford. It was 100lb (45kg) lighter than the V-twin models and the flat-twin engine was mounted longitudinally, as opposed to the more familiar side-to-side layout popularized by BMW. It had a diamond-shaped

tubular frame, trailing link front forks and big valanced front mudguard. The low centre of gravity meant it handled well. But none of this was particularly appealing to US buyers, particularly in view of its $325 price tag. In 1921, the country was in the throes of a national recession and, despite it being short-lived, the majority of Model-W production was exported. The Model-W also lacked the looks of the V-twin, where the engine filled the frame. By 1923, the W-series flat-twins had been discontinued, with only a few hundred having been built.

The Model-W had been something of a distraction and, although the flat-twin concept would reappear in 1942 during the Second World War as the XA dispatcher's bike, the company preferred to concentrate on its V-twins. Back in 1915, Harley-Davidson offered five V-twin options that were available with a combination of the three new innovations. These were a three-speed gearbox with chain drive (although a single-speed transmission could still be specified), a mechanical oil pump and an electric lighting system. One of the stalwarts of the range was the Model-F, which incorporated two of these new features, marking it out

1922 Model-W5 'Sport'	
Engine model:	Horizontally opposed Flathead twin
Engine capacity:	35.64 cu. in. (584 cc)
Cases:	Harley-Davidson
Carburation:	Harley-Davidson
Air filter:	Harley-Davidson
Ignition:	Magneto
Pipes:	Combined intake and exhaust manifold
Transmission:	Three-speed, chain drive
Frame:	Tubular perimeter/cradle
Suspension:	Front: leading-link springer forks Rear: hardtail
Brakes:	Front: none Rear: hub
Wheels:	Wire-spoke front and rear
Mudguards (fenders):	Valanced pressed steel
Handlebars:	Pull-back
Risers:	Integral with bars
Headlight:	None
Tail-light:	None

as a significant model in terms of on-the-road practicality. Clearly a three-speed gearbox made greater speeds possible and hills could be climbed that were previously impossible. Factors of engine reliability and longevity were addressed by the mechanical oil pump, which ensured more thorough lubrication. The Model-F did not come with the electric light package, but it was available as an optional extra. Acetylene lighting was often fitted on bikes that were not equipped with electric lights at the factory.

By this time, footboards were regular fitment, as pedal power was only necessary for getting the bike in motion. There was a rear drum brake, operated by a right-hand foot pedal, and mudguards and a luggage rack were also fitted. The sprung saddle was still hardly any better than that of a bicycle, but the Model-F did come with leading-link front forks that offered a modicum of suspension.

Below: The Model-W 'Sport' featured Harley-Davidson's first side-valve engine, albeit in a flat-twin guise. It also used combined inlet and exhaust manifolding, while the transmission was positioned above the engine.

In standard form, the Model-F cost $275. Alongside it was marketed a commercial tricycle, powered by the same 11hp V-twin, although, rather oddly, it had a cargo box and two wheels up front instead of the conventional bike forks and single front wheel. Along rather different lines, the company introduced sidecars as part of its model range in 1914. Instead of just the one pillion passenger, an entire family could now be transported by Harley-Davidson. Later on, specially adapted engines were built for hauling sidecars, as standard machines had some difficulty coping with the extra weight. Combinations were popular throughout the 1920s and 1930s, featuring prominently in police and military applications, but competition from the three-wheeler cycle-car brigade and cheap mass-produced cars such as the Model T Ford to an extent had a limiting effect on the civilian sidecar market. Harley-Davidson's sidecars were built by the Rogers Company until 1925, when Rogers ended production. From this point, Harley-Davidson made its own chairs and machines so equipped were listed in the catalogue as special sidecar models until 1952.

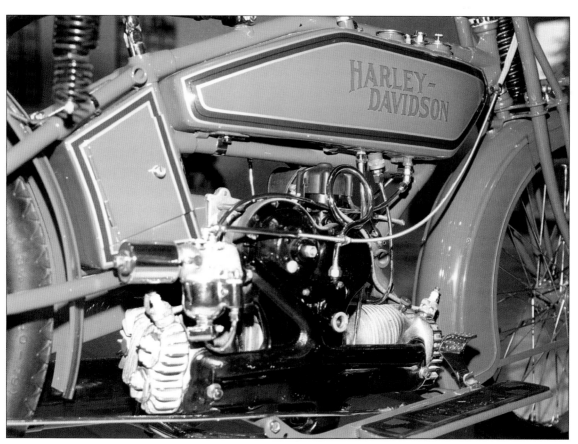

Model-J

Although the company built a prototype V-twin engine in 1907, its first production V-twins did not appear until 1911. The J-series engine's pushrods were operated via a single camshaft, with cam-followers that restricted engine revs.

The Model-J was fitted with 28in (71cm) clincher tyres mounted on 22in (56cm) diameter lace-spoked wheel rims. White-wall tyres declined in popularity due to cleaning difficulties.

The F-head was so-named on account of the positioning of the inlet valve in the cylinder head relative to the exhaust valve, which was on the side of the cylinder, thus forming an F-shape.

Reverse view

Front suspension was by leading-link forks, with a pair of springs located below the steering yoke. Typically, rear suspension was absent.

The 61 cu. in. (1000 cc) V-twin sits snugly in the Model-J's tubular cradle frame, which loops underneath the engine. By 1916, a kick-starter had been adopted, and three-speed transmission was fitted.

With 61 cu. in. (1000 cc) and 11hp on tap from its F-head V-twin engine, the Model-J of 1918 was a powerful machine, capable of hauling a sidecar.

The Model-J line first appeared in 1916, the year that Harley-Davidson's identification system changed to a letter-based rather than a numerical designation. In that year, the three 61 cu. in. (1000 cc) Flathead V-twin lines were the Model-E, the Model-F and the Model-J. Although the standard colour scheme for the Model-J was initially grey, there was a number of colour options available at extra cost. By 1928, olive green was the standard hue, with extra-cost options of black, cream, azure blue, police blue, green, maroon or fawn.

The Model-J was always fully specified. Its leather saddle was mounted on Harley-Davidson's patented sprung seat post, which, along with the voluminous balloon tyres (25 x 3.86in/635 x 98mm), cushioned the rider from potholes and undulations. There were two rear brakes: a contracting band and a hub brake, operated via a rod from the right-hand pedal. A front-hub drum brake was introduced in 1928. The Model-J's optional speedometer was mounted on top of the fuel tank, which, in common with all models, doubled as fuel and oil container. There was electric lighting front and rear, and a dual headlight system was introduced in 1929. It had an electric air horn mounted between the forks, along with a cylindrical tool box and puncture repair kit. There were footboards, of course, generously valanced mudguards, a parcel rack, rear stand and a battery box. A rear-view mirror was a sensible optional extra.

The Model-J was joined by the 74 cu. in. (1200 cc) Model-JD in 1922 and endured until 1929 when, like all the long-running F-head big twins, it was discontinued in favour of the Model-V and a series of nine permutations on the 74 cu. in. (1200 cc) Flathead V-twin theme.

Among the last of the Model-J derivatives was the two-cam JDH version that was powered by a race-derived engine. There is a well-worn adage that racing improves the breed and it is an established fact that technical

Below: The 61 cu. in. (1000 cc) F-head Model-J was equipped with a foot-pedal and hand-lever (right) for clutch operation, plus a hand-shift to work the three-speed transmission. The pressed-steel primary-drive case is embossed with the Harley-Davidson logo.

improvement in racing machinery filter through to the machines that we ride on the road. Nowhere is this more true than with racing bikes, which have almost always represented cutting-edge technology. Publicity accruing from race success has invariably enhanced a company's reputation and had a favourable effect on showroom sales.

Officially, however, Harley-Davidson was not so eager to get involved in competition and did not participate in racing until 1914. At this point, board-track racing was becoming very popular in the United States and was attracting sizeable crowds. Like modern indoor stadium cycle tracks, board-tracks were constructed of thin planks laid edge-to-edge on a wooden frame, which could be steeply banked at corners. Speeds of 120mph (193km/h) were attained on the banking and, unsurprisingly, injuries and fatalities were not uncommon as the smooth wooden surfaces acquired a potentially lethal patina of oil and rubber. As it transpired, board-track racing was a relatively short-lived affair, being superseded in the 1920s by the outdoor cinder tracks of the speedway.

The Wrecking Crew

Harley-Davidson's own team of KT racers immediately began to achieve significant results on the boards and, in September 1915, a Flathead Harley-Davidson set a 100-mile (161km) record of 89.11mph (143.46km/h) on the Chicago board-track. The work's race team also won a number of 100-mile (161km) and 300-mile (483km) endurance events in 1915. The following year, the company introduced the eight-valve racer. These purposeful-looking machines were built exclusively for the use of the factory's own race team, and therefore in very limited numbers, until 1927. A light weight was paramount and most board-track racers did not have brakes – apart from back-pedalling on early versions – and certainly not a front mudguard. The saddle was set lower than normal and drop handlebars enabled the rider to adopt a crouching attitude at speed to minimize wind resistance. A friction damper on the front forks made the suspension movement more containable.

In the same way that doubling up on the number of cylinders increases the potential of the engine's power output, so having two inlet valves and two exhaust valves per cylinder provides better access for gases to flow into and out of the engine than in a regular four-valve unit. This was the formula adopted by Harley-Davidson for its Eight-Valve racers that first appeared in 1916. The barrels and cylinder heads were designed for Harley-Davidson by the celebrated British engineer Sir Harry Ricardo.

Above: Even the earliest machines used coil and dry-cell battery ignition, and by 1916 the electrical system consisted of magneto or generator and battery. Thus, one vital component was the battery box, pictured here on the Model-J.

Ricardo's firm provided similar input to companies such as Triumph motorcycles in the United Kingdom for its 1922 Type IR Fast Roadster and is still at the forefront of racecar technology today. Ricardo's main modification was to install a hemispherical combustion chamber in the heads of the Harley-Davidson eight-valve engine.

Harley-Davidson's works racing team became known as 'The Wrecking Crew' and, in the process of racking up an enviable record of race wins, four evolutions of the eight-valve racer emerged between 1916 and 1927. The classic version was based on a Keystone tubular loop frame with leading-link suspension, powered by a 15hp, 61 cu. in. (1000 cc) overhead-valve V-twin unit. These were very much machines in the raw. There were no exhaust pipes, simply open exhaust ports, which emitted scorching blasts of flame as the engine backfired. There was no clutch or gearbox either, just a single rear sprocket that could be swapped to suit different venues. The machine was slowed by a compression-release mechanism that was effectively an engine kill-switch and the rider's boots.

The concept of the race replica is not a modern phenomenon confined to fans of World Superbikes. A significant proportion of riders have always yearned to emulate the achievements and style of racing machines and the heroes that rode them. With an eye on such a market, Harley-Davidson released the KR Fast Roadster way back in 1915. It was heavily based on the KT board-track bike, using a shortened 'close-coupled' tubular frame with leading-link forks and powered by the 61 cu. in. (1000 cc) inlet-over-exhaust V-twin. It used a single-speed transmission and chain drive, and was capable of 80mph (130km/h). The KR Fast Roadster was fitted with Clincher wheel rims shod with beaded tyres, which had to be inflated to very high pressures so that they would stay put on the rims. The bike's control cables were made of single-strand piano wire, wound round with a metal outer cable and leather-sheathed for extra protection. To make it usable on the road, it was equipped with mudguards, chain-guard and conventional pull-back handlebars. Just over 100 units were built, making the Fast Roadster something of a rarity.

Above: The Harley-Davidson logo on the Model-J's fuel tank was typical of the period. Bored out to 74 cu. in. (1200 cc) in 1922, the big twin was designated the Model-JD, and its rocker gear was accommodated in semi-circular edifices in the tank.

One sure-fire route to increased performance is the time-honoured scaling up of cubic capacity. By 1922, Harley-Davidson could see that the long-serving 45-degree F-head motor was due for retirement and it launched the 74 cu. in. (1200 cc) V-twin in the new JD model. Suddenly, by the simple expedient of raising engine size by 13 cu. in. (200 cc), here was a high-performance motorcycle that was as quick as almost anything else on the US highway. It had a top speed of 75mph (121km/h). It was no surprise then that these new big-bore bikes found popularity with US police departments, giving two-wheeling patrolmen a new lease of life in the war against criminals and speed merchants. Power output for the Model-JD was 9.5bhp at 4500rpm, which was transmitted via a three-speed gearbox with hand-shift and foot-operated clutch. Like the earlier KT board-track racer, the Model-JD had a pair of cut-outs in the lower portion of the fuel tank to allow clearance for the F-head rocker gear.

The Model-JD retained the standard tubular cradle frame and leading-link front forks and was quite the most popular Harley-Davidson of all by 1926, when more than 9000 units were built. Two years later, Harley-Davidson brought out the pair of high-performance roadsters called the JH and JDH, which were replicas of the factory's two-cam race bikes and based on lower and narrower frames than the regular J and JD models.

Front-wheel Braking

Prior to 1928, punters and pundits believed that front brakes were potentially dangerous, liable to lock up and cause skids and all manner of mayhem. Front brakes were fitted at this point, however, bringing the long-in-the-tooth Model-J up-to-date, and instituting one of the biggest changes to the Harley-Davidson specification for some time. The run-out F-head models included the 61

Below: The Model-J was the most popular machine in the range in the mid-1920s, and was correspondingly well equipped, with electric lighting, air horn and tank-mounted speedo.

1923 Model-J	
Engine model:	Inlet-over-exhaust F-head V-twin
Engine capacity:	74 cu. in. (1200 cc)
Cases:	Harley-Davidson
Carburation:	Harley-Davidson
Air filter:	n/a
Ignition:	Points
Pipes:	Two-into-one
Transmission:	Three-speed, chain drive
Frame:	Tubular cradle
Suspension:	Front: leading-link forks Rear: hardtail
Brakes:	Front: drum Rear: contracting band and expanding band
Wheels:	Wire-spoke front and rear
Mudguards (fenders):	Valanced pressed steel
Handlebars:	Pull-back
Risers:	Integral with bars
Headlight:	Single electric
Tail-light:	Electric

cu. in. (1000 cc) JH and 74 cu. in. (1200 cc) JDH, which featured two camshafts. Ironically, once the company had pulled out of board-track racing, its publicity strove to distance itself from competition activity, yet the JH and JDH were among the fastest vehicles on the road at the time. These bikes were deliberately aimed at sports and race-oriented riders, seduced by the notion of two cams and 'exceptional speed and tremendous power,' as the Harley-Davidson publicity department put it. It was even possible to get an 80 cu. in. (1300 cc) version to special order. But although the two-cam machines helped restore the company's image as far as the enthusiast market was concerned, their introduction was in reality more of a marketing-driven reaction to falling markets, which in the late 1920s saw the factory operating at half-capacity.

In 1930, Harley-Davidson stopped making the big F-head twins and, instead, introduced the Model-V range of side-valve machines. This was seen by many as a retrograde step, since the new Flathead engines were not only slower but at first, they were no more reliable than the old F-head units.

Model-RL

Flamboyant two-tone paint schemes were the order of the day, with detailed coachlining. The matching mudguards (fenders) were flared to cover much of the upper tyre area. Rear mudguard folded up to aid wheel changing.

The Model-RL had a hard-tail frame with no rear suspension, the rider having to make do with the tractor-like saddle and the 'Ful-Floteing' sprung seat post.

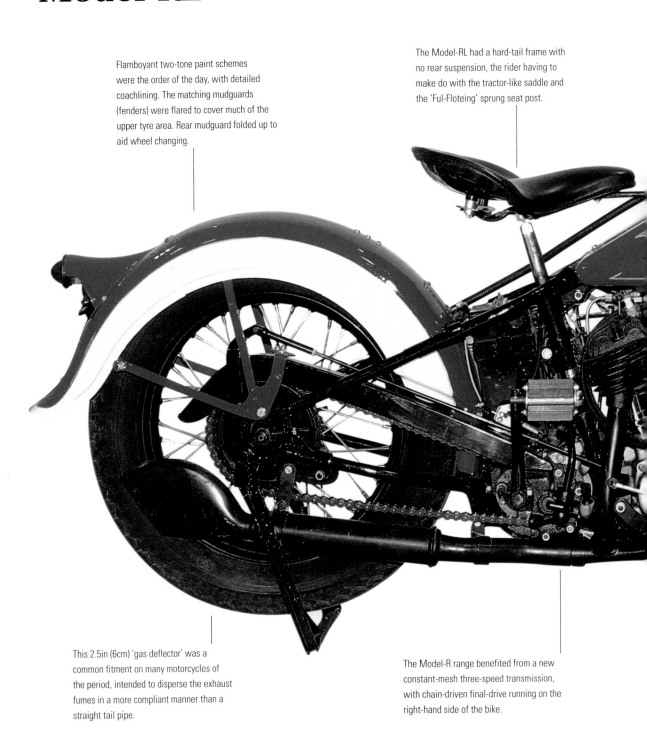

This 2.5in (6cm) 'gas deflector' was a common fitment on many motorcycles of the period, intended to disperse the exhaust fumes in a more compliant manner than a straight tail pipe.

The Model-R range benefited from a new constant-mesh three-speed transmission, with chain-driven final-drive running on the right-hand side of the bike.

The Harley-Davidson logo was worked up into a complex art deco design for the Model-RL's fuel tank. It was used in this format just for 1934 and 1935 model years.

Launched in 1932, the Model-R series' engine was given a comprehensive makeover. The 45 cu. in. (738 cc) side-valve V-twin received new barrels, pistons, conrods, flywheel, crankcase and oil pump.

The Model-R was introduced in 1932 as a replacement for the relatively short-lived Model-D that had itself come out in 1929. The Model-R was powered by the 45 cu. in. (740 cc) Flathead V-twin and there were four variants: the R, the high-compression RL, the sidecar-carrying RS and the RLD. It was not an auspicious time to launch a new model, with the country languishing in the aftermath of the Wall Street Crash and subsequent Depression. Harley-Davidson was in fact fortunate to survive and lay-offs and diminished production volumes were inevitable. The Model-R series also survived, spawning additional variations, but was finally axed in 1936 (along with the

Below: The Model-R's beautifully finished mudguard sported the 'airflow' tail light, introduced for the 1935 model year. The lower portion of the mudguard could be hinged up to make wheel-changing less of a chore.

74 cu. in./1200 cc Model-V) in favour of the similar-powered Model-W range.

In 1929, Harley-Davidson was inspired to produce the Model-D as a response to the success of its rival Indian Motorcycles' offering, the Scout. However, the Model-D lacked the appeal of the 45 cu. in. (740 cc) Scout and Excelsior's Super X – the Scout was the market leader at that time. Indian was enjoying a strong position, having recently taken over Ace Motorcycles, which produced Henderson fours (Bill Henderson left Indian in 1919 to set up on his own). When Harley-Davidson's Model-D series came out, the bike quickly earned the nickname of 'the three-cylinder Harley', on account of its upright generator which gave the appearance of a third cylinder. This, of course, was anything but the case, although Harley-Davidsons have always benefited from the fore-and-aft V-twin engine layout (rather than the BMW-style flat-twin or east-west V-twin of the Moto Guzzi), which makes for a more slender machine and ensures the weight is along the bike's centre line.

Frame Upgraded

The most significant difference between the Model-D and Model-R was the new tubular cradle frame unveiled in 1932. Gone was the straight down-tube at the front, replaced by a curved swan-neck shape. This facilitated the horizontal mounting of a generator in front of the engine, as opposed to the vertical siting on the Model-D. Mechanical updating was unseen, but no less significant at the time. For 1932, the Model-D's 45 cu. in. (740 cc) engine was given a thorough makeover. Hardly any of the casings remained unchanged, with alterations made to the crankcase, barrels, flywheel, conrods and oil pump. These served the Model-R well enough through its four-year life span – only minor upgrades to the engine were made up to 1935.

The Model-RL's power output was rated at 22bhp, transmitted through a new constant-mesh three-speed gearbox with hand-operated shift. Its maximum speed was about 65mph (105km/h). In common with other makes, the RL could be fitted with a fish-tail exhaust that was meant to disperse gases more efficiently.

By the mid-1930s, motorcycle manufacturers in both Europe and the United States had begun to smarten up their products' liveries, using bright colours and coachlined detailing on the fuel tanks and mudguards, and chrome-plating the silencers. This was very much the way things were going at Milwaukee. In 1935, a typical Model-RL featured the Harley-Davidson logo on its tank sides as a gold-edged winged diamond set against a pastel-blue or teak-red background, thrusting into the contrasting cream- or black-painted front area. The broad valanced mudguards were beautifully painted to match, with delicate gold coachlines. Such colour schemes were modified or renewed with successive model years.

Nor was rider comfort ignored. The Model-RL came with the patented sprung seat post and the I-beam forks featured exposed coil sprung suspension at the steering yoke. The bikes were fitted with broad pull-back handlebars, with ignition control on the left-hand grip. The speedometer was positioned on top of the tank and a large electric air horn took the place of the tool box in 1935, the same year that a stylish airflow tail-light was fitted on the back of the mudguard. The aft section of this could be folded up to make wheel changes easier and a quick-release hub was available as well. A stand was also fitted, as were crash bars and mud flaps.

There's no question that the Model-RL was a handsome bike. It couldn't fail to impress with its elaborate duo-tone paint finish, and extras such as crash bars and saddle bags added substance to the basic machine. Yet despite all the revisions that had gone into the 45 cu. in. (740 cc) sidevalve V-twin, it was not actually that much quicker than the overhead-valve single-cylinder 21 cu. in. (330 cc) BA model of almost a decade earlier.

In 1936, the Model-R series was replaced by the Model-W line, with which it had much in common mechanically. The new range, however, tended to mimic the 61EL with its Knucklehead engine, which had also been launched in 1936, and upon which the company's future success would be based. In retrospect, the Model-R can therefore be seen as one of the last of the veteran Harleys.

Right: Complex detailing of the headset and steering yoke of the Model-RL, including coil springs, headlight, electric horn and wide-angle pull-back-style handlebars.

1935 Model-RL

Engine model:	Side-valve V-twin
Engine capacity:	45 cu. in. (740 cc)
Cases:	Harley-Davidson
Carburation:	Harley-Davidson
Air filter:	Chrome Harley-Davidson
Ignition:	Points
Pipes:	Two-into-one
Transmission:	Three-speed, chain drive
Frame:	Tubular cradle
Suspension:	Front: I-beam, leading-link springer forks Rear: hardtail
Brakes:	Front: drum Rear: hub
Wheels:	Drop-centre wire-spoke front and rear
Mudguards (fenders):	Valanced pressed steel
Handlebars:	Wide-angle pull-back
Risers:	Integral with bars
Headlight:	Harley-Davidson
Tail-light:	Airflow

Model-VL

The Model-V had new heavy-duty forged I-beam fork legs from 1932, with dual springs augmenting the front suspension. It remained a hardtail frame – reworked along with the engine after teething troubles.

Drop-centre wire-spoke laced wheel rims were shod with up-to-date beaded tyres, while bulbous balloon-type tyres measuring 19 x 4in (48 x 10cm) were optional fitment.

The new big-twin engine had removable cast-iron cylinder heads, fed by a Schleber die-cast carburettor with chrome air filter, while the high-compression VLE version used magnesium-alloy pistons.

Reverse view

Launched in 1930, the Model-V was powered by a 74 cu. in. (1213 cc) side-valve V-twin, but the initial output had to be recalled to rectify a number of problems with engine cases and internals.

Five colour schemes were available in 1933, but the base-model in the V-series looked relatively dowdy compared with the VLE, which featured the eagle logo on its fuel tank. The entire machine could be chrome-plated for an additional $15.

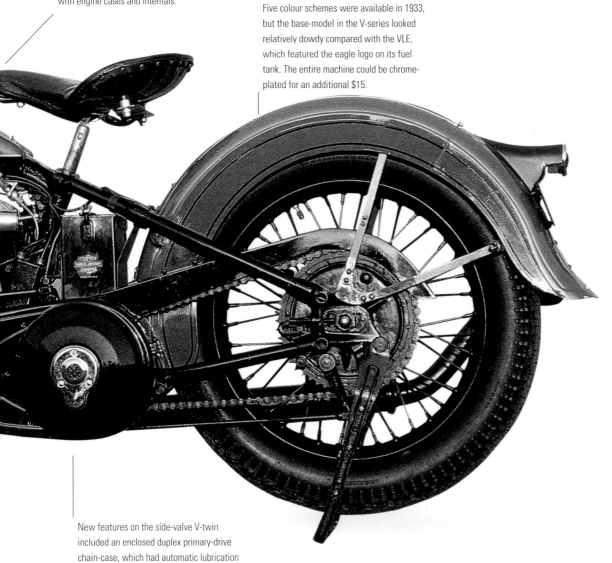

New features on the side-valve V-twin included an enclosed duplex primary-drive chain-case, which had automatic lubrication system for longer life.

Above: The art deco style graphic incorporating the Harley-Davidson logo had connotations of a flying diamond. The base-model was quite restrained, compared with its two-tone coachlined siblings.

Introduced in August 1929 for the 1930 model year, the all-new VL was brought in to replace the F-head V-twins. Although in fact some saw it as little more than an enlarged 45, the V-series was the first Harley-Davidson to use the 74 cu. in. (1200 cc) side-valve V-twin engine. It was at this point in time merely following a number of precedents as, when it first appeared in 1930, it was 14 years after its chief rivals Indian Motorcycles had first built their own side-valve big twins. The Harley-Davidson V-series was not an instant success, however, because the bike suffered from a number of teething problems. This was not unusual, as virtually all new vehicles require some post-launch adjustment. In the case of the V-series, however, the first two months' production had to be recalled for what amounted to a comprehensive rebuild, as everything from frames, flywheels and engine cases to valves, valve-springs and kick-start mechanisms had to be changed. The work was naturally carried out for owners free of charge, but it was a costly exercise that did little to promote the reputation of the new V-series. After such an unpromising start, the side-valve machines recovered lost ground and swiftly evolved into rugged, dependable bikes. With 22bhp on tap and weighing in at 390lb (177kg), they were capable of a modest turn of speed, too, being capable of reaching 65mph (105km/h).

Registrations Falling

To give some idea of the volumes that Harley-Davidson was making when the Model VL was in production, only 5689 bikes were invoiced by the company in 1933. This still, however, accounted for some 60 percent of all motorcycles sold in the United States that year, when total motorcycle registrations fell below 100,000 for the first time in 30 years.

The V-series was based on a tubular steel cradle frame, with leading-link springer front forks and a rigid rear end. The rider sat on a leather saddle with seat post springs available for the first time on the V-model. A buddy seat could be ordered for carrying pillion passengers and other extras were also available. The battery box was positioned beneath the saddle within the triangle of the rear frame.

Other new features included the duplex primary chain, which was enclosed in a casing with the benefit of a hand-operated oiling facility. This prolonged chain life and, along with the chain guard, was a major step towards cleaning up the oily image that motorcycling had at that time. There was a tool box on the front of the fork yokes, with horn attached, and there was also a steering head lock and heavy-duty I-beam forged fork legs. The removable cylinder heads were in cast-iron and a Schebler die-cast carburettor was fitted. The twin headlights and the klaxon horn were carried over from the 1929 model. There was a drum brake at the front and drop-centre wheel rims allowed modern beaded tyres to be fitted, although 19 x 4in (48 x 10cm) balloon tyres could be fitted as optional extras. VLs were normally equipped with three-speed transmission, but reverse gear was an option. Heavy-duty front forks were introduced on the V-series from 1932, when the chrome air filter was first fitted. The VLE of 1933 was the high-compression model in the series, with magnesium-alloy pistons providing the extra power. A VLE went on to establish the US production bike speed record in 1933, achieving 104mph (167km/h). As the years passed, however, it gradually became apparent that piston failure in the

Below: The Model-V often had twin headlamps mounted on the head-stock, with an electric horn fastened to the tool box ahead of the front springs. The chrome air filter belongs to the Schleber carburettor.

1930 Model-VL	
Engine model:	Side-valve V-twin
Engine capacity:	74 cu. in. (1200 cc)
Cases:	Harley-Davidson
Carburation:	Harley-Davidson
Air filter:	Chrome Harley-Davidson
Ignition:	Points
Pipes:	Two-into-one
Transmission:	Three-speed (optional reverse), chain drive
Frame:	Tubular cradle
Suspension:	Front: I-beam, leading-link springer forks Rear: hardtail
Brakes:	Front: drum Rear: hub
Wheels:	19in (483mm) drop-centre wire-spoke front and rear
Mudguards (fenders):	Pressed steel
Handlebars:	Wide-angle pull-back
Risers:	Integral with bars
Headlight:	Harley-Davidson
Tail-light:	Harley-Davidson

big side-valve engine was a not uncommon occurrence.

The eagle tank graphics appeared in 1933 on VLD models only, but that was the start of the use of the enduring eagle symbol in Harley-Davidson graphics. Although auxiliary components like the chain guard were painted black, the entire machine could be chrome-plated for an additional $15 charge. The bike's colour scheme was generally the traditional olive green with vermilion striping, and edged in maroon and centred in gold, which could be very attractive. The VL side-valve V-twin was significant in so far as it transcended a difficult economic period in the company history, during the Depression, but while it was a cleaner design than its F-head predecessors it probably fell short of expectations in terms of performance.

Despite its origins in Sir Harry Ricardo's laboratories, the Model-V's side-valve combustion chamber was prone to unreliability, manifest at worst in piston melt-down. Its labyrinthine conduits meant high compression and effective breathing were strangers, while the hot exhaust valve next to the cylinder barrel caused the pistons to melt.

Model-61EL

Virtually everything about the Model-61EL was new, apart from its mudguards and generator, carried over from the Model-V series. There was now an integral tank-mounted dash with built-in instruments.

Proportions of the Model-61EL rely on traditional Harley-Davidson architecture – hardtail tubular cradle frame, teardrop fuel tank, tractor-style saddle, wide-angle pull-back bars and, perhaps most significantly, the new overhead-valve Knucklehead engine.

The prototype 61EL incorporated a refined four-lobed camshaft arrangement and new recirculating oil system, devised by William Harley and patented in 1938.

A couple of late modifications to the Model-61EL's V-twin engine in 1936 were cup enclosures around its valve springs and return oil lines running to the rear of the rocker housing.

The oil tank is horseshoe shaped, and wraps around the battery, stowed neatly between the twin down-tubes of the rear frame.

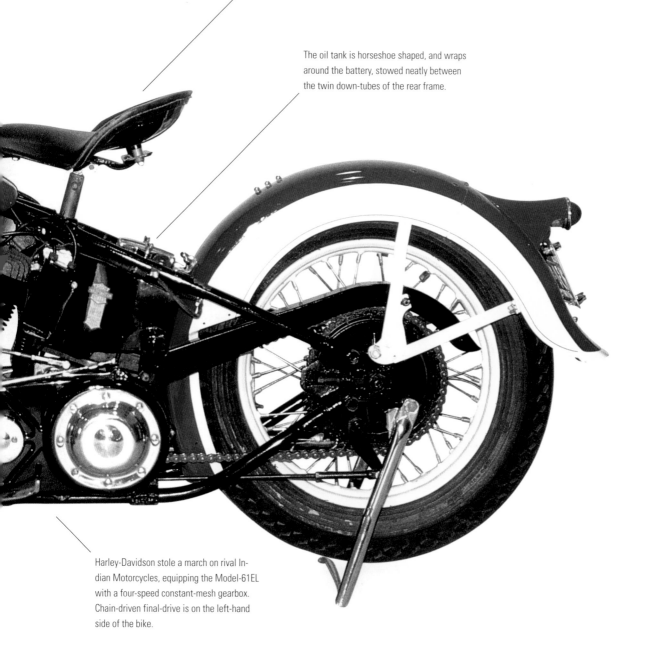

Harley-Davidson stole a march on rival Indian Motorcycles, equipping the Model-61EL with a four-speed constant-mesh gearbox. Chain-driven final-drive is on the left-hand side of the bike.

As Harley-Davidson emerged from the economic gloom of the Great Depression, it came out with a masterpiece. That was the Model-61E range, incorporating the standard 61E, the high-compression 61EL Special Sport Solo, and the medium-compression 61ES with sidecar.

The Model-61E line was introduced in 1936 and powered by the new 61 cu. in. (1000 cc) overhead-valve Knucklehead engine, which developed 40bhp at 4800rpm. Not only did the Knucklehead engine go on to acquire legendary status, but also the 61EL was the first truly modern Harley – the characteristic Harley-Davidson look had arrived. It is still considered by many to be the best motorcycle that the company ever produced, and indeed, historically, one of the best in the world. It also provided the cornerstone of all subsequent Harley-Davidson big twins. Designers of the 61EL were the celebrated bike racer and engineer Joe Petrali, William Ottoway and race engineer Henry Syvertson. The 61EL retained the classic

Below: The Model-61EL was fundamentally a new machine, with the brand new overhead-valve Knucklehead engine at its heart – so-called because of the appearance of the alloy rocker boxes.

Harley-Davidson V-twin architecture with its overhead-valve layout. It ushered in many contemporary design elements, including dry-sump lubrication, a system that was derived from car and motorcycle racing, whereby engine oil was stored in an independently located tank or sump. This enhanced oil flow and reduced the chance of starving the engine during hard cornering. On the EL, the horseshoe-shaped oil tank that would become a regular Harley-Davidson feature was wrapped around the battery. A tough new four-speed transmission was also included, although the shift mechanism remained hand-operated on the left-hand side of the fuel tank, as opposed to the more ergonomically sound foot-operated gearshifts and hand-lever clutches that were starting to appear on some of the more advanced European makes. Final drive was by chain.

Rocker Boxes

The 61EL was based around a low-slung frame and a shapely teardrop fuel tank with bright graphics and chrome fittings. As it came on to the market, customers nicknamed it the Knucklehead, based on the four knob-like bolt housings protruding from the polished aluminium valve covers on the engine's right-hand side. Suspension was by leading-link springer forks, now in chromed molybdenum rather than the previous forged I-beams from the VL, with a friction suspension damper that was fronted by the klaxon horn, plus the patented sprung saddle, of course. The instrument binnacle was located on top of the fuel tank, and, in addition to the shapely front mudguard, the rear one was now styled and given a duck-tail curve at its trailing edge. An art deco style streamlined tail-light was mounted on it as well. The 61EL used drum brakes and rode on colour-coordinated 18in (46cm) interlaced wire-spoke wheels, which were interchangeable front and rear. The control cables ran inside the handlebars,

Above: The Model-61EL was the first Harley-Davidson to feature the chrome-plated tank-top instrument console, flanked by the fuel and oil tank fillers. Speedo reads somewhat optimistically to 120mph.

and a large-diameter headlight, fold-away footboards and Burgess fishtail silencer completed the specification.

Although the 61E was well conceived, early tests revealed an unwelcome propensity to leak oil from the valve train. Petrali and others recommended further development before the model was released to the public, but Walter Davidson insisted that dealers took them. Warranty and service claims were minor considerations throughout the automotive industry in those days, with dealer and customer expected to make do with flawed products and makeshift repairs. However, Petrali and Ottoway worked throughout 1936 and 1937 to fix the leaky valve gear and dealers meanwhile were provided with repair kits. When Joe Petrali quit the company, largely because of its miserly attitudes (such as the premature launch of the EL), and went to work for the enigmatic billionaire Howard Hughes as a flight engineer on the Spruce Goose project, Bill Ottaway became chief engineer after William Harley died in 1943.

By 1939, the 61 cu. in. (1000 cc) Knucklehead EL, with its improved valve-train assembly and modified oiling system, was capable of 100mph (160km/h), as its test riders had confirmed out on the back roads of Wisconsin. It was relatively nimble, well balanced, and nicely finished. Motorcycle clubs were beginning to spring up in the United States, and Hollywood stars of the calibre of Clark Gable, Randolph Scott, Tyrone Power and Robert Taylor rode Harley-Davidson 61ELs. Motorcycling drill teams were also popular, one such being the Motor Maids of America,

a team of uniformed female enthusiasts who entertained the crowds at public functions.

In many ways, the 61EL represented a minor renaissance for Harley-Davidson. Not only was almost everything new about it – only the generator and mudguard styling were carried over from the previous Model-V line – but in the new overhead-valve Knucklehead engine and four-speed gearbox, the bike could take on all comers.

A grand total of 11,000 61ELs were built, around half of which were exported. The machine was joined in 1941 by its larger-capacity sibling, the 74 cu. in. (1200 cc) FL range, and superseded by the Panhead-engined Hydra Glide in 1949. Understandably, original 61EL Knuckleheads from the pre-war years are among the most sought after by classic motorcycle collectors around the world, and immaculate examples can sell for $30,000.

1936 61EL Knucklehead	
Engine model:	Knucklehead overhead-valve V-twin
Engine capacity:	61 cu. in. (1000 cc)
Cases:	Harley-Davidson
Carburation:	Linkert
Air filter:	Diagonal
Ignition:	Points
Pipes:	Two-into-one
Transmission:	Four-speed
Frame:	Tubular cradle, twin down-tube
Suspension:	Front: springer forks, friction damper Rear: hardtail
Brakes:	Drum front and rear
Wheels:	18in (457mm) wire-spoke front and rear
Front wheel	18in (457mm) wire spoke
Front brake	Drum
Rear wheel	18in (457mm) wire spoke
Rear brake	Drum
Mudguards (fenders):	Valanced EL type
Handlebars:	Pull-back
Risers:	None
Headlight:	6in (152mm) Harley-Davidson
Tail-light:	Airflow

Model-WLA (Military)

Twin tail lights and front-mudguard mounted passing light are blacked out for wartime use. Sometimes these bikes also had canvas leg shields and windscreens fitted, as well as the US Army logo on the fuel tank.

The WLA was powered by the 45 cu. in. (738 cc) side-valve V-twin engine, envisaged as cheaper and potentially more robust and reliable than the relatively new ohv Knucklehead unit.

As befits its military role, the Model-WLA carries a set of leather panniers on its luggage rack, and, like other army vehicles, the whole bike is painted khaki drab for camouflage.

Normal features on the WLA include the tool box, kick-start, points case alongside the timing-gear case, and fishtail-type exhaust pipe.

Mostly used for dispatch duties behind the lines, WLA riders had the protection of a 45mm Tommy gun mounted on the forks and mudguard, as well as a trenching shovel if they got bogged down.

Certain modifications apply to this military mount, such as a metal plate under the engine and gearbox, which also protects the exhaust system on rough ground.

It had been shown in the First World War and other conflicts that battlefield mobility and communications were vital for waging a successful military campaign. As war clouds loomed, the United States began to upgrade its hardware, and the WLA was a military version of the WL, fitted with the 45 cu. in. (737 cc) Flathead V-twin engine. It was produced for the US military in the Second World War, and some 80,000 units were delivered. Clearly, you don't go to war on a gloss-painted chromed up machine, and the WLA was finished in khaki for better camouflage. More fundamentally, the US Army's mobilization involved a new divisional structure. Each division was to consist of three independent Infantry Regiments and support units with sufficient motorized transport to move regimental-sized groups. In addition, reconnaissance troops would ride at the front of each division, equipped with trucks and motorcycles. Of the latter, there were eight single motorbikes and three motorcycle combinations per troop. Unlike the German Army, which favoured machine-gun-mounted sidecar outfits, the US Army saw the motorcycle as a modern replacement for the horse, the idea being that the motorcycles would carry the scouts forward to where dismounted reconnaissance could be carried out. This structure was quickly modified as other technology became available. The Jeep, which was introduced in 1941, was active in all theatres of operation, and rivalled the motorcycle in this respect, in a similar way that the Model T Ford had two decades earlier. The bikes became the workhorses of both dispatch riders and military policemen and were in sufficient demand for Harley-Davidson to continue building military motorcycles for the duration of the war.

Favoured Manufacturer

The history of the W-series machines from which the WLA was derived went back to 1937, by which time Harley-Davidson had supplanted Indian as the favoured 45 cu. in. (737 cc) side-valve manufacturer. They were the smallest machines built by Harley-Davidson at the time, and the W-series replaced the R-series, but there were many features in common. Apart from the horizontal fins on the timing case that identified W-series from R-series engines,

Below: The most obvious aspect of the Model-WLA, apart from its drab colour scheme, is the amount of extra weight it has to carry in the shape of luggage and ammunition. The seat is mounted further forward for better balance.

4600rpm, sufficient to propel it to a maximum of 65mph (105km/h), although fully laden, 50mph (80km/h) was more realistic. It was heavy, though, at 576lb (262kg), which was its only drawback in an off-road situation. Otherwise, its reliability, ease of maintenance, strength and simplicity made it an excellent military machine.

Among the other modifications that Harley-Davidson made to the 45 WL to turn it into a war machine were the fitment of 18in (457mm) wheels, which were more appropriate for rough terrain, wide mudguards and a large air filter. The engine was also protected underneath by a large steel sump guard, while the transmission was fitted with an extra-low-ratio bottom gear to make slow, cross-country riding possible. It received special blackout-type lights that made nocturnal forays particularly hazardous, twin tail-lights, a sturdy luggage carrier that could accommodate leather panniers and a military radio, windscreen with canvas fairing, canvas leg shields, and a holster on the front mudguard for carrying a rifle and ammunition. The WLA was also equipped with new synthetic tyres with knobbly treads instead of rubber ones, and the front forks were extended to provide better ground clearance. The cut-

Above: The WLA used the 45 cu. in. (738 cc) side-valve V-twin engine, capable of 65mph (105km/h), given its power output of 23bhp at 4600rpm. Its weight penalty, plus use over uncertain terrain, meant a much more modest rate of progress in reality.

the main difference was the adoption of new styling cues that mimicked the previous year's 61 cu. in. (1000 cc) Knucklehead. The smaller Flatheads now sported teardrop-shaped fuel tanks that had an integrated instrument panel on top, curved mudguards and lavish paint finishes. In addition to the basic W, there were also the WL, WLD, WLDR, WLA and WLC variants.

The months leading up to the production of the WLA were full of tension. Since 1939, when war broke out in Europe, both Harley-Davidson and Indian had received orders from Europe for military motorcycles, as production there had either been halted by bombing or given over to other armaments and munitions. It was supplied to the British Army after the Triumph factory was bombed and production interrupted, and the Canadian military also used a version called the WLC that had a slightly different specification. Based on a tubular cradle frame, the WLA had three-speed transmission with chain drive, and had leading-link front forks with a rigid rear end. This lack of rear suspension was in part compensated for by a large and commodious saddle, positioned further forward than on the regular WL. Power output for the WLA was 23bhp at

Above: In times of hostilities, a WLA dispatch rider in trouble had a 45mm Thompson sub-machine-gun at his fingertips, whilst the bike's front end was further burdened by wartime blackout lighting and an ammunition box.

close replica of the BMW R75, although they were quite different visually. The advantage of shaft-drive was that, unlike a chain, the shaft was enclosed and not so easily compromised by mud and stones. Like the WLA the XA was fitted with a protective guard under the engine and a front mudguard that made it resemble a modern off-road machine. It also had plunger-type rear suspension damping, and the first productionized telescopic forks on any Harley-Davidson. Like the WLA, the XA was equipped with a rifle holster, front and rear racks and saddle bags or field radio. Oddly, the throttle control was via the left-hand twist-grip on the basis that the rider's right hand needed

Above: No top box here. The leather panniers are slung as low as possible off the luggage rack on this military-issue Model-WLA to keep the bike's centre of gravity as low as possible, too. Note the rear stand and blackout rear lights.

down mudguard was also raised to prevent clogging up in muddy conditions. A brass plaque on the top of the fuel tank provided the rider with lubrication details.

When the US Army's orders started flooding in after the Japanese attacked Pearl Harbour in 1941, the company had to rent additional factory space and recruit new workers to cope with increased production. The US military had also been impressed by the performance of BMW's flat-twins used by the German Army during General Erwin Rommel's campaign in the north African desert. The US motorcycle industry was lobbied to come up with something similar, and in 1942 Harley-Davidson responded with the XA 45. Like the BMW, it had a transverse (horizontally opposed), side-valve, 45 cu. in. (750 cc) flat-twin 'boxer' engine, so-called because of the punching motion of the pistons. It featured wet-sump lubrication, requiring no external oil tank, and the fins on the engine block were reckoned to keep the oil temperature far cooler than on the WLA. The XA had a foot-operated four-speed transmission, the company's first foot-shift, a hand-operated clutch, and Cardan shaft. The only Harley-Davidson to have a driveshaft, it was in this respect a

1942 Model-WLA	
Engine model:	Flathead side-valve V-twin
Engine capacity:	45 cu. in. (750 cc)
Cases:	Harley-Davidson
Carburation:	Linkert
Air filter:	Oil bath
Ignition:	Points
Pipes:	Two-into-one with fishtail silencer
Transmission:	Three-speed
Frame:	Tubular cradle
Suspension:	Front: springer forks Rear: hardtail
Brakes:	Drum front and rear
Wheels:	18in (457mm) wire-spoke front and rear
Mudguards (fenders):	Pressed steel, military specification
Handlebars:	Flat
Risers:	None
Headlight:	Military specification
Tail-light:	Twin military lights

to be free to fire his sub-machine-gun. Disappointingly perhaps, the US military's interest in the project evaporated when problems developed with the lubrication system and valve gear, and just 1,000 units were built. A rival shaft-drive prototype from Indian was also dropped.

Another Harley-Davidson derivative that featured in the theatre of war was the 74 cu. in. (1200 cc) side-valve Model-U. Released in 1937 as a replacement for the V-series 74 cu. in. (1200 cc) and 80 cu. in. (1300 cc) twins, its redesigned Flathead motor had a recirculating lubrication system and was mated to a four-speed gearbox, fitted in the 61E Knucklehead frame that came out the preceding year. It was ideal for sidecar work, and, being simple and rugged, was also ideal for military use. Fewer U-series bikes were drafted than WLAs, just 580 units in fact, but they were similarly equipped, with raised mudguards, blackout lights, and the sub-machine-gun and holster. The U-Navy version was appropriately finished in pale grey-blue, and the 74 cu. in. (1200 cc)

Below: Like its civilian counterparts, the army WLA also carried its instrumentation in the binnacle mounted on top of the fuel tank. The only difference was, it was matt olive drab rather than chrome-plated.

model remained in production and in service until the late 1940s.

There was no way of predicting when the Japanese would capitulate, so production was maintained at full capacity. Therefore when the war ended in 1945, Harley-Davidson still had the parts to make 33,000 more machines in its warehouse. Along with the machines abandoned in Europe and the army surplus bikes disposed of by the military, WLAs were sold off to private motorcyclists and were 'civilianized' by their new owners.

Death of the Founders

Sadly, however, all was not well with the founders of Harley-Davidson. The company president Walter Davidson had become seriously ill during the war, and he died in February 1942 aged 65. At first it wasn't clear who would be his successor, and there was a considerable delay before William Herbert Davidson was appointed. He was the son of the vice president William A. Davidson who had died in 1937, and not only was this new president of the Harley-Davidson Motor Company a business management graduate, he was also an enthusiastic motorcyclist, too. More sadness was to follow. In September 1943, another founder, William Harley also died, aged just 63, having had a heart attack in the bar of a Milwaukee club. Harley had been a diligent engineer and technical designer, whose hobbies extended to painting and drawing. His position as chief engineer was taken over by Bill Ottaway at first, and then by his son William J. Harley, who had been his father's assistant for two years. Of the four founders of the Harley-Davidson Motor Company, only Arthur Davidson survived the Second World War. In recognition of an outstanding contribution to the nation, the company was given the 'E Award' by the US Army and Navy for its 'Excellent' services.

WLC Civilianized

When peace returned in 1945, many military-issue machines were converted to civilian spec. This was most simply achieved by a smart paint job and chromium-plating various ancillaries such as exhausts, crash-bars and tool-box cover.

Although the W-series machines were mostly fitted with regular tractor-style seats, they could accept the more ample 'buddy' seat, which could accommodate a pillion passenger.

True to form, the WLC ran with three-speed transmission, with chain-driven final-drive taken down the right-hand side of the bike. At the time, the W-series was the smallest machine that Harley-Davidson built.

The front end of the WLC is adorned with headlight and passing lamps, plus air horn. The decorative running light on top of the front mudguard is a factory optional extra.

The Model-WLC was powered by the 45 cu. in. (740 cc) Flathead V-twin engine, a robust and reliable unit that was ideal in times of post-war austerity, yet could be fixed with army surplus parts if necessary.

The WLC runs with chromed wire-spoke laced wheels, shod with 16 x 5in (41 x 13cm) tyres. They are interchangeable, front and rear, with 8in (20cm) front drum brake.

Above: The WLC in both military and civilian forms used the hand-shift transmission control. The rider pushed it forwards from neutral into first gear, then pulled it back for second and third ratios.

In 1945, in the wake of the Second World War, motor-cycles were in great demand, especially in the United States. For the vast numbers of troops returning home, there were reasons for motorcycle ownership other than purely as a means of transport. Many of the de-mobbed soldiers were still fuelled by adrenaline, and bent on peacetime adventure that would to some degree match the experiences of the past few years. They were fortunate that their needs coincided with the disposal of thousands of redundant military machines. In the aftermath of war, large quantities of military surplus machines, some of them brand new, were sold off to regular riders and this temporarily satisfied demand. The army sold something like 15,000 WLA models with the 45 cu. in. (737 cc) V-twin engine for $450 each, while the much scarcer XA flat-twin machines could be bought for $500. They were also bought by dealers in large numbers, and offered for sale again in their showrooms, either in their military camouflage guise or repainted and fettled according to civilian spec. The Harley-Davidson factory retained sufficient components

to make another 33,000 military WLAs, plus plentiful reserves of spares. These were released as civilian products, and not for another two years could the factory focus on the production of normal stock again.

Peace-time Variants

Meanwhile, apart from the civilianized WL models, there were other peace-time variants of the W-series. One was the WLD Special Sport Solo, a machine with high-compression alloy cylinder heads delivering 25hp and 95mph (150km/h) potential from its 45 cu. in. (750 cc) Flathead V-twin. There was even a racing derivative designated the WLDR. The WLD was understandably quite rare, since its introduction coincided with the switch-over to a war footing. Its factory specification included a valenced front mudguard, plus a new rear light introduced in 1939. It had a rear mudguard that folded up to facilitate removal of the rear wheel, which was reduced in 1940 to 16in (40cm) diameter to improve ride quality. Front and rear wheels

Right: On its flared rear mudguard, the WLC carries the post-war tail-light known as the 'tombstone' because of its characteristic shape. Behind the number plate is the join where the mudguard hinges.

Left: All quirky designs soon get a nickname, and the WLC's instrument binnacle was no exception – it was known as the 'cat's eye' dash because the warning light lenses resembled feline eyes.

were interchangeable. Also that year the WLD received tubular forks, while the new recirculating lubrication system incorporated the oil tank on the left-hand side of the fuel tank. There were thus two filler caps – the oil went in the left and the fuel on the right. The instrument panel was integrated into the top of the teardrop tank as well. On early WL models the tank-top dash panel was known as the 'cat's eye' dash. There was a rear stand, a factory-fitted exhaust guard and a new streamlined tool box within the frame below the saddle. A standard fish-tail silencer was fitted. It came complete with footrests, but chromed safety bars, chrome spotlights and a running light on the front mudguard were optional extras.

Both versions of the WL, military and civilian, used the same three-speed transmission, albeit with different gearing on the military spec bikes, with hand-shift operation, The gear lever was moved forward from neutral into first gear, and back through neutral into second and third.

1942 Model-WLC Civilianized

Engine model:	Flathead side-valve V-twin
Engine capacity:	45 cu. in. (750 cc)
Cases:	Harley-Davidson
Carburation:	Linkert
Air filter:	Pancake
Ignition:	Points
Pipes:	Standard fishtail silencer
Transmission:	Three-speed
Frame:	Tubular cradle
Suspension:	Front: springer forks
	Rear: hardtail
Brakes:	Drum front and rear
Wheels:	16in (406mm) wire-spoke front and rear
Mudguards (fenders):	Stock Harley-Davidson
Handlebars:	Buckhorn
Risers:	None
Headlight:	Chromed WL
Tail-light:	Tombstone

Model-WL

Harley-Davidson motorcycles have always made excellent long-distance touring machines, and tall windscreens take much of the hardship of wind and insects out of it, at the expense of streamlined aerodynamics, however.

Customizing has become a prominent part of Harley-Davidson ownership since 1945, with high-quality paint jobs, chrome accessories, and factory-spec saddlebags, studded and tasselled and redolent of the Wild West.

Back in 1941, the W-series received a new recirculating lubrication system, requiring the oil and fuel to switch sides in the fuel tank – with fuel now poured in on the right-hand side.

Like the rest of the W-series, this 1947 Model-WL is fitted with the 45 cu. in. (750 cc) side-valve Flathead V-twin engine, developing around 25bhp at 4600rpm. It is easily distinguished from the earlier R-series unit by the horizontal ribs on the timing-gear case.

Reverse view

Although the WL's mudguards and fuel tank were like those of its pre-war ancestors, they took on a confident new post-war look. Some components were sourced from newer models to update the bike.

One of the hallmarks of Harley-Davidson motorcycles is their side-stand, a device that hinges forwards from underneath the left-hand side of the frame and, contrary to one's perception, props the bike up quite effectively.

When Harley-Davidson production returned to civilian mode in 1947, the WL models were essentially unchanged from their pre-war incarnation. There were sound reasons for this, and it was common practice at the time throughout the automotive industry as well. The US economy was greatly affected by a wide-ranging economic collapse in war-torn Europe, where even in victorious Britain, food and other necessities were rationed, making the purchase of brand new motorcycles simply out of the question for the majority. Thus, an important market had been temporarily lost to the export-driven US economy. To assist with recovery in western Europe, the US administration elected to give the economy a boost with the Marshall Aid scheme. Part of the solution was to ship significant quantities of North American raw materials such as steel, iron and aluminium to Europe to stimulate industry, while simultaneously lowering import duty on manufactured goods. This had a knock-on effect on US industry, and in order to provide a degree of security, the government guaranteed US producers a supply of raw materials that matched what they had received in the run-up to the war. Manufacturers like Harley-Davidson were hard pressed as it was, unable to concentrate on new lines and having now to face competition from growing numbers of European imports. British bikes in particular were in demand, and in 1946, nearly 10,000 foreign machines were sold in the United States. Ironically, a fair number of newly established importers were former Harley-Davidson employees who were conscious of Milwaukee's weak spots, although a broader spectrum of machines was now available in the United States, which opened up the market and made a wider sphere of potential buyers receptive to motorcycle ownership.

Given limited supplies of raw materials, the collapse of export markets and growing threats from competition in its home market, there was every good reason why Harley-Davidson elected to begin only limited production of its three pre-war models. These were the two 61 cu. in. (1000 cc) and 74 cu. in. (1200 cc) ohv models and the 45 cu. in.

Below: The Model-WL features an extensively chromed front end, with springer front forks, headlight and passing lamps, windscreen stays and mudguard motif. Colour schemes and tank badges change with each model year.

Above: The WL's 45 cu. in. (740 cc) Flathead engine uses a Linkert carburettor with chromed circular air filter, and points housed on the timing cover. This side-valve engine remained in use up to 1972 in the GE ServiCar trike.

(750 cc) with its side-valve engine. Apart from these, the 74 Flathead could be manufactured on request, but no longer appeared in the official range, and the same applied to the ServiCar, various combinations with sidecars and delivery vehicles. Since demand on the motorcycle market exceeded the number of available motorcycles, the factory supplied dealers on a quota basis.

Long-running Engine

The WL of 1947 retained the 45 cu. in. (740 cc) side-valve V-twin that had powered the model on its introduction back in 1937. It wasn't as fast as its chief rival the Indian Sport Scout, but it proved rather sturdier and more reliable. A measure of its dependability was that the 45 cu. in. (740 cc) side-valve engine carried on being fitted to the

ServiCar tricycle right up until the beginning of the 1970s.

The post-war WL came with valenced mudguards and chrome-plated parts like tool boxes, hubs, wheel rims, headlights, silencers, handlebars and crash bars. The dash panel and rear light cluster were redesigned and upgraded to match post-war trends. The tail-light was dubbed the 'beehive' because of its characteristic shape. But while the basic specification of WL models remained the same for over a decade, the tank badging chrome trim and colour schemes were altered each year. One way of ensuring custom without having to go to the major expense of releasing new models was to offer a range of accessories with which to personalize and improve existing model ranges. The expanding Harley-Davidson range of bike accessories extended to leather saddlebags and chrome spotlights in the late 1940s, and it was not uncommon for the WLs to be specified in this way. Particular attention was paid to the accommodation of a pillion passenger so that motorcycling would appeal as a hobby for couples. For example, extended footboards and 'buddy seats' could be ordered, and luggage carrier, panniers and top box could be mounted over the rear wheel.

1947 Model-WL	
Engine model:	Flathead side-valve V-twin
Engine capacity:	45 cu. in. (740 cc)
Cases:	Harley-Davidson
Carburation:	Linkert
Air filter:	Circular, mesh element
Ignition:	Points
Pipes:	Two-into-one, fishtail muffler
Transmission:	Three-speed, chain drive
Frame:	Tubular cradle
Suspension:	Front: springer forks Rear: hardtail
Brakes:	Drum front and rear
Wheels:	16in (406mm) wire-spoke front and rear
Mudguards (fenders):	Valanced steel
Handlebars:	Chromed pull-back
Risers:	None
Headlight:	Chromed 6in (152mm)
Tail-light:	Beehive

Model-61E

Much effort has been spent on this 61E, with its chrome-plated horseshoe oil tank, 'tombstone' rear light, chrome laced wheels, crash-bars and tasselled saddle bags.

The carburettor manifold lies in the V between the pair of cylinder heads, fronted here by the 7in (18cm) diameter chromed circular air filter.

This 61E runs on 16in (41cm) chromed wire-spoke laced wheels, shod with 16 x 5in (41 x 13cm) tyres, while mudguards are typically flared and curvaceous.

The Knucklehead name was derived from the polished nuts visible on either side of the rocker covers and those which retain the rocker arms. They are said to resemble a clenched fist – the pushrod tubes look a bit like the veins in the top of your hand.

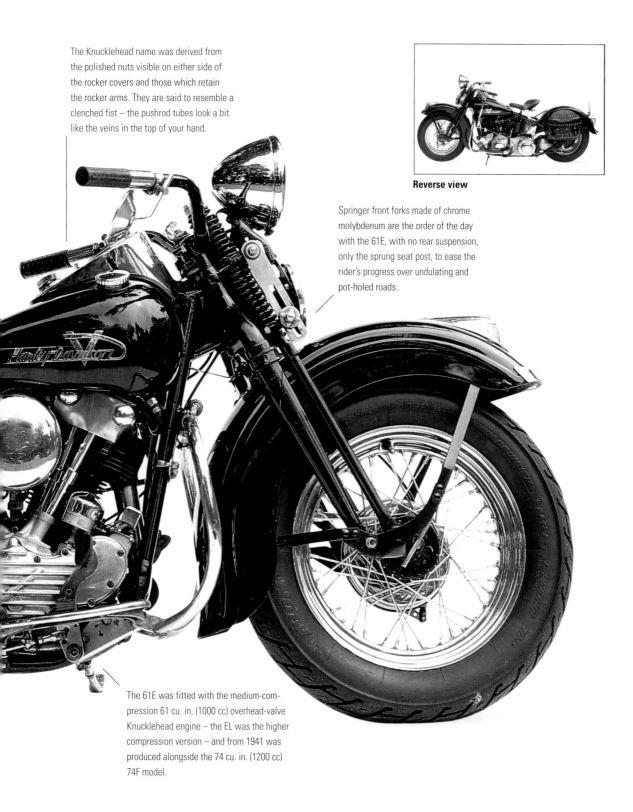

Reverse view

Springer front forks made of chrome molybdenum are the order of the day with the 61E, with no rear suspension, only the sprung seat post, to ease the rider's progress over undulating and pot-holed roads.

The 61E was fitted with the medium-compression 61 cu. in. (1000 cc) overhead-valve Knucklehead engine – the EL was the higher compression version – and from 1941 was produced alongside the 74 cu. in. (1200 cc) 74F model.

Above: The front mudguard (fender) of this 61E is embellished with trim that was very fashionable in the late 1940s. The stock running light resembles the cockpit of a contemporary aircraft and the eagle is a direct piece of Harley-Davidson iconography.

Undoubtedly one of Harley-Davidson's most significant models, the ground-breaking 61E Knucklehead was viewed with some apprehension when it was announced in 1936. Despite the fact that here was Harley-Davidson's first proper production overhead-valve twin, the two more highly evolved big Flathead models were far more readily accepted than the Knucklehead, especially by hard-bitten touring enthusiasts. The new 61E, of which 2,000 units were produced in 1936, was also prone to teething troubles. These centred on its new engine's dry-sump lubrication system, which suffered from leaks, coupled with damage to bearings and problems with valve gear. Although US motorcycle journalists, especially those writing for The Motorcyclist, a magazine closely associated with the American Motorcycling Association, hailed the 61E and its contemporary 61EL and 61ES variants as something special even before the first road test was carried out, dealers and customers were slow to place orders, however, preferring to wait for teething troubles to

be sorted. Nevertheless, there is a school of thought that believes the 61E Knucklehead to have been the saviour of the company, if not the machine that actually put the rival Indian concern out of business.

Economic Recovery

By this time, the US economy, and with it the motorcycle market, was slowly recovering from the widespread economic crisis. It was time to introduce something new. Harley-Davidson's enlarged 80 cu. in. (1310 cc) Flathead engine may have been impressive, but the new Model-61E was a technical sensation. It was a completely new design of engine, with valves suspended in the cylinder head. In this way it was an overhead-valve configuration like the single-cylinder AA and BA models of the 1920s. It also featured a single camshaft arrangement that provided the precedent for the next 60 years of Harley-Davidson big-twin production. The Knucklehead engine's rocker covers had a pair of prominent exposed bolt heads that gave rise to its nickname, because they were reminiscent of the knuckles of a clenched fist. This machine developed 36hp from its 61 cu. in. (1000 cc), which was about twice as much as its predecessor, and provided a top speed of 90mph (145km/h). It was fitted with a recirculating forced lubrication system, which, unlike the total loss system, did not need to be constantly topped up with oil. At last Harley-Davidson was on a par with Indian and certain European manufacturers, who had fitted this system as standard for some time. This recirculating form of lubrication worked on a dry-sump system, based on an oil tank containing about one gallon (4 litres) of oil located beneath the rider's seat. However, it was not just the engine of the 61EL that was new. The same could also be said of its four-speed constant mesh transmission, multiple-disc clutch, sturdy double-loop frame and front forks.

Viewed as one of the best-looking bikes that Harley-Davidson ever built, the 61E Knucklehead featured the teardrop fuel tank incorporating the dash panel, and streamlined mudguards front and rear finished in a choice of five different colour schemes with colour-coordinated wheel rims. The exhaust ended in a Burgess fish-tail silencer, and other neat styling touches included the air-flow tail-light. Crash bars were fitted as standard. It was no lightweight, however, and when fuelled up, the Knucklehead weighed some 600lbs (275kg). Much of the credit for the 61EL was due to Harley-Davidson's development shop under the direction of Bill Harley and Bill Ottaway, while testing and development work had been carried out by Joe Petrali and Hank Syvertson, former stalwarts of the old Harley-Davidson racing team. William J. Harley, the son of the company's founder, had also played a part in test riding it, having also studied engineering at Wisconsin and working as a designer in the factory.

During the late 1930s, the 61E came in three different specifications. The 61E was medium compression, the 61EL was the high-compression Special Sport Solo, and the 61ES ran the medium-compression engine with a sidecar attached. In the autumn of 1940, the sensation for the following season was unveiled. This was a 74 cu. in. (1200 cc) version of the overhead-valve V-twin Knucklehead engine, designated the 74FL, which generated more than 48hp. It was offered alongside the 61 cu. in. (1000 cc) model. The

Below: When production of the 61E resumed after the war, a new instrument binnacle was fitted atop the fuel tank, commonly known as the 'two-light dash' to distinguish it from the earlier 'cat's eye' and later 'three-light' version.

1947 61E Knucklehead

Engine model:	Knucklehead overhead-valve V-twin
Engine capacity:	61 cu in (1000 cc)
Cases:	Harley-Davidson
Carburation:	Linkert
Air filter:	Circular pancake
Ignition:	Points
Pipes:	Two-into-one
Transmission:	Four-speed
Frame:	Tubular cradle, twin down-tube
Suspension:	Front: springer forks Rear: hardtail
Brakes:	Drum front and rear
Wheels:	16in (406mm) wire-spoke front and rear
Mudguards (fenders):	Valanced steel
Handlebars:	Chromed pull-back
Risers:	None
Headlight:	Chromed 6in (152mm)
Tail-light:	Beehive

frame was stronger and the transmission was improved, and wheel diameter dropped from 17in (432mm) to 16in (406mm) to give better ride quality. Cosmetic changes included chromed exhaust pipe covers, a streamlined tool box, boat-tail rear light and a metal tank badge. Harley-Davidson had commissioned the hugely influential Studebaker stylist Raymond Loewy to come up with these enhancements to the machine's visual appeal. Some of his other masterpieces included the Lincoln Continental Derham of 1941, the Studebaker Commander of 1947, and the Studebaker Starliner coupé of 1953. However, the 74F and 61E were virtually suspended as Harley-Davidson production lines geared up for a war footing in 1941; and it was not until 1946 that manufacture of these models resumed in any number. Specification remained unchanged until the advent of the Panhead engine in 1948. There were a few minor alterations, including the tank-mounted instrument panel that was known as the two-light dash in order to differentiate it from the earlier cat's-eye dash. The front mudguard's running light and leading-edge trim were typical emblems from that era, as was the revised tank badge.

Chapter 2

Through Boom to Gloom 1946–1980

In some respects, the post-war period represented the halcyon days of Harley-Davidson, since much of the style and imagery attached to the marque was born in those times. But faced with a tidal wave of foreign imports, especially from Japan, the company was all set to buckle under the strain.

Production of civilian motorcycles resumed at Harley-Davidson after 1945, but only returned to a semblance of normality in 1947, when raw materials became more freely available again. It was the start of an optimistic period in the United States, the time of the baby boomers who would help bring about the company's renaissance in the 1980s. Business flourished, and in 1948 Harley-Davidson sold 31,163 bikes. It was too good to be true, and the home-grown machines began to face serious

Left: One of Harley-Davidson's all-time greats was the 74FLHB Electra Glide, which made its debut in 1965. What marked it out as something special was its electric starter, which meant fitting a larger battery and 12-volt electrical system.

challenges from imported bikes from Europe that were lighter, faster and handled better. They might not have suited the vast distances that a Harley-Davidson could swallow up, but they were an attractive proposition to sports-minded riders. In the face of this competition, Indian Motorcycles bowed to the inevitable and the last machines rolled off the line in 1953. On the other hand, Harley-Davidson preferred to compete head on with the imports, and introduced a range of motorcycles that would take them on.

The Model-K was one such machine, a curious mixture of old and new components. The last 45 cu. in. (740 cc) W-series Flathead was made in 1951, but a new Flathead engine was fitted to the Model-K. It resembled its foreign competitors in styling, with its swing-arm rear-suspension assembly, telescopic forks, foot-shift gear-change and neat compact lines. The side-valve engine was of unit construction but was vastly slower than the imports and, as a result, the Model-KK was developed. A couple of years later, the Model-KH was introduced, with a larger capacity

Below: The 1946 Knucklehead-powered 74FL used the 74 cu. in. (1213 cc) version of the overhead-valve V-twin, with ancillaries including a streamlined tool box, air filter and exhaust benefiting from styling input from design guru Raymond Loewy.

54 cu. in. (883 cc) engine that was capable of 95mph (153 km/h). By the late 1950s, side-valve engines were decidedly old-fashioned and in 1957 Harley-Davidson upgraded the motorcycle to accommodate overhead valves and re-designated it the XL. It was also known as the Sportster, a name still used on Harleys today. The engine had been designed with the Chevrolet slogan in mind, which was 'one horse-power per cubic inch.' The Sportster developed 55hp and weighed just 440lbs (200kg) giving quite a sensational power-to-weight ratio that endeared it to sports-minded customers. From 1958 onwards, the Sportster was known by the letters XLH, and a sportier version was the XLCH.

Panhead Follows Knucklehead

The big V-twin Harleys were also sequentially upgraded. The Panhead superseded the Knucklehead in 1948 but retained the E and F designations for both 61 cu. in. (1000 cc) and 74 cu. in. (1213 cc) models. The Panhead was essentially a new top end on the existing Knucklehead bottom end and, as the nickname implies, its rocker covers looked like upturned cooking pans. The cylinder heads were cast from aluminium after problems with the all-iron Knucklehead, while hydraulic lifters contributed to a quieter running engine and a larger oil pump was used to

Above: Perhaps the three most obvious things about this 54 cu. in. (883 cc) XLH Sportster from 1959 are its rear suspension damper, the alloy primary-drive cover, and the streamlined aluminium fork nacelle housing the headlight.

improve lubrication. Upgrades did not end there, though. In 1949 the springer forks were replaced by hydraulic telescopic units on the Hydra Glide, the rigid frame was improved to swingarm rear suspension on the Duo Glide and the electric start that appeared in 1965 saw the big twin renamed the Electra Glide.

The Panhead engine gave way to the Shovelhead in 1966 and once again it was a new top end on an existing crankcase. The new engine became known as the Shovelhead because the rocker covers bore a resemblance to the backs of shovels. Most of the models had designations that started FL, with bikes such as the FLH, FLT and FLHB. The Shovelhead was to take Harley-Davidson through the 1970s and the years of AMF ownership.

By the mid-60s Harley-Davidson's share of the US domestic motorcycle market had contracted considerably, and it soon became clear that Harley-Davidson would go the way of Indian unless it received a substantial injection of capital. After negotiating with various potential buyers, Harley-Davidson was bought by American Machine and Foundry (AMF) on 7th January 1969. The takeover was not an entirely happy affair, beset by job losses and walkouts over quality-control issues. Despite these difficulties, the early 1970s were boom years for motorcycle sales and the AMF-controlled company was able to increase production considerably.

AMF has been frequently criticized for its style of ownership, but if AMF had not bought out Harley-Davidson, the company would not have survived. In 1971, a new Harley-Davidson emerged – the FX Super Glide. This was a Shovelhead equipped with an alternator and with the slimmer Sportster front end. In many ways it was the first factory custom model and was also an attempt to compete with the unauthorized chopper-builders who thrived on customizing the dresser-style machines. There was a succession of FX models, including the FXE, FXWG, FXDG, FXR, EXEF and FXB. Despite the popularity of the new model with Harley-Davidson enthusiasts, the 1970s belonged to the new generation of Japanese superbikes that effectively sank the British motorcycle industry. AMF began to reconsider its involvement in Harley-Davidson.

FL Hydra Glide

This FL model is fitted with a factory-option 'buddy' seat, capable of carrying rider and a pillion passenger. Grab-handles are fitted for the pillion, with extra support from a pair of sprung supports to the frame tubes.

The livery of this Hydra Glide is relatively restrained, with an absence of coachlines and two-tone paintwork, and just a subtle trim on the front mudguard. The tank-badge was liable to vary from year to year.

The FL Hydra Glide ran on 16in (41cm) wire-spoke laced wheels, shod with 16 x 5in (41 x 13cm) tyres. The front drum brake was 8in (20cm) diameter.

The FL was the high-compression version of the 74 cu. in. (1200 cc) big twin, and was the company's best-seller during the early 1950s. This 1953 model is fitted with the height-adjustable windscreen and tinted lower section.

The FL Hydra Glide was introduced in 1949, ushering in the new hydraulically damped front suspension forks in place of the long-serving springer variety. At a stroke, Harley-Davidsons embraced modernity.

The FL came with the new Panhead engine, which was equipped with larger rocker covers intended to prevent the oil leaks that had dogged its Knucklehead predecessor. They were so-named because they resembled upturned cooking pans.

The FL Hydra Glide was the first Harley-Davidson to be fitted with hydraulic telescopic front forks, instead of the springer leading-link forks that had taken the pot-holes in their stride since 1907. There was still no rear suspension, and the Hydra Glide relied on the massive springing of its saddle for rider comfort. In this case the bike is fitted with a 'buddy' seat that is sufficiently capacious to accommodate a passenger, who is provided with grab handles. Introduced in 1949, the Hydra Glide came in two versions, the 61 cu. in. (1000 cc) and 74 cu. in. (1200 cc), both based on the Panhead engine that had appeared a year earlier. By the standards expected of Harley-Davidson there was not too much wrong with the Knucklehead, apart perhaps from excessive engine noise and oil leaks. The introduction of the Panhead engine changed all that. They took the bottom end of a Knucklehead and grafted on a revised top end, which incorporated fully enclosed valve gear with fully hydraulic valve lifters. The effect was to render the engine quieter and cleaner, and cut down on maintenance. The new aluminium cylinder heads were crowned by large pan-shaped rocker covers from which the new engine derived its name. Not only did they look like upturned skillet pans, they acted like oil pans too, in that the pressed steel rocker covers were lined with felt and sealed by an alloy collar and secured to the cylinder

Above: This Hydra Glide is fitted with period panniers and a dual exhaust system, with chromed lockable tool box and a more efficient mellow-tone muffler, which came out in 1950.

head by a series of screws. The golden fluid was thus safely retained. A third cylindrical shape, the 7in (175mm) diameter chromed air filter located between the cylinder V supplemented the cooking pan analogy. However, even the Panhead had its teething troubles. In the initial running phase it sometimes happened that the oil pump did not build up enough pressure to ensure that the hydraulic pushrods functioned, resulting in rattling valve gear and a drop in performance due to altered timings.

Larger Engine Casings

The Panhead was generally a neater looking engine than the Knucklehead, and it remained in its 1948 configuration until 1955 when larger engine casings were used. Both capacities - the 61 cu. in. (1000 cc) and 74 cu. in. (1200 cc) – were available as medium- or high-compression versions, and the 61 cu. in. (1000 cc) was phased out in 1953. By 1951, the 74FL had become Harley-Davidson's best-selling model, with more than 6,000 units invoiced that year. Helping to quieten down the staccato V-twin, a new

silencer called the Mellow-Tone was fitted from 1950, while an optional foot-shift and hand-lever clutch were available in 1952. The revamp of 1955 to the Panhead engine meant that the hydraulic lifters that had originally been located in the cylinder head were placed beneath the pushrods, and a camshaft with different timings was used. The big twin was also available on request with foot-operated gear change and hand clutch instead of the tank gearshift and foot clutch that had previously been the norm. With this new Panhead, the ohv twin at last became a reliable, robust and powerful engine, which the company proudly compared on its 50th anniversary in 1953 to the contemporary V8 engines of the automobile manufacturers Ford, Chrysler and General Motors.

A little earlier, Harley Davidson had acquired the premises of a propeller maker, A.O. Smith, on the edge of Milwaukee,

thus doubling factory capacity. They were now turning out the best part of 30,000 motorcycles a year, and the company tried to match the competition with improved quality and by employing a strict policy on dealerships. To provide protection against corrosion, the steel parts of the bike were subjected to the Parker Process, a form of protection devised by Edward Parker in premises that were rented from Indian. In addition, Harley dealers were required to swear allegiance to the Harley-Davidson marque and promote the company image. They were even forbidden to maintain or repair other makes of motorcycle in their workshops, and in a bid to get rival machines off the road, they were encouraged to take in a part-exchange machine that very often they were saddled with. The factory line was the purist pursuit of traditional motorcycling American style, and indeed, it was a view that appealed to many motorcyclists,

who were keen to uphold American tradition and support US industry. However, an event of far-reaching importance for motorcycling in the United States and the motorcyclist's image in general was just around the corner.

The General Clubmen's Meeting

The General Clubmen's Meeting was held for the first time on 4th July 1947 in Hollister, California; it's an event that now takes place on an annual basis. Back then, more than 4,000 motorcyclists gathered there, and among them was a relatively small group of outlaw bikers made up of the Booze Fighters and the Pissed off Bastards of Bloomington (POBOBS), bent on creating anarchy. Street races and heavy drinking were commonplace among this hardcore pack, and although some 47 arrests were made, it required the presence of 500 police officers to augment the regular five-man squad to keep matters in check. The incident was to an extent exaggerated, and the only photograph was the shot of a single rider sprawled on his Harley-Davidson outside Johnny's Bar and Grille on San Benito Street, raising a bottle of beer in salute and surrounded by empty beer bottles. Most likely, these

Above: The 'buddy' seat was an optional extra for those wishing to carry a pillion. This one has extra springs and grab-handles, and is decorated with western-style fringes and concho studs.

were props, probably placed there for effect by the San Francisco Chronicle photographer Barney Peterson, who got there too late to record any of the real brawling. The 'rider' may not even have been the bike's owner. At any rate, the photo was featured on the cover of Life magazine accompanying a detailed report on the outlaw clubs. The events at Hollister served to arouse a largely unjustified prejudice against motorcyclists, and had the effect of promoting the outlaw clubs – of which there were a growing number – as a haven for the dysfunctional and dropouts. The machine of choice for these types was the Harley-Davidson big twins, which were relatively plentiful and had the attributes of sturdiness and reliability that imports did not have. It became fashionable, particularly in California, to strip the machine of extraneous hardware and replace cycle parts with lighter-weight items. This was carried out both for visual impact and to make the bikes handle better and go faster. These machines were known as 'bobbers'. On the other hand, the members of straight motorcycling clubs went in the opposite direction, and added copious accessories to their machines, and indulged in chrome-plated fests and flashy paint schemes. These bikes became known as 'dressers', and were accessorized with panniers, wind-shield, crash bars and extra head- and spot-lamps. The outlaw ethics ran totally contrary to Harley-Davidson company policy, and dealers and service outlets were forbidden to work on so-called outlaw machines, Harley or not. The effect was the establishment of scores of alternative workshops that specialized in bobbers and provided a haven for this particular clientele. It was the beginning of a tributary of the Harley-Davidson movement from which would spring the significant elements of the company's volume production from the 1980s onwards.

Below: The Panhead engine was available in two capacity sizes – 61 cu. in. (1000 cc) and 74 cu. in. (1200 cc) – and as a medium- or high-compression unit, although the smaller engine was dropped in 1953. Kick-start was still the old-fashioned pedal.

1953 FL Hydra-Glide	
Engine model:	Overhead-valve Panhead V-twin
Engine capacity:	74 cu. in. (1200 cc)
Cases:	Harley-Davidson
Carburation:	Linkert
Air filter:	Circular chrome
Ignition:	Points
Pipes:	Right- and left-hand two-pipe system
Transmission:	Four-speed
Frame:	Tubular cradle frame
Suspension:	Front: telescopic forks Rear: hardtail
Brakes:	Drum front and rear
Wheels:	16in (406mm) wire-spoke front and rear
Mudguards (fenders):	Valanced FL-type, pressed steel
Handlebars:	Dresser
Risers:	None
Headlight:	9in (229mm) chrome and visor
Tail-light:	Tombstone

At the time the Hydra-Glide was taking off, the company's sales were set against a backdrop of domestic optimism as the US economy was taking off. On the world stage, as far as the United States were concerned, the Korean War began in 1950. In 1952 Dwight D. Eisenhower was elected 34th president, and the following year the Korean War came to an end. It was succeeded by the Vietnam War, which the United States became involved in in 1955. Unlike earlier conflicts of the 20th century, this was predominantly a war characterized by jungle fighting, where the helicopter was more influential than a motorcycle could possibly be. There was little scope in trying to win military contracts to supply motor bikes here.

Harley-Davidson was to lose its last remaining founder as 1950 drew to a close. Somewhat ironically, on 30th December a motorcyclist travelling at high speed strayed on to the wrong side of the road and crashed head-on into an oncoming car occupied by Arthur Davidson and his wife. They were thrown from their vehicle and died of their injuries. Arthur Davidson had shepherded Harley-Davidson through difficult times, and his successor as general sales manager was his nephew, Walter Davidson Jr.

KH900 Sportster

An important introduction inherited by the Model-KH was the swing-arm rear suspension and shock-absorber or damper. The sprung seat post for the saddle was retained.

The oil tank on the KH Sportster was located below the saddle and ahead of the damper on the right-hand side of the bike, while the matching battery case was on the opposite side.

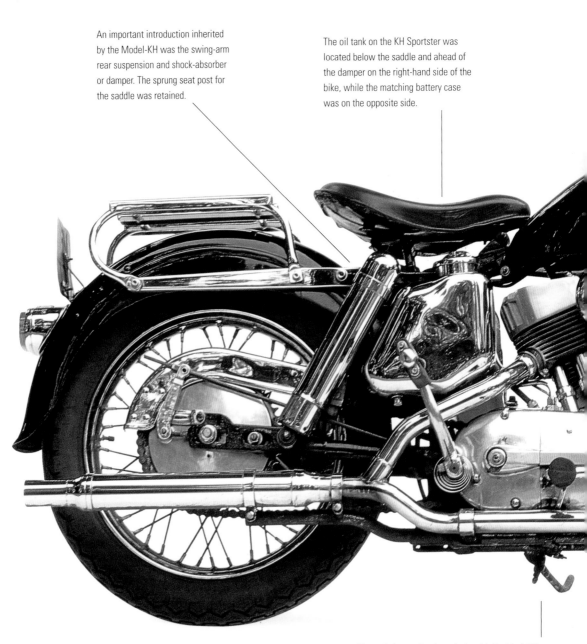

The main innovation brought in with the Model-K was the unit-construction engine and gearbox, now manufactured as a single casing.

The K-series machines that evolved into the Sportster model were fitted with smaller 4.5-gallon (20.5-litre) fuel tanks, too small for the instrument dash, which was relocated to the handlebar clamp.

Reverse view

The large, 9in (23cm)-diameter headlight blended well with chromed shrouds of hydraulically damped front forks.

In 1954, the KH Sportster was fitted with the bored-out 54 cu. in. (883 cc) version of the earlier 45 cu. in. (738 cc) Model-K's side-valve V-twin engine.

They say that racing improves the breed, and in 1952, the 45 cu. in. (738 cc) Model-K Roadster benefited from improvements to Harley-Davidson racing machines. The forerunner of Harley-Davidson's Sportster series, its main features were a four-speed transmission, which was located in a joint housing with the engine's crank mechanism (a layout known as unit construction), cast alloy cylinder head, hydraulically damped telescopic forks as on the Hydra Glide, and rear wheel swing-arm suspension. The Model-K was based on a cradle frame, with drum brakes, optional crash bars, steel mudguards and a hand-lever clutch and right-side foot-shift. It ran on 19in (483mm) wheels that were taller and narrower than normal. A smaller fuel tank meant there was not enough space for the dash panel, so on later models the speedo was housed in a bracket attached to the handlebar clamp.

The Model-K's comfortably sprung chassis was a concession to the spirit of the age, but powered as it was by an obsolete side-valve V-twin engine, which in principle dated back to the 1920s, the Model-K did not prove an instant success. By now though, even conservative US

Above: The Model-KH was pitched against some strong competition from British imports, and its single leading-shoe front drum brake gave it stopping power to match the opposition.

motorcyclists demanded more performance from their machines, and the Model-K was sadly underpowered. The evidence of what was possible was on display in the import showrooms. So, to give the motorcycle at least an acceptable level of performance, the cubic capacity was increased two years later by lengthening the stroke, from 45 cu. in. (738 cc) to 54 cu. in. (883 cc), to become the KH900 model. Now this really was the most significant advance in the Harley-Davidson product line since the Knucklehead. The KH900 was a realistic response to the influx of British twins from BSA, Triumph and Norton, also incorporating new flywheels, cylinder barrels, and a new clutch. It was in production from 1954 to 1956, when it was superseded by the Model-XL, the first of the Sportster series. The 54 cu. in. (883 cc) engine capacity is the same as for Sportsters in the early 21st century.

Return to Motorcycle Racing

Although it had run a factory race team in the distant past, namely the Wrecking Crew of around 1917, Harley-Davidson had kept out of racing until the late 1940s. Part of a new marketing strategy was to increase its involvement in motorcycle sport. The dealers were called to Milwaukee and encouraged to increase their sponsorship, while the factory also announced that it would be increasing production of the WR racing machine and asked dealers to do everything possible to prevent foreign marques dominating. As far as the AMA's regulations were concerned, Harley-Davidson was still able to exert a powerful influence, and promising sport bikes such as the Ariel Red Hunter and the Triumph

1956 KH900 Sportster

Engine model:	Side-valve V-twin
Capacity:	54 cu. in. (880 cc)
Cases:	Harley-Davidson
Carburation:	Linkert
Air filter:	Circular chrome
Ignition:	Points
Pipes:	Two-into-one
Transmission:	Four-speed, unit construction
Frame:	Tubular cradle
Suspension:	Front: telescopic forks Rear: swing-arm and dampers
Brakes:	Drum front and rear
Wheels:	Front: 19in (483mm) wire-spoke Rear: 18in (457mm) wire-spoke
Mudguards (fenders):	Pressed steel KH
Handlebars:	Buckhorn
Risers:	None
Headlight:	9in (229mm) chrome
Tail-light:	Stock Harley-Davidson

Speed Twin were prevented from competing with the side-valve Harley-Davidsons by clever additions to the rules. Road races on asphalt were dismissed as too dangerous, despite the fact that they were commonplace in Europe, so European manufacturers could be expected to have an advantage when it came to expertise. For the next two years the formula worked. Harley-Davidson riders won 19 out of 23 victories in the 1948 national championship races, and in 1949 it took 17 out of the 24 first places in the championships. Only the victory of a Norton ridden by Billy Matthews at Daytona ended the run of Harley-Davidson victories in 1950 and plunged the race department into feverish activity. A new, more competitive racing machine had to be developed.

Harley-Davidson had not been blind to the shortfall in performance of the Model-K when it was first released. Their racing involvement ran to the construction of a variant called the KR, which appeared at the same time

as the Model-K itself. However, its engine was still the outdated side-valve little twin, and victories proved elusive. It took until 1954, and required the assistance of the tuner Tom Sifton, before Harley-Davidson rider Joe Leonard regained the national championship, which was held that year for the first time according to a new AMA points scheme. The KR engine possessed all the tweaks known to the competition world, including bigger valves, high lift cams, race bearings, polished ports and cylinder head. Races were staged on a variety of surfaces, so the KR was available with either sprung or hardtail frame. For a dirt-track racer, for example, the suspension and brakes would be omitted. But a black-top speedway machine, such as the KRTT of 1961, was fully equipped. The KR used alloy rimmed spoke wheels, with block-tread race tyres screwed on for safety. The primary drive cover was in pressed steel rather than aluminium. Riders who enjoyed success racing the KR during the 1950s and 1960s included Brad Andres, Joe Leonard, George Roeder, Roger Reiman, and the legendary Carroll Resweber, who won almost every race he entered and secured the championship for Harley-Davidson from 1958 to 1961, until he suffered a bad accident in 1962.

Below: The KH side-valve V-twin was the first of the unit-construction Harley-Davidson engines with 54 cu. in. (883 cc), and the Sportster has remained at that capacity ever since.

FL Duo Glide

When Harley-Davidson fitted rear suspension to the Electra Glide's tubular cradle frame in 1958, the bike was renamed the Duo Glide – a reference to its two suspension systems.

The power-unit for the FL Duo Glide was the 74 cu. in. (1213 cc) Panhead big-twin, which had been uprated in 1955, allied to four-speed transmission with chain-driven final drive on the left-hand side.

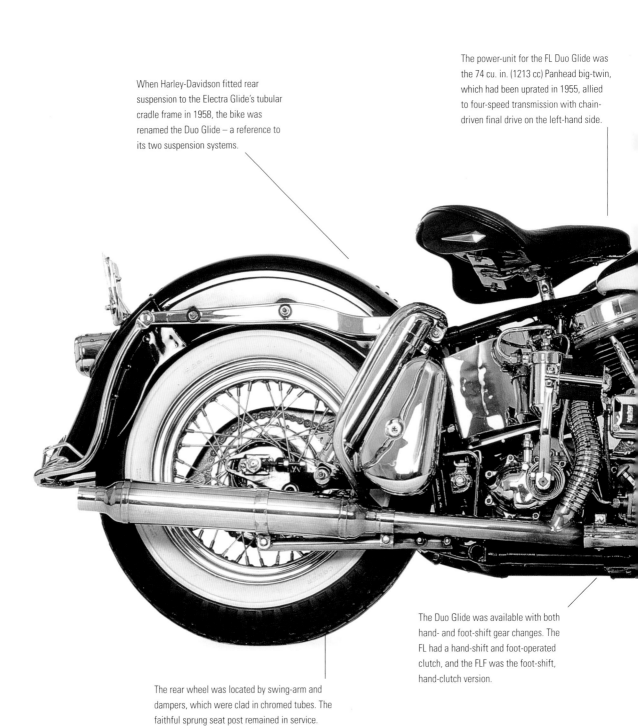

The Duo Glide was available with both hand- and foot-shift gear changes. The FL had a hand-shift and foot-operated clutch, and the FLF was the foot-shift, hand-clutch version.

The rear wheel was located by swing-arm and dampers, which were clad in chromed tubes. The faithful sprung seat post remained in service.

Reverse view

The FL Duo Glide was bedecked with a plethora of chromed ancillaries and accessories, including the mudguard bars, exhaust muffler, tool-box cover, air filter and klaxon air horn.

While items like the crash bars, spot-lights and mudguard embellishments were optional factory-made accessories, the foot boards, stand and tool box were normal fitment.

As the 1950s wore on, Harley-Davidson's big V-twins had built up a reputation for torquey comfortable touring machines. But there was still something lacking in the comfort department, in spite of the heavy-duty saddles. So in 1958, the Hydra Glide, which until then still had a rigid rear frame, was endowed with hydraulically damped rear swing-arm suspension, and became known as the Duo Glide. The name came from the fact that it had two sets of suspension. There were two levels of specification. The FL Duo Glide was the medium-compression version, while the FLH was the high-compression model. This designation had been introduced in 1955 for the top-of-the-range models following the overhaul of the Panhead motor. The low-compression E and F base models were dropped at this point. A more efficient block resulted in increased horsepower, and the H in the title showed that the heads had polished ports and Victory camshafts that gave another ten percent more power. The FLF designation showed that the bike had a foot-shift gearchange, otherwise the FL had a hand-change set-up. All FL variants used the tubular cradle frame and were based on the 74 cu. in. (1213 cc) ohv Panhead engine, which, in the case of the

FLH, delivered some 55bhp at 7200rpm via a four-speed transmission. Top speed was 100mph (160km/h), and the task of hauling the weighty beast down from these speeds was now carried out by a single drum at the front and a hydraulically operated cast-iron brake at the rear.

The FL Duo Glide proclaimed its identity via a chrome badge on either side of the front mudguard bars. It was slap in the middle of the chrome-plated era, when the entire automotive industry was preoccupied with chrome, fins and jet fighter styling cues. The Duo Glide sported many chromed items including the rear shock absorber cases, grab rail for the passenger, leg shields, forks, headlamps, air horn and sundry engine components like the silencer and horseshoe oil tank. The chromed wheel rims were complemented by white-wall tyres, another hallmark of the 1950s. There was a new streamlined cast alloy headlamp nacelle, and the instrument binnacle still resided on top of the fuel tank. Optional extras included

Below: The hand-shift gear lever on the left-hand side of the fuel and oil tank indicates that this Duo Glide is an FL model, with foot-operated clutch.

special two-tone paint schemes, windscreens, mirrors, and stylish fibreglass rear panniers, so that by the turn of the decade hardly any two Harleys looked the same. Owners showered their mounts with accessories, either specified with their order or as aftermarket extras, and bikes thus equipped came to be known as 'dressers'.

Indian Closes Its Doors

Meanwhile, there was one less threat to Harley-Davidson's hold on the big-twin market. Its seminal rival, Indian, the only US manufacturer to have challenged Harley-Davidson's dominance in the US motorcycle market, closed its doors for the last time in 1953. Indian had produced V-twins (and big fours) along similar lines to Harley-Davidson, and sometimes more audaciously, since 1901. Its last offering, the Chief, from 1953 was not so different visually from a contemporary Hydra Glide. The Indian name was bought in the late 1990s, first by an Australian, then a Canadian businessman, bent on introducing a new V-twin powered Indian Chief. Back in the era of the Hydra Glide, Harley-Davidson was facing stiff competition

Above: Now that the Duo Glide had rear suspension, with the chrome-sheathed damper prominent here, the teardrop-shaped tool box was re-orientated in a vertical position.

1958 FL Duo Glide	
Engine model:	Overhead-valve V-twin Panhead
Engine capacity:	74 cu. in. (1200 cc)
Cases:	Harley-Davidson
Carburation:	Stock Harley-Davidson
Air filter:	Circular chrome
Ignition:	Points
Pipes:	Two-into-one
Transmission:	Four-speed
Frame:	Tubular cradle
Suspension:	Front: telescopic forks
	Rear: swing-arm and dampers
Brakes:	Drum front and rear
Wheels:	16in (406mm) wire-spoke front and rear
Mudguards (fenders):	Valanced pressed steel FL
Handlebars:	Dresser
Risers:	None
Headlight:	9in (229mm) chrome and spotlights
Tail-light:	Stock Harley-Davidson

from Europe, but what was to confront them from Japan could not even have been guessed at. The Japanese two-wheeled assault was at first couched in softer tones. An advertisement from 1953 in the November edition of the motorcycle magazine Cycle carried the copy-line: 'You meet the nicest people on a Honda'.

By contrast, Harley-Davidson riders were not considered to be the nicest people by the average law-abiding American, and the company's image was still suffering as a result of the Hollister outrage and the long-running backwash it produced. The outlaws' bikes were by this time known as 'choppers', which was apt because they often looked as though parts had simply been chopped off in the stripping down process. It was not exactly beneficial to the Harley-Davidson image that many Harley-Davidson riders liked and copied these choppers and the macho image of the outlaw, without in fact belonging to this shady group. Significantly, these mobile desperadoes were known in the 1950s as 'bikers', a name by which almost every motorcyclist likes to be known today. Gradually the term 'custom bike' began to be applied to the bikers' individually prepared machines, as they were custom-made by a backyard specialist or by the customer himself.

FLH Electra Glide

This 1972 FLH model is fitted with the Shovelhead version of the 74 cu. in. (1200 cc) V-twin. The engine is so-called because from the right-hand side of the bike, its rocker boxes resemble inverted shovel blades, viewed end on.

While accessory-bedecked machines were known as 'dressers', some bikes were kitted out for touring with top-box, matching panniers, and bulbous fairing with windshield up front.

The battery for the FLH Electra Glide is carried beneath the upper frame tube, concealed behind the square chromed box. The oil tank is located in the corresponding position on the other side of the bike.

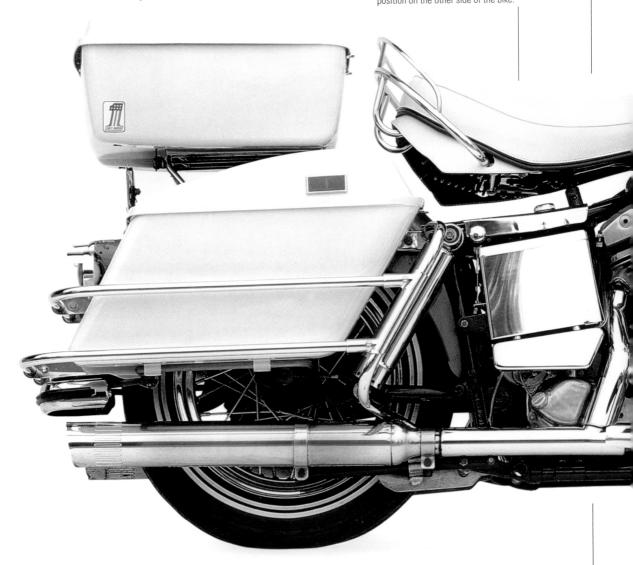

Probably the best-known of all Harley-Davidson models, the Electra Glide was announced in 1965. It got its name because it was equipped with an electric starter, a year after the facility was tried out on the GE ServiCar trike. Early models retained the kick-start.

Reverse view

This Shovelhead engine has nine black cooling fins, indicating that it's the 74 cu. in. (1200 cc) version and not the 80 cu. in. (1312 cc) model, which had ten cooling fins.

One of the distinctive hallmarks of the Shovelhead V-twin, introduced in 1966, was its oval air filter, known as a ham-can and invariably chrome-plated. Behind it lurks the carburettor.

Right: The dual saddle, as applied to this FLH
Electra Glide, has underlying springing, but still
relies on the solitary sprung seat post. The rider
is obliged to adopt a somewhat elevated riding
position with the seat so far forward.

In the mid-1960s Harley-Davidson was
struggling to defend itself against the
growing pressure of competition from
Japanese and British imports. At this
point it had three models in its range
with the two Sportster versions and the
Duo Glide. It was time to join the high-
tech party and, following the ubiquitous
Japanese examples, the Duo Glide
was given an electric starter in 1965,
and from then on it was known as the
Electra Glide. The push-button electric
starter was first fitted on the ServiCar
tricycle in 1964 and after it proved to be
reliable, the system was installed on the 74FL. As part of
the improvements to the 74 cu. in. (1213 cc) motorcycle,
and more specifically to run the starter motor, the electrical
system was converted from 6 volts to 12 volts, necessitating

Below: This particular motorcycle still retains its original factory-
fit Goodyear tyres, complete with their dual white-wall bands. The
chromed disc-brake cover and mudguard bars were typical extras of
the period.

Above: By the time this machine was built, the company was in the hands of AMF (American Machine and Foundry), whose logo was displayed on the timing gear case of the Shovelhead engine, now fitted with an alternator rather than a dynamo.

a redesigned oil tank that was moved to the left-hand side of the bike. As a precautionary measure, Harley-Davidson continued to fit the kick-start lever for a limited time, just in case the bike's electrical system failed. On the FLH model the hand-shift was optional up to 1973, which had the foot-clutch on the left hand side and the shift lever on the left-hand side of the tank. The front-brake lever was on the left-hand side of the handlebars, and the electric start button was on the right. The tubular steel cradle frame was unchanged from the previous Duo Glide, but the power output of the 74 cu. in. (1200 cc) Panhead engine was boosted from 52hp to 65hp at 5400rpm by changing the timing and increasing the compression, although this added considerably to the engine's vibrations. The Electra Glide used the tried and tested hydraulically damped telescopic forks and a rear swing-arm system that invariably featured a chromed damper case. Again, lashings of chrome were applied, and the exhaust silencer often featured a Cadillac-style fin, and the air cleaner, battery box, front forks, wheel rims and crash bars were also fitted to improve the product. They revised the 74 cu. in. (1200 cc) big twin with a view to a further increase in power output, designing new cylinder heads with new ports and more compact combustion chambers that contributed to higher compression. In addition, they installed new camshafts that made for longer valve opening sequences, and a year after its introduction, the Electra Glide was fitted with this new engine. In customary fashion, it was named after the shape of its revised rocker box covers, which

were seen as resembling the up-turned blade of a shovel. It was an engine that would see the company through to 1984. Electra Glides built after 1966 were fitted with Shovelhead engines.

Ownership Profile

The model was immortalized in the 1973 movie Electra Glide in Blue, featuring Robert Blake as an Arizona Highway Patrol Officer. This was post Easy Rider, but further proof, if any were needed, that the Harley-Davidson was well established as a household icon. Nowhere was it better exemplified than by the contemporary TV programme Happy Days, featuring Harry Winkler as the Fonz, an improbable dumbed-down rocker who rode a Harley-Davidson. There are few other machines that can claim to appeal to such a wide disparity of people. The contrasts are startling – from the hard-bitten cop to the Hell's Angel, the dirt-track racer to the flamboyant dresser brigade. Go into any Harley-Davidson dealership, and a cross-section of humanity will most likely be there.

1972 FLH Electra Glide	
Engine model:	Shovelhead
Engine capacity:	74 cu. in. (1200 cc)
Cases:	Harley-Davidson
Carburation:	Stock Harley-Davidson
Air filter:	Harley-Davidson oval
Ignition:	Points
Pipes:	Two-into-one, left and right silencers
Transmission:	Four-speed
Frame:	Tubular cradle
Suspension:	Front: telescopic forks
	Rear: swing-arm and dampers
Brakes:	Front: single disc
	Rear: drum
Wheels:	16in (406mm) wire-spoke front and rear
Mudguards (fenders):	Stock FLH
Handlebars:	Dresser
Risers:	None
Headlight:	9in (229mm) Harley-Davidson with visor
Tail-light:	Stock Harley-Davidson with spotlights

FX Super Glide

Rear suspension was by swing-arm and coil-over damper shock absorbers, while the bike was fitted with a regular dual seat that placed the pillion's weight over the rear wheel.

The power-plant for the FX Super Glide was the Shovelhead V-twin, with 74 cu. in. (1213 cc) capacity sufficient to produce 65bhp at 5400rpm. The cone cover for the alternator came out in 1970.

One aspect of the FX Super Glide that lent a hard edge was its kick-start lever. This meant that the bike needed a smaller battery as there was no electric starter.

A combination of Sportster and Electra Glide, the FX Super Glide of 1971 was the brainchild of Willie G. Davidson. It blended the comforts and running gear of the big-twin with the raw edge of the Sportster.

Drum brakes were fitted front and rear, with a chrome cover over the master cylinder for the back brake.

The chopper-look of the FX Super Glide was achieved partly by fitting a larger diameter 19in (48cm) laced front wheel and using raked Sportster front forks.

Like many home-built choppers, the FX1200 introduced in 1971 was a hybrid machine. This one, however, had genuine factory provenance, as the FX appellation was sourced from the 'F' of the FLH Electra Glide and the 'X' from the XLH Sportster. Thus, it was a straight cross between the two earlier models. It had the character of a stripped-down 61 cu. in. (1000 cc) twin with the telescopic forks and front wheel of the Sportster, but without the electric starter, and foot pegs rather than ungainly footboards.

Left: The FX1200 combined the rakish stance of a Sportster with the refinements of the Electra Glide, plus the big-twin's 74 cu. in. (1200 cc) Shovelhead motor.

Below: For one year only – 1971 – the FX Super Glide was equipped with the boat-tail design incorporating the round rear light. The glass-fibre dual seat unit combined the rear mudguard and was devised by Harley-Davidson's golf-cart division.

Inspiration and backing for the new model came from William (Willie) G. Davidson, who worked in the Milwaukee design office. In contrast to his hard-edged predecessors – and, indeed, most other members of the Harley-Davidson management at that time – Willie G. blended artistic sensitivity with considerable technical ability. A keen rider himself, he was wont to wear biker leathers or jeans in public, attending biking events and race meetings where he would happily chat with riders and potential customers. As a result, he was well aware of what motorcyclists thought and what kind of bikes they wanted. And that was something with a raw edge to it, hence the chopperesque attitude of the bike. The FX Super Glide became a success and, as well as spawning the FX series, it was – if you discount 'race replicas' – the originator of the 'factory custom' genre. In an attempt to cash in on the Easy Rider type of lifestyle, the company advertised the FX Super Glide as the 'All-American Freedom Machine'.

Dealer Dismay

Behind the up-beat imagery, all was not going so well at the factory. In 1972, the production lines at the Juneau Avenue plant were updated and output rose from 30,000 units in 1970 to more than 70,000 in 1973. As volumes increased, however, price tags went up in the showrooms, much to the dismay of Harley-Davidson's dealers. Build quality suffered and warranty claims were rife; to make matters worse, the company handed the problem to dealers, who became responsible for final pre-delivery checks, meaning that the dealer had to honour any warranty claims. The issue was exacerbated when the AMF management began to weed out dealerships that were felt to be operating below Harley-Davidson standards, in terms of showroom, workshop premises and location. Those that did not comply were axed, resulting in a spate of anti-AMF feeling and the removal of the AMF logo that adorned Harley-Davidson bikes from 1971.

Dismayed by the changes within the company, some of the older Harley-Davidson workforce opted for early retirement and, in 1971, William J. Harley died, aged 58. Vice president Walter Davidson Jr left the company the same year, disgruntled at having to toe the AMF line.

The FX Super Glide may have opened up a new market for Harley-Davidson, but the company was still struggling against the foreign competition that was swamping the burgeoning motorcycle market; by 1973, its market share had fallen to below six percent. Unable to tolerate AMF policies any longer, company president William H.

1971 FX Super Glide	
Engine model:	Shovelhead
Engine capacity:	74 cu. in. (1200 cc)
Cases:	Harley-Davidson
Carburation:	Stock Harley-Davidson
Air filter:	Ham-can
Ignition:	Points
Pipes:	Two-into-one
Transmission:	Four-speed
Frame:	Tubular cradle
Suspension:	Front: Sportster telescopic forks Rear: swing-arm, coil-over dampers
Brakes:	Front: single leading shoe drum Rear: drum
Wheels:	Front: 19in (483mm) wire-spoke Rear: 17in (432mm) wire-spoke
Mudguards (fenders):	Front: Sportster Rear: Harley-Davidson custom boat-tail
Handlebars:	Buckhorn, chromed
Risers:	Integral with bars
Headlight:	Sportster
Tail-light:	Circular, integral with tail fairing

Davidson also resigned in 1973. His successor was AMF's own man, John H. O'Brien, and, for the first time in its existence, Harley-Davidson was headed by an outsider.

AMF then invested heavily in converting a former munitions factory in York, Pennsylvania, for chassis manufacture. For the foreseeable future, engines and gearboxes would continue to be made at Milwaukee and plastic parts at the Tomahawk plant.

The FX Super Glide evolved along with the rest of the model range, keeping close to the trends introduced by customizers and one-off dealer specials. Fundamentally a stripped-down Electra Glide shorn of its touring kit, the FX Super Glide was always powered by the stock 74 cu. in. (1200 cc) factory engine. Succeeded by the FXE with electric starter from 1974, which itself gave rise to the FXS1200 Low Rider in 1977, the FX line ran out in 1978. From this point, the Super Glide line-up branched out in all directions into Wide Glides, Fat Bobs, Sturgis and Super Glide II. Willie G. Davidson's vision had been acute.

FLH Shovelhead Custom

Further customizing is revealed by the 7in (18cm) diameter Screamin' Eagle circular air filter cover, plus crash bars that bear the impact in the event of a spill.

The lines of the Fat Bob fuel tank and the chrome-plated instrument binnacle dash are almost as timeless as Harley- Davidson itself. The badges fitted are circa 1965, while the dash is 1970s.

By 1976, when this bike was manufactured, the tractor saddle had long since been dispensed with. However, the owner has chosen to return to the traditional type of seat in the interests of a retro look.

Although this machine is an Electra Glide, it also has a kick-starter. The cone-shaped timing gear case indicates this is the post-1970 AC alternator Shovelhead engine.

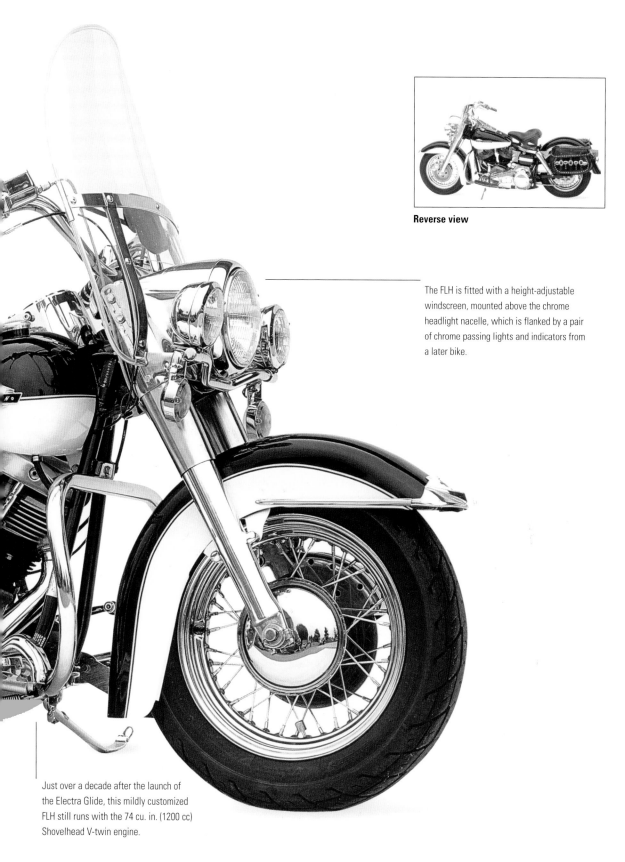

Reverse view

The FLH is fitted with a height-adjustable windscreen, mounted above the chrome headlight nacelle, which is flanked by a pair of chrome passing lights and indicators from a later bike.

Just over a decade after the launch of the Electra Glide, this mildly customized FLH still runs with the 74 cu. in. (1200 cc) Shovelhead V-twin engine.

In cash-strapped times, Harley-Davidson resorted to improving its existing product, since developing completely new models was out of the question. It was a formula that always worked very well for the British sportscar maker Morgan, which, even in the 1990s was building its wood-framed cars more or less as they had been made in the mid-1930s. That's how their customers wanted them, traditionally hand crafted and with traditional looks. Harley-Davidson's customer base was not dissimilar. So, as much to empower the ever-increasing bulk of its big Electra Glide cruisers as to appease a market now accustomed to ever-changing Japanese designs, the archaic 1937 EL engine went through yet another incarnation and received its third cylinder head. Viewed horizontally, the cast-alloy rocker boxes on the revised cylinder heads looked like the top edges of a pair of shovels, and that was what the engine was called – the Shovelhead. It had the desired effect, being cleaner, quieter, more efficient and a bit more powerful

than the Panhead. The new cylinder heads were based on those of the Sportster. Until 1970, the bottom end of the Shovelhead was virtually identical to its predecessor, and then the electrical system went over to alternator from generator. The changeover dispensed with the external four-finned timing case and the forward mounting position of the generator, and instead, Shovelheads post 1970 had a smaller cone-shaped timing gear case. Because of the easy interchangeability and availability of parts, many early Shovelheads were upgraded to alternator spec.

When the Shovelhead was young in the late 1960s, Harley-Davidson's corporate affairs took a dramatic turn for the worse, compounded by the lack of a lucrative export business, which, having previously flourished, had never recovered after the Second World War. In the 1968 financial year, exports accounted for a meagre three percent. The management saw that joining forces with a larger, healthier concern was the only means of saving the company. Two companies showed an interest in such a merger, and they were AMF, the American Machine and Foundry Company, which began by making railway rolling stock, and the Bangor-Punta group. Apart from producing

Below: The rear quarters of this mildly customized FLH Electra Glide include chromed rear suspension damper case, twin slash-cut exhaust pipes, chromed oil tank, and leather saddle bags.

Above: The front brake calliper fitted to Harley-Davidsons of the AMF era in the 1970s was also used on aircraft, although the actual front brake disc was introduced as late as 1971.

industrial machines for a wide range of commercial applications, both companies were into manu- facturing leisure equipment, including boats, sports equipment and camping requisites.

Soaring Share Prices

Meanwhile, Bangor-Punta was buying up all the Harley-Davidson shares it could get hold of in order to achieve a majority shareholding as quickly as possible, which had the effect of causing the Harley-Davidson share price to soar. However, company president William H. Davidson advised shareholders to accept AMF's offer. It may have helped that AMF's president Rodney Gott was a time-served Harley rider. The scheme was to allow a tax-free exchange of Harley-Davidson shares against AMF shares, whilst retaining the existing management. Part of the deal was that they would also be permitted to work independently. The plan was accepted by shareholders, and AMF officially took over Harley-Davidson for $21.6m on 7th January 1969. The company structure remained largely unchanged, in order to maintain continuity. William H. Davidson remained president, William J. Harley was vice president and head of engineering, and Walter Davidson Jr was second vice president and head of sales. The third generation of the founding families was already rep-resented within the management by the president's two sons, John A. Davidson and William G. Davidson.

Thankfully, Harley-Davidson had been saved, but AMF soon began a critical analysis of the family business and uncovered numerous aberrations in its running. The introverted management consisted almost entirely of members of the founders' families, who had risen to key positions whether they were qualified or not. The Juneau Avenue plant in Milwaukee was still an outdated pre-war factory, but modernization had been out of the question as it would have meant securing a loan from a commercial bank, a course of action the company's management had repeatedly rejected. The prevailing marketing plan was based on the idealized notion of a traditional motorcyclist such as the member of a dresser-riding touring club. This vision eliminated all but a perceived elite group, and alienated the custom fraternity even though custom bikers were the staunchest Harley-Davidson cult members. The AMF programme began with an advertising campaign to promote Harley-Davidson motorcycles, and a modernization of plant and equipment was put in hand, with a far-sighted plan to increase production and sell the bikes with new strategies.

1976 FLH Shovelhead	
Engine model:	Shovelhead overhead-valve V-twin
Engine capacity:	74 cu. in. (1200 cc)
Cases:	Harley-Davidson
Carburation:	Screamin' Eagle
Air filter:	Screamin' Eagle
Ignition:	Points
Pipes:	Slash-cut over-and-under
Transmission:	Four-speed
Frame:	Tubular cradle
Suspension:	Front: telescopic forks Rear: swing-arm and dampers
Brakes:	Front: single disc Rear: disc
Wheels:	16in (406mm) wire-spoke front and rear
Mudguards (fenders):	Valanced pressed-steel FLH-style
Handlebars:	Dresser
Risers:	None
Headlight:	9in (229mm) nacelle mounted
Tail-light:	Harley-Davidson with blue dot

XLCR Café Racer

The XLCR's tubular cradle frame differed from normal Harley-Davidson practice in having a triangulated rear section derived from the XR750 race bike.

The traditional hue for the Café Racer was mean-and-moody gloss black, with the exhausts in matt-black. The tank badge was the Harley-Davidson bar-and-shield dating from 1910.

Launched in 1977, the XLCR Café Racer was a deliberate attempt to cash in on the long-established fashion for racing between hostelries and bars, and incorporated styling cues from XR race bikes.

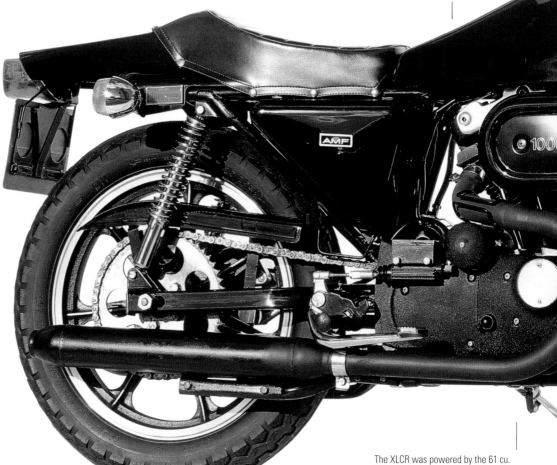

The XLCR was powered by the 61 cu. in. (1000 cc) version of the Shovelhead V-twin, displaying the capacity on its ham-can air filter cover. A siamesed twin exhaust system was fitted.

Reverse view

Flat handlebars were fitted, with the
headlight contained in a bikini fairing
with tinted screen and clocks behind. The
elongated, sculpted fuel tank had a 4-gallon
(15-litre) capacity.

Up front were Kelsey-Hayes twin disc
brakes allied to a Morris seven-spoke
19in (48cm) aluminium alloy wheel.
Telescopic forks had chromed shrouds.

Above: The XLCR was equipped with a race-inspired solo seat, although a dual saddle was available. The rear coil-over damper unit was located close to the back axle, with rear disc brake and Morris alloy wheel prominent.

Conveniently, the initials XLCR sound like Excelsior, which harked back to the long-running British make of the same name, but more pertinently to Excelsior-Henderson, another American icon that went bust in the Depression. In truth, the XLCR had nothing to do with any product emanating from Excelsior – the reality lay in the CR of its designation. That stood for Café Racer. Launched in 1977, the XLCR was an obvious extension of the Sportster concept, a retrospective take on the type of machine beloved of the tearaways who literally raced from café to café, not in search of refreshment, but for kicks.

It was the inspiration of the shrewd Willie G. Davidson, who doubtless had some personal experience of the genre. The Café Racer was a stripped-down road bike, with much time and money lavished on tuning the engine and making it look as mean as possible, not unlike the XR flat track race bike. In fact, the XLCR might have looked the part, but its 61 cu. in. (1000 cc) Shovelhead V-twin power-unit was completely standard. It was the bike's frame and

siamesed exhaust system that were new; otherwise it was a pastiche. Building an authentic Café Racer generally involved its creator many minor hassles, so the XLCR was a convenient means of achieving the look without the tears.

The XLCR was finished in brooding black, with the company's bar-and-shield logo from 1910 riveted on the 4-gallon (15-litre) fuel tank. The engine was also finished in crinkle-effect matt black and its size – 61 cu. in. (1000 cc) – was identified on the battery cover. The shape of this item was defined by the triangulated rear frame section that was derived from the XR750. The oil tank on the left-hand side was tucked in, thanks to this frame design. The XLCR used the four-speed transmission with chain drive, and was good for 105mph (170km/h). A shortened racing mudguard was fitted at the front, while the back end consisted of a fibreglass moulded tail piece, which also served as a mudguard, and a rectangular rear light. The single headlight was shrouded by a bikini fairing, while the rider crouched behind a tinted screen and grasped the flat handlebars. The foot pegs were also set further back than normal. Part of the secret of the XLCR's appearance lay in the lowered handlebar height and positioning the seat further back. It came with a solo saddle, although a dual seat was available. The upside-down forks were chromed, and there was a box-section swing-arm at the rear, while the coil-over damper lower mounting was located close to the axle. An oil cooler was fitted to the front of the frame, and twin Kelsey-Hayes front discs retarded its progress as the next bar sign appeared. The whole effect was set off by smart, contemporary Morris seven-spoke alloy wheels, 19in (48cm) diameter at the front and 18in (46cm) at the rear.

York Factory

In the grand scheme of things, meanwhile, IBM launched the personal computer (or PC) in 1981, and the former film star Ronald Reagan was elected 40th president of the

United States. Harley-Davidson was still not yet out of the woods. Back in 1973, in order to expand and improve production, the AMF group spent millions converting an ammunition factory in York, Pennsylvania, to the requirements of motorcycle production. The idea was also that it would circumvent disputes with a frustrated workforce at Juneau Avenue. In 1974, Harley-Davidson announced that part of the manufacturing process would move from Milwaukee to York, and henceforth only engines and transmissions would be produced in Milwaukee. The plastic componentry would continue to be made in Tomahawk, while chassis production and final assembly would be carried out in York. Parts coming from Milwaukee and Tomahawk would be transported to York in the company's own trucks. Things did not go according to plan. Straight away, the York plant was hit by a three-month long strike, terminated by substantial wage rises. Harley-Davidson also suffered from the world oil crisis of 1974, which affected sales and caused transport costs to escalate. To maintain profitability it was necessary to exploit the production capacity and hike the price of the bikes. Neither of these measures was good for quality or the marketability of the machines, especially in the face of dynamic Japanese competition. In 1975, Honda came out with its top tourer, the 61 cu. in. (1000 cc) shaft-drive Gold Wing, powered by a flat-four water-cooled engine fed by four carburettors, developing 80bhp at 7000rpm. Bizarrely, the fuel tank was under the seat, and the dummy tank contained the electrics, but it was the opening salvo in a barrage of evolutions that would go the whole distance in the fight with Harley-Davidson for top tourer.

In the mid-1970s, even Highway Patrol officers, who had traditionally been equipped with Harley-Davidsons, were now getting astride Kawasakis on the basis that they were faster, more reliable and cheaper. Both Honda and Kawasaki established bridgeheads in the United States, as factories on US soil exempted them from import restrictions. By contrast, Harley-Davidson was unable to bring out new models and sales figures continued to fall. In 1976, a total of 61,000 units were produced, including the limited-edition machine released to mark the United States' bicentenial. But by 1977, output had fallen to 45,000. Along with the XLCR Café Racer, Willie G. Davidson introduced the Super Glide. He came up with the Low Rider, too, which was so-named because of its extremely low seat and custom styling. It turned out to be very popular, which was also true of the XLCR . This motorbike was not produced in great numbers, however, and by 1979 it had been dropped. Some 3,200 units were made, and it has become very collectable in recent times.

Above: Much of the XLCR's Shovelhead engine, including barrels and primary-drive cover, was finished in crinkle-effect matt black, with the redesigned oil tank (right) in gloss black. Foot-shift and foot-peg are at bottom right.

1978 XLCR Café Racer

Engine model:	Shovelhead overhead-valve V-twin
Engine capacity:	61 cu. in. (1000 cc)
Cases:	Harley-Davidson
Carburation:	Stock Harley-Davidson
Air filter:	Black Racetrack oval
Ignition:	Points
Pipes:	Siamesed two-into-one
Transmission:	Four-speed
Frame:	Tubular cradle
Suspension:	Front: telescopic forks Rear: swing-arm and coil-over dampers
Brakes:	Front: Kelsey Hayes twin disc Rear: disc
Wheels:	Front: 19in (483mm) Morris seven-spoke cast-alloy Rear: 18in (457mm) Morris seven-spoke cast-alloy
Mudguards (fenders):	Front: racing type Rear: integral with tailpiece
Handlebars:	Flat-track
Risers:	None
Headlight:	Fairing-mounted
Tail-light:	Integral with tailpiece

Renaissance and Respectability 1980–2001

The fight back to respectability and a return to the company's true identity and independence began with a management buyout in 1981, with a consolidation of production and workforce. Before long, Harley-Davidson was embraced by a vast new market of wealthy middle-class motorcyclists.

The solution for a bemused AMF was the appearance of a determined management buyout. In 1981, a group of 13 senior Harley-Davidson executives, led by Vaughn Beals, raised $100m and bought the company from AMF.

The Harley-Davidson renaissance was not without its difficulties. Between 1980 and 1982, it had to lay off some of its workforce, and the management appealed to the government to increase tariffs on imported Japanese motorcycles of over 43 cu. in. (700 cc). The Reagan

Left: The FXSTD Super Glide of 2000 came with Harley-Davidson's Softail rear suspension system, which was subtly concealed within the frame to give this lean, retro model the appearance of a classic hardtail chassis.

administration imposed tariffs of up to 50 percent on any Japanese imports and the president visited a Harley-Davidson plant and posed on a Harley.

As the yuppie brigade embraced the Harley-Davidson in its acquisitive search for traditional icons of respectability, the company's turnaround was assured. In 1983 another new engine was announced. It was officially called the Evolution but was soon dubbed the Blockhead, in the tradition of identifying an engine by the shape of its rocker covers. It is now more generally referred to as the Evo. The Evolution engine was to be Harley-Davidson's salvation, and by 1984 many of the laid-off workers were re-employed. Market share had increased and the company was in profit for the first time for three years.

Below: The shapely XL883C model for 2000. The bike, like many other Harley-Davidsons, gets its name from its engine size, 883 cc (53.9 cu. in.). The engine is actually the smallest capacity in the Harley-Davidson line-up.

The first XL Sportster was a 54 cu. in. (883 cc) V-twin, although by the early 1970s there was a 61 cu. in. (1000 cc) version available in a whole range of models such as the XL, XLCH, XLT and XLX. It remained in production until the introduction of the Evolution-engined Sportsters in 1986. The Sportster was redesigned in 1978, receiving a new frame, although the engine did not change until 1986. At this point, the Evolution-engined Sportster arrived as a 54 cu. in. (883 cc) machine. The range was extended with the addition of a 67 cu. in. (1100 cc) model, with capacity later increased to 74 cu. in. (1200 cc). Transmission was upgraded from four- to five-speed to make the best of the improved engine. The Evolution power-unit was a much improved Shovelhead engine, using alloy cylinder barrels and heads that made for better cooling than the iron and alloy combination of the Shovelhead. Quality control, oil consumption and frequency of maintenance were all factors that received improvement, and all the big twins benefited from the new engine. The range was extended

Above: As well as extending the product range in the cruiser niche market, the water-cooled V-Rod of 2001 was expected to attract a new kind of customer to the Harley-Davidson brand, as it came bristling with new technology and production firsts for the company.

in 1984 with the introduction of a new model, the Softail. These machines were based on a new type of frame, which had the appearance of a classic rigid hardtail chassis, but included hidden rear suspension. The retro look was also applied to the Softail Springer and Softail Custom. The Springer was fitted with anachronistic springer forks, while the Custom was got up to look as if it had after-market parts and paint schemes applied to it.

New models came thick and fast. Alongside the Softail range came the FXR series. The R suffix signified a rubber-mounted engine and a redesigned frame, and this was followed in 1991 by the Dyna Glide and the FXDB Sturgis. Then came the Bad Boy, which was as close as the factory could come to building an authentic chopper. All are based around the 80 cu. in. (1340 cc) Evolution engine, which could be the final air-cooled Harley-Davidson engine, as emissions regulations could require liquid-cooled engines in the future. In the late 1990s Harley-Davidson ran a liquid-cooled race bike – the VR1000.

The VRSCA V-Rod

In July 2001, Harley-Davidson launched its most radical motorcycle for years, the VRSCA V-Rod, and ushered in a new family of performance cruiser motorcycles. The V-Rod was powered by Harley-Davidson's first ever water-cooled engine, known as the Revolution. Developed by the Harley-Davidson Powertrain Engineering team in Milwaukee, in association with the German sportscar makers Porsche AG, the Revolution was the street-legal version of the VR1000 engine. The 60-degree 67 cu. in.(1130 cc) V-Twin could rev freely to the 9000rpm red-line and produced 115bhp at 8250 rpm, with 74 lb-ft of torque available at 7000rpm. That made it comfortably the most powerful production Harley-Davidson engine ever made. It also had an all-new 5-speed gearbox and electronic fuel injection system. The styling was unmistakably Harley-Davidson, with long, dramatic lines giving the V-Rod a dragster look. It used a silver powder-coated perimeter frame and aluminium body parts, running on solid aluminium disc wheels, complemented by a two-into-one-into-two big-bore exhaust that produced that distinctive Harley-Davidson sound-effect.

XR 1000

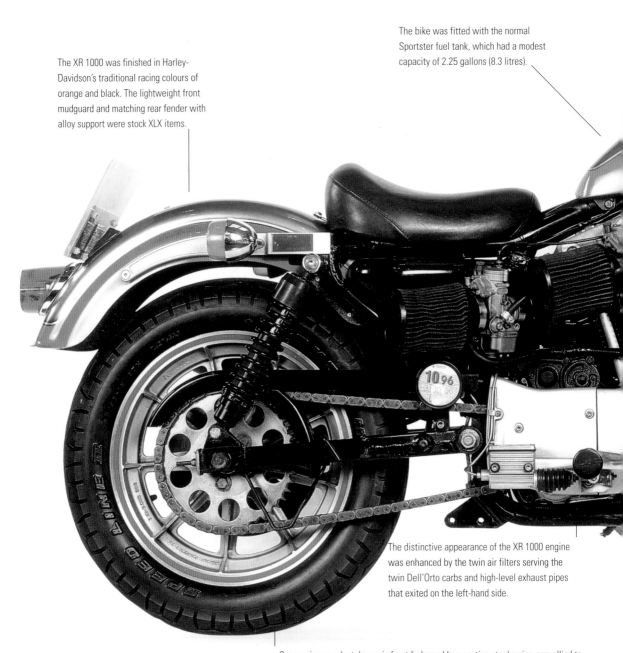

The XR 1000 was finished in Harley-Davidson's traditional racing colours of orange and black. The lightweight front mudguard and matching rear fender with alloy support were stock XLX items.

The bike was fitted with the normal Sportster fuel tank, which had a modest capacity of 2.25 gallons (8.3 litres).

The distinctive appearance of the XR 1000 engine was enhanced by the twin air filters serving the twin Dell'Orto carbs and high-level exhaust pipes that exited on the left-hand side.

Suspension was by telescopic front forks and box-section steel swing-arm allied to coil-over-damper shock absorbers at the rear.

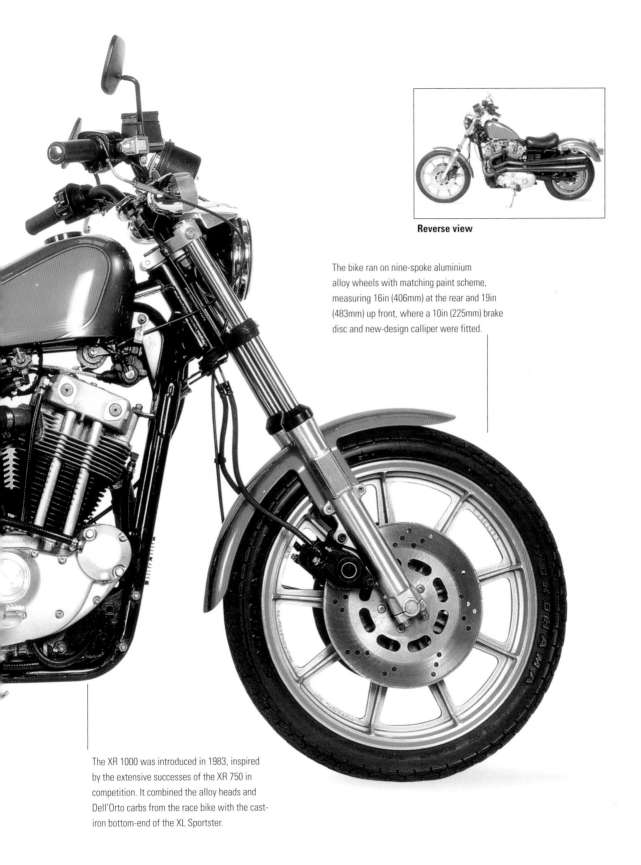

Reverse view

The bike ran on nine-spoke aluminium alloy wheels with matching paint scheme, measuring 16in (406mm) at the rear and 19in (483mm) up front, where a 10in (225mm) brake disc and new-design calliper were fitted.

The XR 1000 was introduced in 1983, inspired by the extensive successes of the XR 750 in competition. It combined the alloy heads and Dell'Orto carbs from the race bike with the cast-iron bottom-end of the XL Sportster.

Above: The XR 1000 was equipped with race-bred alloy heads and cast-iron barrels fed by a pair of Dell'Orto carburettors with stumpy conical K&N air filters that were angled back on the right-hand side.

The XR 1000 was basically a racing machine engineered and produced for road-going use. It was built up around Sportster XL 1000 cycle parts and XR 750 racing componentry. The XR 750 ranks as one of the most successful competition machines ever made, going back to 1970 when it appeared with cast-iron barrels and heads that proved a dismal failure.

In 1972 the XR 750 was relaunched with an aluminium alloy top end, and, confusingly, the rear cylinder of the 45 cu. in. (748 cc) V-twin had a rearward facing inlet port and forward-facing exhaust port. Both air filters emerged behind the rider's right leg, while the high-level exhausts passed up the left of the bike. It was good enough to win the AMA Grand National Championship in its first year, and continual upgrades have kept it in the podium limelight ever since. Gary Scott won the US championship

in three consecutive years – 1975, 1976 and 1977 – and Jay Springsteen was victorious in 1978. These wins undoubtedly carried more weight in the United States than any world championship title.

At this time, Harley-Davidson offered two different versions of the XR 750 for competition riders, one intended for dirt-track racing and a faired version specially set up for racing on black-top race circuits. The XR 750 is to this day acknowledged to be one of the best dirt-track machines ever produced, and the results are there to prove it. However, the XR 750 was more famous – even if it was not widely recognized for the model it was – as the mount of daredevil stunt rider Robert 'Evil' Knievel, who even starred in a movie about his exploits, Viva Knievel, in 1977. The cast extended to such Hollywood stars as Gene Kelly, Leslie Nielsen and Lauren Hutton. A man whose fearlessness was matched only by his capacity to absorb personal physical damage, Evil Knievel used his XR 750 to leap over vehicles in Las Vegas car parks and other similar scenarios. He graduated to a rocket-powered trajectory over the Snake River Canyon, descending somewhat anticlimactically via

Above: The no-nonsense dash of the XR 1000 with speedo and rev-counter is mounted on the steering head. Ancillaries such as indicators, mirrors and the front brake master cylinder are attached to low-level bars.

a parachute, and his association with Harley-Davidson was subsequently terminated after an alleged assault on a colleague involving a baseball bat.

Practicality on the Street

The XR 750 continued to work its magic on the track, however, and by 1983 it looked like it would also be a good bet as a production machine. Harley-Davidson decided that the best way to go was to produce a hybrid that would render the racer more practical on the street. The result was the XR 1000, which consisted of the alloy cylinder heads and twin Dell'Orto carburettors from the XR 750 mated with the cast iron cylinders and bottom end of the XL 1000 Sportster, and fitted in the chassis frame of the XLX model. It was a spectacular-looking machine, with the twin Dell'Ortos and stumpy K&N filters angled back on the right-hand side, a small 2.25-gallon (8.3-litre) Sportster fuel tank, and paired high-rise exhausts exiting, of necessity because of the placement of the carbs, on the left-hand side of the bike. Finished in cool slate grey or orange and black racing livery, it came with a solo race seat as standard, minimal front mudguard, nine-spoke cast-alloy wheels and twin 10in (225mm) front brake discs with a new calliper. This package was good enough

to improve on the standard Sportster performance by ten percent, and was frequently tuned to elicit still more grunt. This could be achieved most simply by applying the manufacturer's tuning kit, which cost a cool $1000, but was said to double the power output. The XR 1000 was a successful race bike too, with Gene Church winning the Battle of the Twins for three successive years at Daytona in 1984, 1985 and 1986, on a modified 112bhp version. It also had the distinction of being the first Harley-Davidson to cover the drag-strip quarter mile in less than 13 seconds. Although such successes ensured that Harley-Davidson products retained a high profile, the XR 1000 itself failed to inspire at the time, probably because its complicated specification meant it was considerably dearer than most other Harley-Davidson Sportsters. Controversially, some claim the 120mph (190km/h) XR1000 to be the best machine that Harley-Davidson ever made, and it certainly commands a premium on the classic market.

1983 XR 1000	
Engine model:	Overhead-valve V-twin (XL 1000 bottom end, XR 750 heads)
Engine capacity:	61 cu. in. (1000 cc)
Cases:	Harley-Davidson
Carburation:	Two XR 750 Dell'Orto
Air filter:	Two K&N
Ignition:	Points
Pipes:	XR 750 competition-type
Transmission:	Four-speed
Frame:	Tubular cradle
Suspension:	Front: telescopic forks Rear: swing-arm and coil-over dampers
Brakes:	Front: twin discs Rear: single disc
Wheels:	Front: 19in (483mm) cast-alloy nine-spoke Rear: 16in (406mm) cast-alloy nine-spoke
Mudguards (fenders):	XLX
Handlebars:	Flat-track
Risers:	None
Headlight:	Sealed beam
Tail-light:	Stock Harley-Davidson

FLST Heritage Softail FLST

The Heritage Softail look incorporates the 4.5-gallon (15.9-litre) Fatbob fuel tank, with the classic flared fenders front and rear giving the bike a timeless appeal.

Although the crankshaft and bottom end were identical to the old Shovelhead engine, the Evolution motor was sufficiently dependable for doubts about reliability to be quashed.

The powerplant is the Evolution version of the 80 cu. in. (1312 cc) big-twin, topped by three-piece alloy rocker boxes covering hydraulic tappets. The engine got its name on account of the new heads, cylinders, flat-top pistons, carb and electronic ignition.

The traditional image of the hardtail cradle frame was endorsed by the fitment of a single retro-look tractor-style saddle.

As well as the tasselled handlebar grips, the FLST has chrome by the shovelful, including horseshoe oil tank, tool-box cover, primary and secondary drive covers, air-filter cover and seat-mounting brackets.

The FLST Heritage Softail was a model from the Electra Glide range, fitted with the concealed Softail rear suspension system that gave the machine the appearance of a rigid hardtail frame.

Post AMF, things changed quite radically at Harley-Davidson. After it became acknowledged by Harley-Davidson that its customer base encompassed several denominations of rider types, the company began to produce machines that paid lip-service to different persuasions. For those bikers who hankered after the 'good old days' – before the advent of such comforts as rear suspension damping – the Softail look was introduced in 1984 with the FLST Softail joining the retrospective Heritage series.

The FLST Softail looked uncannily like a 1950s machine on account of the fact that it appeared to have no rear suspension. This look was achieved by taking a standard tubular cradle frame and substituting a pivoted triangulated rear section in place of the regular swing-arm, while the shock absorber was concealed under the frame. In this way the triangular lines of the hardtail frame were apparent, yet the rider (and pillion) were spared the hard ride and road shocks by virtue of the disguised suspension set-up. The solo saddle reverted to the enormous coil springs last seen a decade earlier. The FLST Heritage Softail was also got up to look the part, with large, valenced FL-type mudguards, two-tone paint scheme and masses of chromed parts, such as the traditional horseshoe oil tank and the visors on the

Above: Although the FLST's nostalgic look is obtained by the duo-tone paint scheme and traditional fenders, its front disc brake and calliper are completely up-to-date.

Below: As befits the retro image, the lighting system on the FLST included headlight and matching spotlights, all with chrome visors, accompanied by pendant traffic indicators.

Above: Marked out in single figures, the FLST Heritage Softail's speedo is really calibrated to 120mph. Flanked by twin filler caps, the instrument dash is in the traditional location on top of the Fatbob fuel tank.

headlight and spotlights. Tasselled leather luggage and bar ends completed the picture.

Evident Anachronisms

However, keen students of cylinder-head configurations would quickly observe that the Heritage Softail was not running a typical Panhead engine, but the Evolution or Blockhead motor. There was also a large disc brake and calliper in evidence at the front wheel, plus another disc at the back, so anachronisms were evident. Not so visible was the electronic ignition, a rarity in the period the bike was meant to recall. The two side-exiting unmuffled exhausts provided a distraction, no doubt, and it was otherwise a convincing pastiche. There were twin filler caps beside the tank-mounted dash panel, a period speedo and, beyond the wide naked bars, twin spotlights flanked the visored headlight. Chromed brackets supported the elegantly flared rear mudguard, surmounted by a chrome number plate, the rear light and indicators, all shrouded in period housings. The Heritage Softail was a hefty-looking package, but a treat for fans of classic motorcycling who preferred to do without the hardships.

1988 FLST Heritage Softail Classic	
Engine model:	Evolution overhead-valve V-twin
Engine capacity:	88 cu. in. (1340 cc)
Cases:	Harley-Davidson
Carburation:	1.5in (38mm) butterfly
Air filter:	S&S
Ignition:	Electronic
Pipes:	Staggered shorty duals
Transmission:	Five-speed
Frame:	Tubular cradle
Suspension:	Front: telescopic forks Rear: Softail
Brakes:	Front: single disc Rear: disc
Wheels:	16in (406mm) wire-spoke front and rear
Mudguards (fenders):	Stock FL
Handlebars:	Wide flats
Risers:	None
Headlight:	9in (229mm) sealed beam
Tail-light:	Stock Harley-Davidson

FXRS Convertible

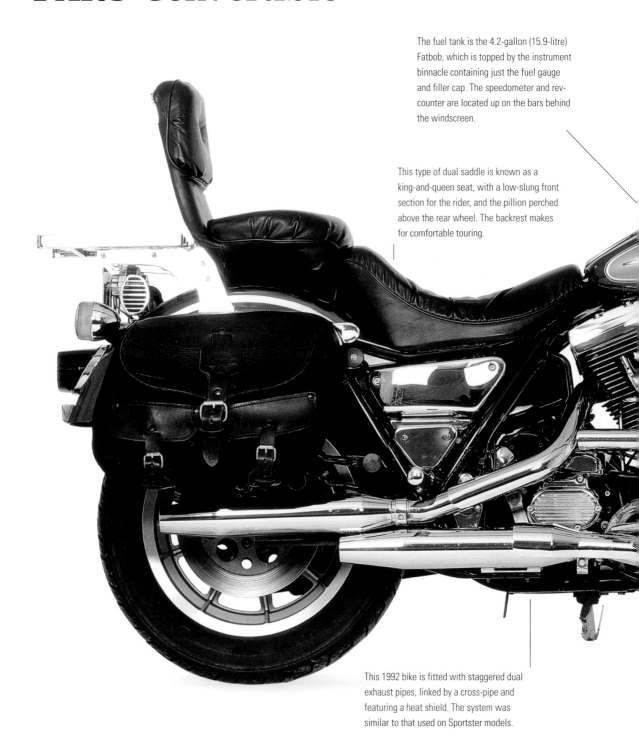

The fuel tank is the 4.2-gallon (15.9-litre) Fatbob, which is topped by the instrument binnacle containing just the fuel gauge and filler cap. The speedometer and rev-counter are located up on the bars behind the windscreen.

This type of dual saddle is known as a king-and-queen seat, with a low-slung front section for the rider, and the pillion perched above the rear wheel. The backrest makes for comfortable touring.

This 1992 bike is fitted with staggered dual exhaust pipes, linked by a cross-pipe and featuring a heat shield. The system was similar to that used on Sportster models.

The idea of the Super Glide-based FXR series of 1982 was to combine modern running gear with custom accessories and come up with a mid-period classic that was not overly retro in appearance. The 1992 FXRS Convertible has sports touring accessories like this wind-shield.

Reverse view

The FXRS was equipped with a lightweight front mudguard and the regular Harley-Davidson stock rear fender, and ran on nine-spoke cast-alloy wheels, measuring 19in (483mm) up front and 16in (406mm) at the rear.

The FXRS was powered by the 80 cu. in. (1312 cc) version of the Evolution big-twin, developing 58bhp at 7200rpm. The round air-filter cover bears the popular legend, 'Live to Ride, Ride to Live'.

The FXRS Convertible of 1983 was a significant introduction in the line of big-twin powered bikes running cruiser or custom chassis because it was built around the Dyna chassis introduced in 1991, and used belt drive instead of chain. The engine mounting points on the Dyna frame were refined with rubber to cut down on vibrations, which can be seen as just one more step in the gradual civilising of the marque.

A year earlier, the FXE Super Glide had been the last of the big twins to receive the 80 cu. in. (1340 cc) engine, and was joined by its two future successors the FXR and FXRS 80 Super Glide II. The latter was equipped with the flexible vibration-damping engine mounts as well as a new five-speed transmission. The primary drive of the FXB 80 Sturgis introduced two years previously had proved problematic and had given rise to warranty claims, so the toothed belt was abandoned for the primary drive, but the FXS 80 Low Rider was given the toothed belt for its secondary drive. In this way they created one model from two and called it the FXSB 80 Low Rider, with roller chain as the primary drive and toothed belt as the secondary drive. The FXRS Convertible was also given the final belt

drive treatment, making it among the smoothest of the big V-twins. Its touring potential was enhanced by the presence of adjustable pneumatic front suspension, which could be programmed via a chamber inside the handlebars for softer or harder damping.

All these innovations came about in the wake of the management buy-out and resurgence of the company a decade earlier. Back then, one of the incentives for AMF to get involved with Harley-Davidson was to take a piece of the action in the motorcycle boom. However, they underestimated the problems within the company and the pressure of the competition from Japan. Although AMF had agreed to the development of new models like the FX Super Glide, there was soon a mood of pessimism surrounding the operation's long-term future. As early as the mid-1970s, AMF began to seek a buyer for Harley-Davidson. Wishing to shift the emphasis of its operations

Below: The FXRS Convertible used the 80 cu. in. (1312 cc) Evolution V-twin engine, with its chromed primary-drive casing bearing the well-known motto 'Live to Ride, Ride to Live'. The bike is also fitted with alternative forward-mounted highway foot-pegs.

Above: The FXRS is finished in two-tone 'victory and sun-glo' paintwork, with removable windscreen, buckhorn handlebars with front-brake master cylinder, and chromed headlight and indicators.

away from leisure goods to heavy industry, AMF decided at the end of the 1970s to sell the company. It appointed Vaughn Beals as a director, giving him the task of finding a buyer or another way of ridding the company of its problematic motorcycle division.

Vaughn Beals

Beals was an arts graduate and a qualified engineer, but not particularly a motorcycle aficionado, yet he resolved to save Harley-Davidson. He reached the conclusion that it would stand the best chance of survival if it regained its independence and stood alone once more. The solution came in February 1981, as a group of Harley-Davidson managers led by Vaughn Beals and including Willie G. Davidson declared that they were prepared to buy back their company and continue to run it. This was accepted by AMF, who netted some $80m, writing off vast sums of money into the bargain. The transaction was completed

on 1st June 1981. The AMF interlude had enabled Harley-Davidson to weather the storms of the 1970s, and transformed it from an outdated, hidebound operation into a company with a knowledgeable, committed management and relatively modern production plants. It is unlikely that Harley-Davidson's old-style management would ever have countenanced the custom bike market and brought out models like the Super Glide and Low Rider. After 1981, the new Harley-Davidson company was split into three divisions. These were identified as Harley-Davidson Milwaukee in Wisconsin, Harley-Davidson York in Pennsylvania and Harley-Davidson International in Connecticut, which was the export division. Vaughn Beals was chairman and Charles Thompson became president, and the marque's rebirth was celebrated with a corporate motorcycle ride from York to Milwaukee. New ground rules were laid down, which allowed for the modernization and expansion of existing model ranges, an improvement of dealer rapport, and litigation over copyright infringements. They undercut non-standard parts producers by setting up the Eagle Iron subsidiary that made aftermarket parts in the Far East.

Below: The tail-end of the FXRS Convertible is fitted with a non-standard rear carrier, sissy bar and air horn, leather saddlebags, plus stock Harley-Davidson back light and traffic indicators.

Above: The 120mph speedometer and 8000rpm tachometer are mounted in a dash located on the FXRS's handlebars rather than in the tank-top dash, which is reserved for just the fuel gauge and filler cap.

They were not in clear water yet, however. A serious slump in the motorcycle market led to a price war among the Japanese manufacturers, leading to nearly 1.5 million unsold imported machines piling up in warehouses in the United States by the end of 1982. The market in used machines was virtually non-existent as new ones were available for less than cost price. On the verge of bankruptcy and with redundancies made, Harley-Davidson asked for help from the state in the form of an import restriction for five years on motorcycles over 700 cc. The plea was successful, and President Reagan signed the Trade Commission's complex draft, with the regulation coming into force on 15th April 1982.

Right: The dual-pillow King-and-Queen seat features a padded backrest for the pillion, which is a welcome support for long-distance touring work, but makes mounting the bike less easy.

Against this background, the revised FXR Super Glide of 1982 was launched. In addition to the new 80 cu. in. (1340 cc) engine, the FXR also got a new frame along with other updates, but in 1984 it was put on ice for a couple of years after the launch of the Evolution engine. The FXR was reintroduced in 1986 with specification upgraded with the new 80 cu. in. (1340 cc) Evo engine, mated to a five-speed gearbox, and it remained in production until 1994. At this point it was replaced by the Super Glide, which also used the rubber engine mount Dyna chassis.

The FXRS Convertible's touring ability could be increased by the fitment of a height-adjustable Lexan plastic screen and removable leather and nylon saddlebags. It could also be specified with chopperesque buckhorn handlebars, and the pillion passenger could be cosseted with a backrest and king-and-queen seat, while the rider was provided with alternative forward mounted foot-pegs. The instrumentation was contained in a binnacle ahead of the handlebars. The fuel gauge and fillet cap, however, lived in a console on top of the fuel tank. The bike could be further personalized, naturally, by fitting customized inspection covers, fuel cap, luggage rack and ornamental indicator housings.

Below: The FXRS Convertible ran with the 80 cu. in. (1312 cc) Evolution V-twin engine, with electronic ignition and 1.5in (40mm) carburettor mated to a five-speed transmission, with the belt drive taken down the right-hand side.

1992 FXRS Convertible

Engine model:	Evolution
Engine capacity:	80 cu. in. (1340 cc)
Cases:	Harley-Davidson
Carburation:	1.5in (40mm) CV
Air filter:	8in (40mm) circular chrome
Ignition:	Electronic
Pipes:	Staggered duals
Transmission:	Five-speed
Frame:	Duplex tubular cradle
Suspension:	Front: telescopic forks
	Rear: swing-arm and dampers
Brakes:	Front: twin discs
	Rear: disc
Wheels:	Front: 19in (483mm) nine-spoke cast-alloy
	Rear: 16in (406mm) cast-alloy spoke
Mudguards (fenders):	Stock Harley-Davidson
Handlebars:	Buckhorn
Risers:	None
Headlight:	Sealed beam

FXDWA Dyna Wide Glide

Being a factory-produced machine, the Wide Glide is obliged to have a front mudguard fitted, which an independent customizer might leave out. The rear fender is a traditional bobbed job.

Apart from the telescopic front forks, this 1995 machine has retro rear suspension consisting of swing-arm and coil-over-damper shock absorbers.

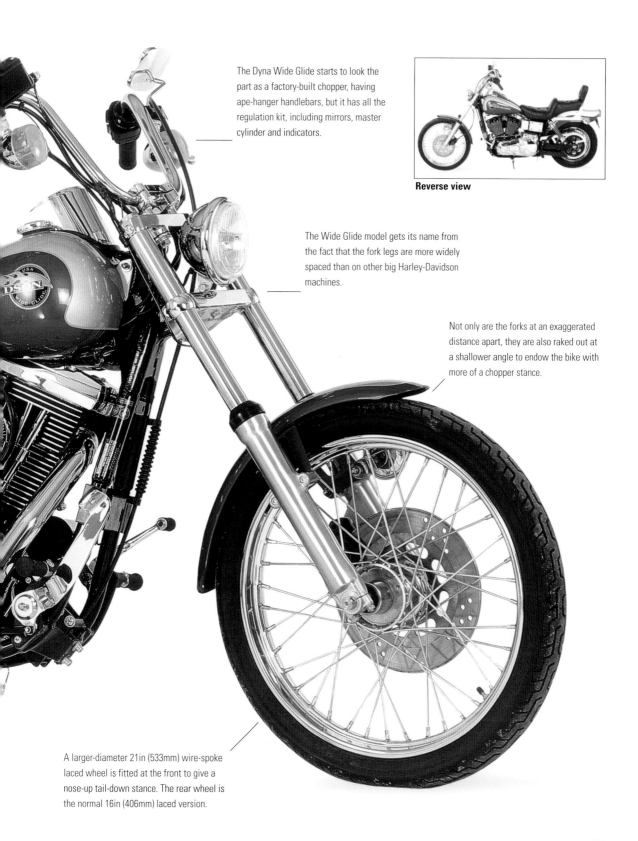

The Dyna Wide Glide starts to look the part as a factory-built chopper, having ape-hanger handlebars, but it has all the regulation kit, including mirrors, master cylinder and indicators.

Reverse view

The Wide Glide model gets its name from the fact that the fork legs are more widely spaced than on other big Harley-Davidson machines.

Not only are the forks at an exaggerated distance apart, they are also raked out at a shallower angle to endow the bike with more of a chopper stance.

A larger-diameter 21in (533mm) wire-spoke laced wheel is fitted at the front to give a nose-up tail-down stance. The rear wheel is the normal 16in (406mm) laced version.

Right: The diminutive sealed-beam headlight emphasizes the broad stance of the Wide Glide's steeply raked fork legs from which it gets its name. The Fatbob tank is painted aquamarine and silver.

What defines the Dyna Wide Glide is, firstly, its frame, which implies that it has the Dyna chassis that was introduced in 1991, with special vibration-free rubber engine mounting points. Secondly, the bike has extra-wide fork yokes, necessary to provide stability and counter the raked front end. The first factory-made Wide Glides came out in 1980 and were very popular for the six years they were in production before being phased out. The model returned in 1993, and essentially it was – and is – an official production version of a chopper.

Every manufacturer of charismatic vehicles has an owner's club, official or otherwise, and another innovation that came in when the Wide Glide was first introduced was the Harley Owners Group (HOG). Every buyer of a Harley-Davidson automatically became a member and was entitled to the first year of membership free. From then on, an annual subscription of $30 entitled the member to take advantage of the services provided by HOG, which consisted of a subscription to The Enthusiast magazine, assistance in case of an accident

Below: The power-plant for the FXDWG Dyna Wide Glide is the Evolution V-twin, which is recognizable by its three-piece alloy rocker cover and, in this case, relatively modest circular air-filter cover and staggered shorty dual exhaust pipes.

or crash damage, and a constantly monitored register of stolen Harley-Davidson machines.

After the import restrictions were in place in 1982, Harley-Davidson gained a breathing space and was able to become competitive once again. Quality control took on greater importance for new models like the Wide Glide, and methodology and working practices were reassessed. This included dispensing with the assembly-line style of production introduced by AMF. Instead, assembly-line workers were reorganized into small groups to assemble motorcycles one at a time. It meant that operators could identify with the product they had created, which had a beneficial effect on quality.

At this time there were three model ranges, each based on the relevant engine size. The XR used the 45 cu. in. (750 cc) V-twin, the XL took the 61 cu. in. (1000 cc) motor, and the FL and FX series that included the FXDWG Dyna Wide Glide (to give it its full designation) were powered by the 80 cu. in. big twin. All three ranges were extended in 1982, when the Sportster was completely revised. It was given a new chassis that reduced its weight to below 500lb (230kg) for better handling. The XLX 61 was added to the XL line-up. It was seen as a reasonably priced solo machine that qualified as an entry-level model.

Easy Rider Style

The FXDWG Dyna Wide Glide came with a tall 21in (533mm) diameter front wheel, shod with a skinny tyre to give it that Easy Rider-style appearance. It would probably look ungainly if we weren't so accustomed to the chopper imagery. There was a suitably diminutive front mudguard, which the factory was legally obliged to fit, whereas a customizer need not, contrasting with the upturned duck-tail or bobbed rear mudguard and tailpiece. The practice of 'bobbing' the rear mudguard was an early customizing trait, in which the front of the mudguard was pruned off and the whole affair shifted round the wheel so the trailing edge was elevated to such an extent that it bobbed up in the air. On the Dyna Wide Glide, it covered a bulbous 16in (406mm) wire-spoked rear wheel that sported a chromed rim. The exhaust pipes were the leery staggered short duals, calculated to make a much racket as legally possible. Another factory twist to the chopper was the exalted stature of the pillion half of the quilted king-and-queen saddle, while the front section occupied by the rider was a low 26.25in (67.95cm).

What makes the Dyna frame special is its unique system of computer-designed engine mounts, coupled with a cleverly engineered frame designed to minimize vibrations from the big twin. The tubular cradle frame's backbone is of rectangular section, welded to a cast steering head, angled to give the desired rake to the forks. High-rise ape-hanger bars soar upwards from the head-stock, featuring wide-bladed levers, mirrors and brake fluid indicator, plus the company's unique traffic indicators. The twin-fork yokes frame the single chrome headlight. Typically, almost all the ancillaries that can be chrome-plated were thus treated, including the battery box, gearbox cover, primary drive cover, coil-over damper, mudguard and seat brace, and air-filter cover. The speedo was housed in the tank-top console and flanked by the filler caps.

The look of the Dyna Wide Glide bordered on the incongruous, combining the spindly front end with a massive power-plant and beefy back wheel, surmounted by a palatial seating arrangement. The exhaust pipes were of larger diameter than the front forks. A single 11.5in front disc brake was fitted, with a disc at the rear. Both were ventilated for lightness and heat dissipation.

1995 FXDWG Dyna Wide Glide

Engine model:	Evolution
Engine capacity	80 cu. in. (1340 cc)
Cases:	Harley-Davidson
Carburation:	Stock Harley-Davidson
Air filter:	8in (203mm) circular
Ignition:	Electronic
Pipes:	Staggered shorty duals
Transmission:	Five-speed
Frame:	Tubular cradle
Suspension:	Front: telescopic forks
	Rear: swing-arm and dampers
Brakes:	Front: single disc
	Rear: disc
Wheels:	Front: 21in (533mm) wire-spoke
	Rear: 16in (406mm) wire-spoke
Mudguards (fenders):	Front: sport
	Rear: bobbed
Handlebars:	Ape-hanger
Risers:	None
Headlight:	Chrome sealed beam
Tail-light:	Stock Harley-Davidson

FLHT Electra Glide

The rider and pillion could luxuriate in supreme comfort on their quilted king-and-queen style dual saddle, which, if any confirmation was needed, showed that the Electra Glide was a big tourer rather than a sports bike.

Maximum luggage-carrying capability aboard the Electra Glide is provided by raked panniers and top box, with rack for additional baggage. Chrome fasteners, reflectors and traffic indicators are incorporated.

The Electra Glide first came out in 1965, and consistent upgrades took it to this highly equipped 1996 configuration, powered by the 80 cu. in. (1312 cc) overhead-valve, fuel-injected Evolution V-twin unit.

The FLHT exhaust system consisted of two-into-one pipes, with both right- and left-hand mufflers. The engine and panniers were protected by crash bars in the event of a spill.

The beautifully sculpted windscreen fairing on the FLHT provides a modicum of streamlining and allows reasonable cruising speeds with minimum buffeting from the airstream.

Like all big Harley-Davidsons, the Electra Glide was built up on the regular tubular cradle frame, incorporating rubber engine mounts to minimize vibration, with footboards for both rider and passenger.

Above: The FLHT Electra Glide of 1996 broke with tradition and had its clocks positioned in the handlebar-mounted fairing instead of the tank-top instrument binnacle, which was instead the location for the fuel filler cap.

Right: The Electra Glide's touring pack comprised a cavernous top box with extra luggage rack and built-in turn indicators, as well as a pillion backrest, fastened to the main luggage rack on the rear fender.

The Electra Glide has been around since 1965, when it ushered in the modern era of electric starter motors. Since then it has passed through numerous evolutions, including the transition from Panhead to Shovelhead to Evolution engine, and from wire-spokes to alloy wheels, so that by the turn of the new Millennium it had become the state-of-the-art Harley-Davidson tourer.

The most important features on a big tourer are rider and pillion comfort, manifest in the size and depth of the seats and the presence of foot-boards for both people. The

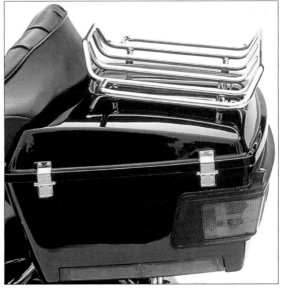

rider's seat is sculpted and quilted for maximum comfort, while the passenger is supported by a backrest more akin to an armchair. But touring and long-distance rides are no fun if it's raining, so the FLHT had a curvaceous fork-mounted fairing and windshield that enveloped the bars. Two substantial panniers were fitted either side of the rear wheel, and a top box surmounted the back rack, with the rear lights built into it and a mini-rack on top of that. The Electra Glide also had the refinement of the pneumatic air suspension system that supplemented the regular dampers and swing-arm. The disc brakes, an Electra Glide first, dating back to 1971, were paired at the front and a single item at the back. The FLHT ran on a pair of 16in (410mm) cast-alloy ten-spoke wheels.

Isolation-mounted Engine

What you don't want when on a long run is too much in the way of mechanical vibrations, and the Electra Glide was fitted with the isolation-mounted 80 cu. in. (1340 cc) Evolution engine. In 1997, the Glide derivative FLHRI Road King's Evo unit was supplied by Weber fuel injection – letter 'I' of the designation. The machine was easy to start, more economical and with lower exhaust emissions. It was mated to a five-speed gearbox with belt final drive. The 80 cu. in. (1340 cc) big twin produced 69bhp, enough to give the bike a maximum speed of 96mph (153km/h).

The Road King went further down the retro road than the standard Electra Glide, featuring wire-spoke wheels shod with whitewall tyres. The Electra Glide invariably had

1996 FLHT Electra Glide Standard	
Engine model:	Evolution
Engine capacity:	80 cu. in. (1340 cc)
Cases:	Harley-Davidson
Carburation:	Stock Harley-Davidson
Air filter:	Harley-Davidson circular
Ignition:	Electronic
Pipes:	Two-into-one, left- and right-hand silencers
Transmission:	Five-speed
Frame:	Tubular cradle
Suspension:	Front: telescopic forks Rear: swing-arm and dampers
Mudguards (fenders):	Stock FLHT
Handlebars:	Dresser
Risers:	None
Headlight:	9in (229mm) sealed beam
Tail-light:	Stock Harley-Davidson

wide-set handlebars, but the Road King's were somewhat high for comfortable long-distance cruising work, and in a sense it was more of a middleweight tourer, equipped with a quick-release screen rather than a fairing. At any rate, the chrome headlight was flanked by a pair of passing lights with suspended indicators below them. On the FLHT the instrument panel was worked into the handlebar fairing, while the binnacle on the 4.5-gallon (15.9-litre) Fatbob tank was the location for the filler cap. The traditional flared front mudguard was very much in evidence on the FLHT Electra Glide and the FLHRI, with such chrome embellishments as befitted any Harley dresser.

Left: The left-hand side of the Electra Glide's Evolution engine, featuring the chromed primary-drive cover. This 45-degree air-cooled V-twin was in production from 1984 to 1999, when it was superseded by the Twin-Cam.

FLHTCUI Ultra Classic Electra Glide

The FLHTCUI enjoyed possibly the longest designation in Harley-Davidson model nomenclature. It came fully loaded with items such as the moulded screen fairing and leg-shield 'lowers'.

The wheels used on the FLHTCUI were ten-spoke cast aluminium alloys, 16in (406mm) at the raear and 18in (460mm) up front, shod with appropriately sized tyres. There was a single disc brake at the rear, with twin discs at the front.

Not only did the rider and pillion of this big tourer have a button-quilted king-and-queen saddle, the passenger was also cosseted with a backrest and side cushions.

The 1996 Ultra Classic Electra Glide used the 69bhp, 80 cu. in. (1312 cc) version of the Evolution V-twin, which produced massive amounts of torque to propel this leviathan towards the horizon with almost indecent haste.

Reverse view

Footboards were present for both rider and pillion, with foot-operated heel-and-toe gear-shift – press down with toe for first, then heel down for the top four ratios.

Matching luggage consisted of panniers protected by crash bars and side rails, plus a rack-mounted top box with built-in traffic indicators. Overhangs were considerable.

Not only did the FLHTCUI have about the longest designation in Harley-Davidson history, by the mid-1990s it was physically the largest machine in the range. The main reason for that was the lengths to which it was accessorized. That's to say, its physical presence was created largely by the proportions of the luggage and the extent of the creature comforts it was endowed with. It come complete with a full set of large-capacity fibreglass touring luggage, and was also equipped with an extravagantly sculpted fork-mounted fairing that was topped by a windscreen. Typically, it came with a pair of passing lamps either side of the headlight, as well as the pendulous traffic indicators. The top box on the rear rack was almost as high as the screen, and it was surmounted by the pillion headrest. The crew of the FLHTCUI travelled in supreme comfort, with the benefit of a built-in hi-fi system, cigarette lighter and more instrumentation than other models. Most of

Below: The Ultra Classic Electra Glide's Evolution engine was fitted with Weber electronic fuel injection and Harley-Davidson V-Fire III electronic ignition. Transmission was via belt drive on the left-hand side of the machine.

the instrumentation was housed in the fairing base, while the tank-mounted module served as the location for the filler cap. These were indeed extraordinary lengths to go to in the quest for rider comfort. The rider was also protected by leg shields, known as 'lowers' by the factory, finished to match the main colour scheme. Not only did they encompass the front crash bars, they also housed the speakers for the stereo system. The rear panniers were also painted to match and were protected by an elaborate system of crash bars and chromed fencing. The pillion passenger was also treated to a set of speakers. The twin aerials for the sound system and CB radio were housed in the rear panniers, which also served as mounting points for the indicator flasher units.

There was no way that such an array of equipment, much of it functional rather than simply decorative, could be ignored, with the result that the machine itself made a huge statement whenever it emerged on the road or at a biker gathering. To pull off this appearance, the rider needed to have some nerve, since such a statement of intent could be viewed as both impressive as well as inviting ridicule from sports-minded motorcyclists.

Above: The Ultra Classic lacked very little in terms of its specification. The front fender was adorned with crash bars and safety reflector, while bar-mounted spotlights and pendant trafficators flank the fairing-housed headlight.

On the positive side, such geared-up machines as the FLHTCUI are, surprisingly, pretty stable.

The Ultra Classic Tour Glide

The closest sibling to the FLHTCUI was the Ultra Classic Tour Glide, which in the mid-1990s was a more modern alternative to the Electra Glide. Its fairing was frame-mounted, making it a more stable machine at high speed, and, like the FLHTCUI, its engine was mounted in the frame using the rubber isolating components. Not only were the levels of equipment supremely high, but the rider and pillion passenger did not feel the engine vibrations as much. The FLHT chassis' revised frame geometry improved the bike's handling, supplementing the regular telescopic forks and rear swing-arm and dampers. The power-plant

was the 80 cu. in. (1340 cc) Evolution engine, running fuel injection and electronic ignition on the FLHTCUI, while the Tour Glide's five-speed transmission included a top gear that was designed as an overdrive. This meant that the engine could run at 3000rpm when cruising at regular speeds, giving the advantage of reduced vibrations, and a quieter and more economical motorcycle. Final drive was provided by the belt drive that first came out in 1985. The split exhaust system fed generous chrome silencers on either side of the bike.

The FLHTCUI Electra Glide was, in fact, a logical progression from the original 1965 electric starter model. A Sport version, the FLHS Electra Glide from 1977, was produced for just one year as a limited edition model, and after a three-year hiatus, it reappeared as the 1980 FLHS. When the Shovelhead motor was dropped in 1984, the FLHS also took a breather, and returned as the Sport version of the Evo-powered, five-speed 'Glide from 1987. The Sport version did without the built-in fairing and top box. While it hardly merited the 'Sport' epithet, it did handle slightly better than its fully-laden stable mate.

1996 FLHTCUI Ultra Classic Electra Glide	
Engine model:	Evolution
Engine capacity:	80 cu. in. (1340 cc)
Cases:	Harley-Davidson
Carburation:	Fuel injection
Air filter:	8in (203mm) circular
Ignition:	Electronic
Pipes:	Dual system
Transmission:	Five-speed
Frame:	Tubular cradle
Suspension:	Front: telescopic forks Rear: swing-arm and dampers
Brakes:	Front: twin discs Rear: disc
Wheels:	16in (406mm) cast-alloy ten-spoke front and rear
Mudguards (fenders):	Stock FL
Handlebars:	Dresser
Risers:	None
Headlight:	9in (229mm) sealed beam
Tail-light:	Stock Harley-Davidson

FLSTC Heritage Softail Classic

The favoured riding position for bikes like the Heritage range built on traditional lines demanded the low-slung front saddle with the pillion slightly raised and above the rear wheel. This leather-upholstered ensemble includes the backrest.

By 1996, motorcycles had graduated from Wild-West style saddlebags to the forefront of technology. But many riders still hankered after traditional styling with modern running gear, hence the market for machines like this Heritage Softail Classic FLSTC.

The colour scheme for this bike is 'patriotic red pearl' with a period-style Harley-Davidson tank badge. The chrome-trimmed items such as the instrument dash and horseshoe oil tank are stock items.

The period look was enhanced by the fitment of classic full-width flared fenders front and rear, with the script on the leading edge proclaiming the Heritage Softail nomenclature.

The Heritage Softail Classic used telescopic front forks, along with concealed dampers substituted for a swing-arm in the Softail rear end, giving it the look of a hardtail Hydra Glide of the 1950s.

The Heritage Softail Classic was powered by the 80 cu. in. (1310 cc) Evolution overhead-valve V-twin motor, delivering 55bhp at 7200rpm. It was mated to a five-speed transmission with belt final drive on the left-hand side of the bike.

Above: The Heritage Softail Classic has a clear windshield with chromed headlight beneath and passing lamps with matched pendant traffic indicators mounted either side.

Below: The FLSTC uses the 80 cu. in. (1310 cc) Evolution V-twin, with an 8in (200mm) circular cover over the carburettor's air filter. The exhaust pipes are known as staggered duals, with a cross-pipe link.

Unveiled in 1987, the FLSTC Heritage Softail Classic was another factory custom, dripping with period paraphernalia that was evocative of a 1950s Hydra Glide. It was based on the Softail chassis from 1984, which concealed the rear suspension under the engine in order to produce the 'hardtail' chassis look. The Softail swing-arm had concealed suspension units, and the lower silencer hid a horizontally mounted shock absorber. The FLSTC utilized the hydraulic telescopic front forks, but its modern equipment meant it was really an up-to-date motorcycle. Unlike the Hydra Glide, it came with electric

starter, front and rear disc brakes, belt drive, and the 80 cu. in. (1310 cc) Evolution V-twin engine. Fuel injection was not an option, however, and it ran a stock Harley-Davidson carb, although it had the benefit of electronic ignition, and staggered dual exhausts. Cosmetically, the front and rear mudguards were only fractionally different from those fitted on FL models back in the 1940s, altered slightly to accommodate different suspension systems, but fundamentally similar. The 4.5-gallon (22.7-litre) Fatbob fuel tank was stylistically similar too, complete with instrument console. The lofty pull-back handlebars were inevitably chrome-plated, with passing lights mounted either side of the sealed-beam headlight, with the trafficators suspended below. In true cruiser fashion, the FLSTC could be equipped with a clear perspex screen, and the bike was generally equipped with period-look leather saddlebags with ornamental studs, as was the saddle, which also included a backrest. Other chromed items included the three-quart horseshoe oil tank, 16in (406mm) spoked wheels, inspection covers and air-filter cover.

Above: Huge flared fenders with chrome trim are one of the hallmarks of this 1996 FLSTC Heritage Classic, with shrouded front forks to locate the windscreen and headlight mounting brackets.

1996 FLSTC Heritage Softail Classic

Engine model:	Evolution
Engine capacity:	80 cu. in. (1310 cc)
Cases:	Harley-Davidson
Carburation:	Stock Harley-Davidson
Air filter:	8in (203mm) circular
Ignition:	Electronic
Pipes:	Staggered duals
Transmission:	Five-speed
Frame:	Tubular cradle
Suspension:	Front: telescopic forks Rear: Softail
Brakes:	Front: single disc Rear: disc
Wheels:	16in (406mm) wire-spoke front and rear
Mudguards (fenders):	Valanced FL type
Handlebars:	Pull-back
Risers:	None
Headlight:	9in (229mm) sealed beam
Tail-light:	Stock Harley-Davidson

The FLSTC Heritage Classic conjures up the spirit of 1950s nostalgia, when stars such as James Dean and Elvis Presley were fast becoming US heart-throbs. It would be surprising if a machine with such a long pedigree hadn't accumulated a fund of myths and legends. One of the more recent concerns a guy who got lucky with an Instants ticket and bought himself a second-hand 1950s Harley-Davidson. He went travelling around Europe on it. Then one day something went wrong, and he was obliged to contact the factory for a replacement part. The factory asked him for the chassis number and then – disbelievingly – instructed him to remove the primary drive inspection cover. He duly complied, and there was a message engraved beneath. It said, 'To Jimmy, love Elvis'. The bike had apparently been given to James Dean by the rock-and-roll singer back in the early 1950s, but the machine had become lost over the years. The factory offered to buy it back, but he thought better of it and sold it through Christie's auction house.

FLSTN Heritage Softail Special

In addition to the neat king-and-queen saddle, the FLSTN carries small leather saddlebags attached via the rear fender supporting bracket. This leaves more of the rear fender visible.

The bike's customized appearance is helped by chrome-plated components such as the horseshoe oil tank, stepped dual exhaust pipes with cross-over, tank-top dash and transmission inspection plate.

Up front, the Heritage Softail Special uses partially shrouded telescopic front forks, with the Softail rear end set-up implicit in its name, with the dampers camouflaged by the specially revised triangulations of the cradle frame.

The bike's duo-tone colour scheme is called mystique green and silver. It's enhanced by a traditional-style Harley-Davidson tank badge.

Reverse view

The FLSTN Heritage Softail Special carries nearly as many 'trad' features, such as the fully enveloping flared front and rear fenders, as the Heritage Classic, making it a showy period dresser.

Typically for a 1996 bike, the engine in the tubular cradle frame is the Evolution version of the big-twin, which was still a year away from sequential fuel injection, fitted with a stock Harley-Davidson carburettor.

Above: This FLSTN dates from 1996, and is fitted with a 16in (406mm) wire-spoke laced wheel, with a single front brake disc on the left and a hub cap on the right.

By the mid-1990s, Harley-Davidson's nostalgia department was in full flood, and among the plethora of offerings calculated to tempt the classic dresser aficionado was the FLSTN Heritage Softail Special. Looking like a latter-day palomino from a Tom Mix western, the FLSTN combined those wistful 1950s design references with modern Harley-Davidson running gear. The overall appearance was suggestive of a Hydra Glide, which took the '50s by storm with its hydraulically damped front forks, although the most obvious difference in the aesthetics department was the substitution of the solo leather saddle and sprung seat post of the fifty-year old bike for the generously padded dual saddle on the 1993 Heritage model. On the modern bike the seat hugged the contours of the cradle frame top rails, merging with the rear mudguard, while the original bike's seat was simply surrounded by fresh air. The mudguards too were virtually identical to the FL Hydra Glide, with a touch of embellishment that proclaimed its Heritage Softail nomenclature. A riding light on the leading edge of the mudguard carried a logo through which the illumination was projected, which was a neat touch. At the rear there was the usual mixture of licence plate, tail light, traffic indicators, reflector and chrome trim.

The original Hydra Glide was launched just after the 74cu in (1213cc) Panhead engine came out, while the modern pastiche was powered by the latest 80cu-in (1340cc) Evolution engine. The difference in power output was not vast. The Panhead developed 55bhp at 4,800rpm, enough to take it to 102mph, while the Evolution motor with its electronic ignition mustered 69bhp, although attention

to efficiency and emissions controls reduced top speed slightly to 98mph (155km/h).

Two Cylinders

One aspect of Harley-Davidson design that lends itself to cosmetic dalliance is the exhaust system. Two cylinders means two manifolds, and they can be merged into one pipe that incorporates a silencer. Or they can remove the gasses from the engine as two individual pipes, more commonly seen on aftermarket systems, which act more efficiently but make more noise. The FLSTN was fitted with an exhaust system that took the best of both options, being a mix of 'shotgun duals' that were linked by a crossover section running below the air cleaner. The relatively high positioning of the upper 'barrel' then, affected the type of luggage that could be accommodated, and therefore the whole character of the bike. There simply wasn't room for the large Tour Pack fibreglass kind of cases, nor the hefty saddlebags of the FLSTC. Instead the FLSTN made

1996 FLSTN Heritage Softail Special	
Engine model:	Evolution
Engine capacity:	80 cu. in. (1310 cc)
Cases:	Harley-Davidson
Carburation:	Stock Harley-Davidson
Air filter:	203mm (8in) circular
Ignition:	Electronic
Pipes:	Staggered duals
Transmission:	Five-speed
Frame:	Tubular cradle
Suspension:	Front: telescopic forks Rear: Softail
Brakes:	Front: single disc Rear: disc
Wheels:	406mm (16in) wire-spoke front and rear
Mudguards (fenders):	Valanced FL type
Handlebars:	Pull-back
Risers:	None
Headlight:	229mm (9in) sealed beam
Tail-light:	Stock Harley-Davidson

Right: Forward-positioned foot controls are easy to operate, with the left-hand side footboard located beneath the gear shift. First is one click down with the toe, while the other four ratios are engaged via back clicks with the heel.

do with altogether more compact leather bags, which showed off the contours of the rear mudguard that clad much of the rear tyre. Also visible was the rear brake disc and the rear frame. Here was one of the Softail's giveaway hallmarks, a hydraulic damper incorporated in the cunningly designed swingarm. So the absence of an external coil-over damper did not mean that the bike had no rear suspension and was therefore an authentic old-time hard-tail, it was all there, only disguised by the incorporation of a different kind of damping system.

The FLSTN had its fair share of chrome-plated glitz, yet it couldn't be described as over-flashy. It didn't have high-rise ape-hanger bars, just regular dresser style items. Apart from the exhausts and 16in spoked wheel rims, the 9in sealed-beam headlight, mirrors and indicator housings were thus treated, while the forks were in polished aluminium. There were no spotlights on the front of the FLSTN, and engine parts receiving the chrome embellishment were the inspection covers and three-quart (2.8-litre) horseshoe oil tank. As might be expected in a bike going for as much of the period look as possible, the instrumentation was carried in the tank-top console. This unit was flanked by twin filler caps, while the 4.5-gallon capacity Fatbob fuel tank and mudguard were finished in a duo-tone colour-scheme.

Left: This FLSTN makes do with a single headlight and no passing lamps. Pendant traffic indicators are mounted towards the ends of the dresser-style handlebars.

FXDS Dyna Glide Convertible

The colour scheme of this FXDS Dyna Glide Convertible is standard Harley Davidson violet pearl, with coachlines where appropriate. All chromed ancillaries, such as the rectangular battery cover, are stock items.

The FX part of the bike's designation stems from the fact that the Dyna Glide Convertible has its origins in the FX Super Glide, which was designed as a custom cruiser.

The power-unit for the Dyna Glide Convertible is the trusty 80 cu. in. (1310 cc) Evolution V-twin, pushing out 58bhp at 7200rpm, driving through a five-speed gearbox.

The FXDS Dyna Glide Convertible was designed as a dual-purpose machine. Fitted with its wind-shield and panniers, it could serve as a touring bike, but with these removed it was transformed into a cruiser.

Reverse view

The FXDS ran on 13-spoke cast aluminium-alloy wheels measuring 18in (483mm) at the front, and 16in (406mm) at the rear. Twin disc brakes were fitted at the front and a single disc operated on the rear.

The FXDS hinted at a sporting potential with its unshrouded telescopic front forks, pull-back handlebars and narrow front mudguard. The rear quarters are heavier set, however, with the coil-over-damper shock absorber prominent.

Riders wishing to use their machine for a more ostentatious cruising role as well as more serious touring purposes might well opt for the Dyna Glide Convertible. Realizing that people don't necessarily want to ride their machines laden down with redundant panniers and their attendant weight penalty when they are on short trips, the factory introduced the FXDS Dyna Glide Convertible in 1994, at the same time as the FLHR Road King.

The original Dyna Glide made its debut in 1991, and what made it special was an innovative two-point rubber mounting system that soaked up engine vibrations. As a result, the ride was improved even more, especially on twisting road sections. This obviously made the prospect of long-distance touring much more appealing, and by the turn of the new century, the compliant Dyna Glide chassis had acquired the all-new Twin Cam 88 power-plant and the engine and transmission had received a more rigid interface. The electronic ignition was a new single-fire design, which was more efficient than previous

1996 FXDS Dyna-Glide Convertible	
Engine model:	Evolution
Engine capacity:	80 cu. in. (1340 cc)
Cases:	Harley-Davidson
Carburation:	Stock Harley-Davidson
Air filter:	8in (203mm) circular
Ignition:	Electronic
Pipes:	Staggered duals
Transmission:	Five-speed
Frame:	Tubular cradle
Suspension:	Front: telescopic forks Rear: swing-arm and dampers
Brakes:	Front: twin disc Rear: disc
Wheels:	Front: 19in (483mm) cast alloy 13-spoke Rear: 16in (406mm) cast alloy 13-spoke
Mudguards (fenders):	Front: XL-style Rear: stock Harley-Davidson
Handlebars:	Pull-back
Risers:	None
Headlight:	Sealed beam
Tail-light:	Stock Harley-Davidson

arrangements. Transmission was by primary drive double-row chain, and the Dyna Glide also came with the cleaner belt final-drive. If further embellishment was required, the factory also offered its own-brand customizing kit, known as Genuine Motor Accessories, and for enthusiasts bent on extracting more performance from their machine, Harley-Davidson offered its Screamin' Eagle performance parts, all of which were available from local dealerships.

The Dyna Convertible was not a hybrid in the sense that it was composed of the chassis of one model, running with the engine from another series of bike. It was simply a stand-alone model that could be converted from one type of riding activity to another. With its rubber-insulation mounted Twin Cam 88 engine, full wind-shield and saddlebags, the bike was capable of matching its big dedicated touring siblings. Yet its luggage was easily detachable. This was achieved by a couple of twists and the saddlebags came off to reveal a traditional Harley-Davidson custom, sparkling with chrome-plated engine parts. Instrumentation was mounted behind the weathershield and in twin binnacles mounted on the handlebars. It included a tachometer, electronic speedometer with odometer and trip meter, and a fuel gauge. Front end, dual-rate fork springs and disc brakes completed the basic package.

Cost of Options

However, the basic Harley Davidson invoice price could begin to stack up once the options list was broached. To give some idea of price, the FXDS cost around $14,600 in 2001, with $240 extra for the pearl finish and another $585 for two-tone paintwork. For a bike specified with California Emission controls, another $285 was required, while the wire-spoke wheels would incur a further $320. Standard wheels were the 13-spoke black painted cast alloys. These prices did not include setting-up, taxes, registration and licensing, and dealer mark-ups could vary. The dimensions of the Dyna Glide Convertible were based on a length of 92.88in (235.90cm), a seat height measuring 27.75in (70.49cm), and ground clearance of 5.75in (14.61cm). The fork rake was set at 28 degrees, and trail at 4.1in (10.37cm). The Dyna Glide wheelbase was 63.88in (162.25cm), with front tyre size of 100/90-19 and rear of 130/90HB16. The fuel capacity of the Fatbob tank was 4.9 gallons (22 litres), which included a half gallon reserve, always reassuring on longer runs. The oil capacity was three quarts (2.8-litres), and the bike's dry weight was 640lb (290kg).

The 1996 model featured ran the 80 cu. in. (1340 cc) Evolution engine, but turn-of-the-century Dyna Glides

Above: The dual-purpose FXDS Dyna Glide Convertible had an all-transparent windscreen, which could be removed along with other touring accessories to transform the bike into a cruiser.

Below: The Dyna Glide's Fatbob fuel tank carries the instrument binnacle, but this contains just the fuel gauge and filler cap. The bike's two clocks are located up behind the pull-back handlebars.

used the isolation-mounted Twin Cam 88 motor. Vital statistics of this engine were a bore and stroke measuring 3.75in x 4.00in, giving a displacement of 88 cu. in. (1450 cc). Torque measured 82lb/ft at 3500rpm. Its compression ratio was 8.9:1, and, as befitted its classic appeal, it still used a carburettor despite the advantages of electronic fuel injection. It was reasonably economical to run, given the size of the engine, and in urban surroundings the Dyna Glide Convertible could achieve 42mpg (15km/l), with closer to 50mpg (18km/l) out on the open road. The stopping distance from 60mph (96.6km/h) was 170ft (51.8m), provided by dual front discs of 11.5in (290mm). The rear disc was the same diameter but slightly fatter. The bike could be laid down in corners at 33.5 degrees to the right, and slightly more to the left – 34.5 degrees – on account of the staggered 'shorty dual' exhaust system on the right hand side of the bike. That's not knee-slider territory exactly, but then the cruiser and tourer fraternity wouldn't want it to be.

FXSTS Softail Springer

In keeping with the bike's retrospective image, it is equipped with studded dual leather seat and saddlebags plus pillion backrest. Buckhorn-style handlebars and headlight visor complement the look.

The colour scheme for this Softail Springer is stock Harley-Davidson vivid black, with gold coachline and traditional logo on the Fatbob tank. A lightweight front mudguard and bobbed rear fender are fitted.

As its name suggests, the Softail Springer uses Harley-Davidson's Softail rear suspension set-up, which gives it the period look of a hardtail frame with no suspension, while concealing its dampers in the frame triangulations.

The FXSTS of 1996 is powered by the 80 cu. in. (1310 cc) Evolution V-twin, with stock H-D carburettor and staggered shorty dual exhausts with connector pipe. The alternator-cover legend reads, 'Live to Ride, Way of Life'.

Reverse view

The most notable aspect of the FXSTS Softail Springer is its front suspension, which features leading-link forks, springs and damper intended to emulate motorcycles from a bygone age.

The Softail Springer has more than a hint of the chopper about it. Heavy-set rear quarters with a 16in (406mm) alloy disc-type wheel are juxtaposed with the airy front end, with its 21in (533mm) laced wire-spoke wheel and single disc brake.

There are many motorcyclists, even non-Harley riders, who, when coming face-to-face with a Harley-Davidson hardtail motorcycle from the 1940s or 1950s find the classic styling irresistible. In order to tempt such people, the factory introduced the retrospective FXSTS Softail Springer. It is fair to say that many have been inspired by the uncluttered American style of the classic era, and the Softail series sets out to recapture the essence of those bygone days in a line-up of modern machines that set fresh standards for styling throughout the latter years of the 20th century.

The Softail hides its wares under the seat, where a pair of gas dampers provide fully four inches of adjustable travel. But what is really special about the FXSTS is the nature of the front forks – from which it derives its name. In 1988, Harley-Davidson brought back the leading-link springer front forks, an archaic design that had last seen the light of day in 1949, after which it was superseded by the hydraulic forks introduced with the Hydra Glide, back in the days of the Knucklehead and Panhead motors. The springer, or leading-link, front suspension system

Above: The FXSTS Softail Springer features curvaceous Buckhorn handlebars, fitted with the brake master cylinder, rear-view mirrors and pendant trafficators. The instrument dash is on the tank top.

consisted of short links that pivoted at the bottom of a solid fork. The axle mounts were on the front of the link, which was controlled by a spring, and it is perhaps hard to comprehend that it was first employed by Harley-Davidson way back on 1907. It is that very longevity that many fans of the marque find attractive. Contrary to veteran 1940s practice, though, the modern incarnations of the springer forks were computer designed and constructed of modern materials, incorporating a single front disc brake and calliper. Further period enhancements included the buckhorn riser handlebars, with an antique-look chrome-plated bullet-style headlight mounted high on the forks. The instrument module contained the electronic speedometer with odometer and trip meter, and was located atop the 4.5-gallon (20.5-litre) Fatbob fuel tank, which featured the company logo on either side, depicted in period graphics. A chromed horseshoe oil tank was fitted, along with a dual stepped saddle and supplementary backrest. Leather saddlebags flanked the passenger.

Sporty Dual Exhaust Pipes

The FXSTS was powered by the 80 cu. in. (1340 cc) Evolution V-Twin, sporting what they called staggered sporty dual exhaust pipes. In 1999, the company fitted a new five-bolt ignition timer cover. The vintage look of the Softail Springer didn't come cheap, at more than $15,000. To that, the buyer had to add $585 to get the two-tone paint job, plus a further $290 to cover the stringent California emissions control system. On this bike, the 21in (533mm) spoked wire wheel was standard at the front, and a 16in (406mm) slotted alloy wheel was fitted at the rear. The forks were raked at a more slanted 32 degrees, while the lean angle was a relatively upright 28 degrees to the right and 29 degrees to the left. That was partly accounted for by the general stance of the bike, with its greater than average fork rake and skinny chopper-style front wheel.

To some motorcyclists, especially those whose main interest is in sports or racing bikes, this type of machine is perceived as something of an anachronism, combining as it does the potent symbols of Harley Davidson's halcyon days. This amounts to no more than indulgent misty-

Below: Ostensibly a hardtail chassis, the Softail frame has its left-hand rear damper positioned on the upper section of the triangle. Also prominent are the bike's belt final-drive and alloy disc rear wheel.

1996 FXSTS Softail Springer	
Engine model:	Evolution
Engine capacity:	80 cu. in. (1340 cc)
Cases:	Harley-Davidson
Carburation:	Harley-Davidson
Air filter:	8in (203mm) circular
Ignition:	Electronic
Pipes:	Staggered shorty duals
Transmission:	Five-speed
Frame:	Tubular cradle
Suspension:	Front: springer forks Rear: Softail
Brakes:	Front: single disc Rear: disc
Wheels:	Front: 21in (533mm) wire-spoke Rear: 16in (406mm) alloy disc
Mudguards (fenders):	Front: springer Rear: bobbed
Handlebars:	Buckhorn
Risers:	Yes
Headlight:	Chrome bullet
Tail-light:	Stock Harley-Davidson

eyed nostalgia, some may say. However, there is no getting away from the fact that the FXSTS Softail Springer is a well-executed blend of old and new, containing a host of traditional elements as fundamental as the sprung leading-link front forks and the hardtail chassis.

To be in any way critical of retrospective-looking machines is to miss the point. The rider of a classic bike takes pride in it, but is always at the mercy of old or outdated componentry. A new or late model retro bike like the FXSTS combines the best of both worlds – classic looks with modern componentry.

FXSTSB Bad Boy

The FXSTSB was fitted with a lightweight front mudguard and bobbed rear fender. The instrument console was mounted on top of its Fatbob fuel tank, while the hand controls were located on the pull-back bars.

Although the Bad Boy's main paint colour was vivid black, it was finished with bright yellow flashes to give an impression of speed. This was also a reference to colour schemes from the 1930s.

The overall appearance of the FXSTSB Bad Boy suggested, in keeping with its name, that it was stripped down and ready for action. The compact running gear was housed in the Softail chassis to give it something of a period look.

This 1996 machine was fitted with the 80 cu. in. (1310 cc) Evolution engine, which had a bore and stroke of 3.5 x 4.25in, fed by a stock Harley-Davidson carburettor and circular air-filter cover. Pipes were staggered shorty duals with a cross-pipe.

Reverse view

The chopperesque look of the Bad Boy was obtained by equipping it with leading-link springer front forks, which were augmented by springs and suspension damper.

The front wheel was a laced wire-spoke item measuring 21in (533mm) in diameter, with a single ventilated disc, while the rear wheel was a 16in (406mm) slotted aluminium-alloy job.

Above: The FXSTSB Bad Boy was powered by the Evolution V-twin allied to a five-speed transmission, with foot-pegs instead of footboards. This engine was so-called because it contained a number of improvements over the old Shovelhead unit.

The provocatively named Bad Boy was introduced to seduce those who fancied themselves as would-be Hollister rebel rousers. Now, surely, the company had openly acknowledged its roots in the low-life biker culture. But that assumption misses the point. The reason why many people, and men in particular (96 percent of Harleys are owned by males), aspire to Harley-Davidson ownership is so that they qualify to attend events like the Daytona Bike Week or Sturgis Rally and countless similar events attended by hundreds of thousands of bikers, at which they can reaffirm their manhood. If this involves behaving badly for a few days, then so be it. Having got it out of their system they return to their everyday lives and ride out at weekends. The Harley-Davidson motorcycle is absolutely fundamental to

this, and ownership of one is not just crucial, it is a true right of passage. Unlike Japanese machines, its patina of evolution and longevity has endowed it with soul, so that for an American rider, nothing else will do. All very well dressing up in Levis and leather, but go to any club meeting in, or on, a vehicle of a make other than that of the host club and see how out of place it feels. The aesthetics of the Harley-Davidson motorcycle and its V-twin motor are so charged with emotion, involving all the folk-tales of rebellion, tradition and escapism, that no other machine can possibly live with it. Long before the management buyout of 1981, the marque had attained iconic status – which is why someone like Elvis Presley could pose for a magazine cover shot, one icon identifying another. By 1990, the whole complexion of the marketplace had been altered by the invasion of yuppie buyers, known as 'Rubies', or 'rich urban bikers', and the market fragmented into much more diverse groups of owners. There were the traditionalists, the outlaw types, the weekenders, family

1996 FXSTSB Bad Boy

Engine model:	Evolution
Engine capacity:	80 cu. in. (1340 cc)
Cases:	Harley-Davidson
Carburation:	Stock Harley-Davidson
Air filter:	8in (203mm) circular
Ignition:	Electronic
Pipes:	Staggered shorty duals
Transmission:	Five-speed
Frame:	Tubular cradle
Suspension:	Front: springer forks
	Rear: Softail
Brakes:	Front: single disc
	Rear: disc
Wheels:	Front: 21in (533mm) wire-spoke
	Rear: 16in (406mm) slotted alloy disc
Mudguards (fenders):	Front: springer
	Rear: bobbed
Handlebars:	Pull-back
Risers:	Yes
Headlight:	Chromed bullet
Tail-light:	Stock Harley-Davidson

At the back was a 16in (406mm) slotted alloy wheel. The power-plant was the 80 cu. in. (1310 cc) Evo motor, with five-speed transmission, belt drive and staggered shorty dual exhausts. With the chassis sorted to look like the archetypal stripped-down Knucklehead, it was time to deal with the cosmetics.

A Distinguished Machine

A minimal front mudguard was fitted, with a bobbed one at the back, which matched the contemporary paint scheme of the Fatbob fuel tank. That gave it the basic mien of an early bobber or chopper, and the effect was completed by the pull-back handlebars and chromed bullet headlight. It was fitted with a stepped dual saddle, but no luggage and, naturally, no screen. The amount of chrome was actually minimal, with the horseshoe oil tank and instrument console painted to match the rest of the bike. It was as distinguished as any home-built custom.

If stereotyping is important, it's fair to say that the FXSTSB Bad Boy was really a cruiser with attitude. In standard form, it lacked the luggage-carrying capability of a touring bike like the Convertible, and eschewed any kind of protection from the elements, as might be expected in a genre which holds that windscreens are for wimps.

Below: Harley-Davidson re-introduced the springer leading-link front forks in the late 1990s, and the Bad Boy was one of the machines it was used on. The hydraulic damper was fitted back in 1947 to control the movement of the forks. It replaced the hand-adjusted ride control.

owners, and numerous splinter groups, all bound by the Harley-Davidson marque. No other man-made machine has ever had this effect, transcending all echelons of society.

Which brings us back to the Bad Boy. Based on a Softail FSXT cradle frame, in which the rear suspension is concealed to promote the fake hardtail appearance, the FXSTSB was fitted with period-look hand-adjustable leading-link springer forks. There was also a more pronounced rake to the forks. The front wheel was a 21in (533mm) wire spoke item, allied to a single disc brake and calliper.

FLSTF Fat Boy

The FLSTF's seating plan involved a low-slung contoured saddle for the rider, 26.5in (67.3cm) above the road, with the pillion perched atop the rear fender, with back rest and matching saddlebags alongside.

The colour scheme for this 1996 Fatboy was standard-issue Harley-Davidson, called 'two-tone wine-berry sun-glo', with gilt coachlines on the Fatbob tank and fenders.

The Softail chassis disguised the rear dampers located almost horizontally in the triangle of the back section of the frame, a direct reference to machines of an earlier, less civilized era.

Reverse view

The FLSTF Fat Boy achieves its looks by means of metal shrouds on its telescopic fork legs, and the use of 16in (406mm) alloy disc wheels front and rear, shod with ample Dunlop Elite tyres.

The Fat Boy's hefty appearance made it an ideal foil for tough guy Arnold Schwarzenegger in the 1991 movie Terminator 2. Flared Hydra Glide-style fenders were fitted front and rear to provide substance as well as a period look.

The big 80 cu. in. (1310 cc) Evolution V-twin engine was complemented by a chromed horseshoe oil tank and imposing shotgun dual exhaust pipes with a cross-pipe link.

1996 FLSTF Fat Boy

Engine model:	Evolution V-twin
Engine capacity:	80 cu. in. (1310 cc)
Cases:	Harley-Davidson
Carburation:	Harley-Davidson
Air filter:	Harley-Davidson
Ignition:	Electronic
Pipes:	Shotgun duals
Transmission:	Five-speed
Frame:	Tubular cradle
Suspension:	Front: telescopic forks Rear: Softail
Brakes:	Front: single disc Rear: disc
Wheels:	16in (406mm) cast-alloy disc front and rear
Mudguards (fenders):	Stock Harley-Davidson
Handlebars:	Wide FLH style
Risers:	Aluminium clamp
Headlight:	Sealed beam
Tail-light:	Stock Harley-Davidson

Back in the days when Harley-Davidsons had no rear suspension, riders relied for their comfort on sprung seat posts and padded saddles that wouldn't have looked out of place on a contemporary agricultural tractor. The tubular cradle frame was known retrospectively as a hard-tail because it lacked suspension, and the look of the frame in this configuration was clean and unadulterated. Customizers of early bikes valued this simplicity of line, and by 1984, the manufacturer was providing factory-built machines that replicated the hardtail look. The FLSTF Fat Boy was one such motorbike, based on the Softail frame on which the rear swing-arm and lower exhaust pipe concealed the suspension dampers. Released in 1990, the Fat Boy looked more of a bruiser than its chopperesque brethren, an effect obtained by keeping it clear of too much extraneous luggage and therefore stripped for action, and by fitting chunky-looking 16in (406mm) alloy disc wheels. Looking more like metal plates, these plain and simple wheels were shod with Dunlop's podgy Elite tyres, as befitting the bike's nomenclature. They were more aerodynamically efficient than wire-spoked wheels, and referred back to wheel discs that were occasionally fitted to Harley-Davidsons in the past, as a means of streamlining. They were also far easier to keep clean even than spoked alloy wheels. The Fat Boy was retarded by a single drum brake at the front and a disc at the rear.

There were plenty of other classic references on board the Fat Boy. The front forks were clad with metal shrouds to further the reference to an FL Hydra Glide from the late 1940s, and the chromed sealed-beam headlamp was mounted on a metal panel across the front of the forks, just like a 1948 FL. The front and rear mudguards were attractively flared in a way that brought to mind the Hydra Glide as well, while running gear such as the traffic indicators was restrained and kept to a practical level. The front ones were mounted on the ends of the simple, wide FLH-style chrome handlebars. The instrumentation comprised electronic speedometer with odometer and trip meter and was housed in the console on top of the 4.5-gallon (20.5-litre) Fatbob fuel tank, so that from the front, the Fat Boy presented a clean-cut image. The rider and pillion travelled on a solo saddle and removable pillion, with a backrest fitted to the latter. The rider's seat was set especially low, at just over 26in (67cm) from the road.

The profile of the Fat Boy was in part dominated by the shotgun dual exhaust system that incorporated the balance tube cross-pipe. The teardrop-shaped tool box and the horseshoe oil tank that curved around the battery were chrome plated, and the rocker covers of the Evolution engine could have a cosmetic job done on them to pick up the bike's main body colour. The air cleaner was fashioned from chromed steel, with a spun aluminium insert, and from 1993, the Evo engine's breather system was modified so that pipes serving the classic filter were eliminated. From the year 2000, the 80 cu. in. (1310 cc) Evolution engine was superseded by the incoming 88 cu. in. (1475 cc) Twin Cam motor.

Vital Statistics

The Fat Boy's vital statistics ranged from a length of 93.85in (238.40cm) and a seat height of 26.50in (67.30cm)

Left: The most striking feature of the FLSTF was the fitment of solid-looking alloy-disc wheels, suggestive of the wheel discs fitted as streamlined covers to laced wire-spoke wheels in the past.

Above: The left-hand side of the Fatboy shows its lockable tool-box cover, rear foot-peg, belt final-drive, and Softail chassis members in which the rear suspension damper is located.

to a ground clearance of 5.47in (13.90cm). The rake of the forks was 32 degrees, and trail was 5.80in (14.73cm). The wheelbase measured 63.89in (162.30cm), while the tyre sizes were MT90B16 at the front, and MT90B16 at the rear. The Fat Boy's dry weight was 631lb [283.95kg]. The bore and stroke of the Evolution engine were 3.498in x 4.250in, and the compression ratio was 8.5:1, fed via a carburettor fuel system. In urban use, the Fat Boy returned 43 mpg (15.2 km/l), against 55 mpg (19.5 km/l) out on the open road. The braking distance from 60 mph (95km/h) was 177ft. (53.1m), and the lean angle was 28 degrees to the right and 29 degrees to the left.

Not surprisingly, the FLSTF Fat Boy caused a stir on its introduction, as there is no question that such a name can only be perceived as derisory. However, like its cousin the Bad Boy, this bike was all about a kind of attitude, which proclaims in no uncertain terms that big is beautiful. Or, at least, that it has substantial physical presence.

XL 1200S Sportster Sport

The XL 1200S Sportster Sport has improved suspension systems, with adjustable telescopic forks and gas reservoirs accompanying the coil-over-damper shock absorbers and swing-arm at the rear.

The 1200 Sportster's peanut fuel tank was larger than previous versions, holding 3.5 gallons (12.5 litres), although it was still not as voluminous as the Fatbob tank. The tank motif incorporated the checkered V-sign that recalled graphics from the early 1960s.

Traditional elements of Sportster styling included the three-cornered oil tank located beneath the low-profile saddle, the chromed ham-can air-filter cover, brake master cylinder, and shallow pressed steel fenders.

With a five-speed gearbox, the Sportster line received belt-driven final-drive in 1991, instead of chain. This was taken down the right-hand side of the machine, unlike its big-twin siblings where it was located on the left-hand side.

Reverse view

The Sportster Sport ran with a 19in (483mm) 13-spoke cast alloy front wheel, and a matching 13-spoke alloy at the back, but measuring 16in (406mm) in diameter with a correspondingly chunkier tyre.

The 1200 Sport model came out in 1996, and was powered by the 73 cu. in. (1200 cc) version of the Evolution V-twin, producing 69bhp. Staggered dual exhausts were fitted and each cylinder head had two spark plugs for improved combustion.

Above: Although the XL 1200S had a larger fuel capacity than previous Sportster models, its tank was not as large as the Fatbob type fitted on the Harley-Davidson big-twins. The standard duo-tone colour scheme is violet and red pearl.

Although the Sportster models have been fitted with a variety of V-twin guises and engine capacities over the years, the machine itself has always stayed pretty close to the original concept. That precedent was the Model-K from 1952, born in the post-war rush to acquire motorbikes that promised more sporting performance and more exciting handling than had previously been on offer. The original Model-K used the long-serving 45 cu. in. (738 cc) side-valve V-twin, and, being less encumbered than the bigger Knucklehead models, it had more of a sporty nature, even if it wasn't exactly in the same league as some of the British imports. As capacity increased in 1954 to 54 cu. in. (883 cc), the Model-K gained in performance, but it wasn't until it was transformed into an overhead-valve model in 1957 that the Sportster was born. The XL was the first true Harley-Davidson Sportster, which now had styling to match its capability. It was also available with luggage, screen and crash bars, which transformed it into a touring machine, if so desired. It was not uncommon for owners to go the opposite way and remove superfluous components to achieve a more sporting appearance and create a lighter, better handling bike. This was not quite the same thing as customizing or chopping, because the

real object was to improve the performance. Competition versions of the Model-K, such as the KRTT of 1961, provided inspiration, if any were needed. This out-and-out dirt track racer used the reliable 45 cu. in. (738 cc) side-valve motor with four gears and chain drive, with special cams and big valves installed, and had a lengthy race-winning pedigree to back it up. The XR 750 Sportster also provided the basis for a number of successful flat track racers and carried on winning for some 25 years. It was also the model chosen by dare-devil stunt rider Evil Knievel. By 1972 there was a road-racing version of the XR, called the XRTT. This was generally fitted with a full-race fairing and aerodynamic race hump, clip-on bars and a

Right: The rear suspension set-up of the XL 1200S Sportster Sport, showing 13-spoke alloy wheel, ventilated brake disc and calliper, swing-arm and coil-over-damper shock absorber with attached gas reservoir cartridge.

1996 XL 1200S Sportster 1200 Sport

Engine model:	Evolution
Engine capacity:	74 cu. in. (1200 cc)
Cases:	Harley-Davidson
Carburation:	Stock Harley-Davidson
Air filter:	Racetrack oval
Ignition:	Electronic
Pipes:	Staggered duals
Transmission:	Five-speed
Frame:	Tubular cradle
Suspension:	Front: telescopic forks
	Rear: swing-arm and dampers
Brakes:	Front: twin disc
	Rear: disc
Wheels:	Front: 19in (483mm) cast-alloy 13-spoke
	Rear: 16in (406mm) cast-alloy 13-spoke
Mudguards (fenders):	Stock XL
Handlebars:	Flat-track
Risers:	Aluminium
Headlight:	Sealed beam
Tail-light:	Stock Harley-Davidson

massive ventilated Cerani drum brake up front. The whole ensemble was not so different in concept or appearance from modern road- or circuit-racing machines. Soon afterwards the company came out with the XR 1000, the engine of which was composed of the alloy heads and Dell'Orto carbs from the XR 750 grafted on to the bottom end of the XL 1000 Sportster engine. It was the fastest production Harley-Davidson ever – 70bhp from 61 cu. in. (998 cc) and 120mph (190km/h) potential – but it was not the quantum leap that some customers had been anticipating. That came with the installation of the 54 cu. in. (883 cc) version of the Evolution engine in the XLH chassis in 1986. It wasn't long before the 68 cu. in. (1100 cc) and 74 cu. in. (1200 cc) versions appeared.

A Modern-spec Harley

The XL1200S was exactly that, a top-of-the-range Sportster fitted with the 74 cu. in. (1200 cc) V-twin, with a twin-plug cylinder head for optimum combustion. The exhaust system was a staggered dual set-up, each pipe linked by a balance tube that helped the engine comply with federal noise regulations. The oval air-cleaner cover displayed the engine's cubic capacity – in this case 1200cc.

The suspension consisted of adjustable cartridge-type damper valving on the telescopic front forks, head shock in the head stock, rear swing-arm with coil-over dampers and gas reservoirs, adjustable for pre-load and damping. Up front, twin floating discs with two-piston callipers and

a single rear disc brought it to a halt, and it ran on 13-spoke cast alloy wheels, 19in (483mm) at the front and 16in (406mm) at the back. The XL 1200 was equipped with flat-track type bars, with twin instrument binnacles containing speedo and rev-counter mounted in the centre, and a sealed beam headlight with anti-glare peak. The graphics on the 3.5-gallon (12.5-litre) fuel tank harked back to the racing logo of the early 1960s. A pressed-steel front mudguard was fitted, with a regular rear mudguard surmounted by the pillion half of the seat. For fans requiring a modern spec Harley, the Sportster Sport was the optimum choice.

XLH 883 Sportster Hugger

The fenders on the XLH 883 are standard-issue Sportster, with a slender pressed steel mudguard at the front and the rear one carrying the tail-light and registration plate. The dual saddle ends in a backrest, with tool roll attached.

Introduced in 1957, the Sportster range was lighter and had better handling than its big-twin siblings. Central to the model's image was the 2.5-gallon (10-litre) peanut fuel tank.

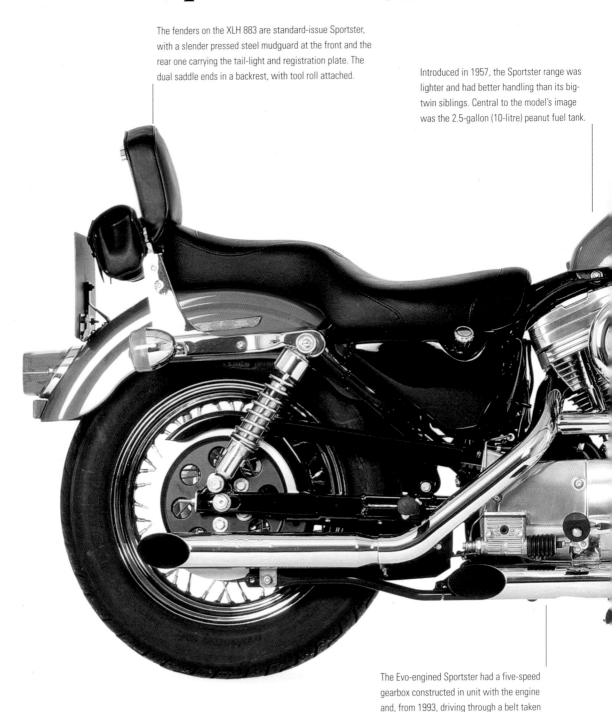

The Evo-engined Sportster had a five-speed gearbox constructed in unit with the engine and, from 1993, driving through a belt taken down the right-hand side of the bike.

From 1912, a lever-operated rear hub clutch enabled the bike to be brought to a halt without having to stall the engine, although this was an optional extra.

Reverse view

The Sportster Hugger runs on a 19in (483mm) laced wire-spoke wheel at the front, with a single 11.5in (290mm) ventilated brake disc, and a similar 16in (406mm) laced wheel at the back.

The XLH 883 Sportster Hugger gets its designation from the engine capacity, which is 53.9 cu. in. (883 cc), making it the smallest power-unit in the Harley-Davidson line-up. The Evolution engine was used in Sportsters from 1986 to 1999.

The lean, street-fighter styling of the XLH Sportster Hugger was unmistakable. A derivative of the marque's longest-running series, the XL Sportster line, the 883 Sportster Hugger had the smallest displacement of any Harley-Davidson motorcycle. At 53.9cu in, the model was referred to by its engine's cubic capacity, which was 883cc. It was also the smallest bike in the range in terms of its weight and length. It weighed 486lb and measured 88.0in (223.52cm) long, with a seat height of 27.12in (68.8cm) and ground clearance of just 4.7in (11.94cm). The wheelbase was 59.0in (149.86cm). There were six models in the Sportster line-up in 2000, including bigger displacement 73 cu. in. (1200 cc) versions. All have the traditional look about them, with no protective plastic fairings to hide the classic V-twin. The drivelines and running gear have been upgraded through the Sportster's 40-year history.

The 1996 model featured here was fitted with the 54 cu. in. (883 cc) version of the overhead valve Evolution engine, operated by electronic ignition and 1.5in (40mm) CV carburettor. It delivered 52lb/ft of torque at 4500rpm. The

883's exhaust system consisted of staggered shorty duals. Internal measurements are a bore and stroke of 3.0in x 3.8in, and a compression ratio of 9.0:1. The powertrain was of unit construction, with the lower engine and gearbox casing manufactured as a single unit. There was five-speed transmission, via triple-row primary drive chain and, from 1993, final belt drive. Unlike many chain-driven final drive bikes, the Sportster's belt drive was taken off the right-hand side of the gearbox.

The 883 Sportster Hugger had telescopic front forks and rear swing-arm allied to coil-over dampers. The steering rake was 30.1 degrees and trail was 4.7in (11.94cm). Tyre sizes were 100/90-19 at the front, and 130/90HB16 at the back. Another feature that rendered the 883 Sportster Hugger different from its heavyweight siblings was the smaller 3.3 gallon (15 litre) fuel tank, with a half-gallon reserve. The oil tank capacity was 3 quarts (2.8 litres).

Fuel Consumption

Economy was pretty good, at 48 mpg (17km/l) in town and 57 mpg (20km/l) on the open road, while the stopping distance from 60 mph (95km/l) was 160ft (50m). This 883 ran on a 19in (483mm) wire-spoked wheel at the front and a 16in (406mm) spoke wheel at the rear. Standard wheels were 13-spoke cast aluminium alloy, but wires were optional fitment. A single disc brake served at the front, measuring 11.5in. x 0.20in (29.21cm x 5.08mm) with a slightly wide disc at the back, 11.5in. x 0.23in (29.21cm x 5.82mm). The bike could be leant over in corners at a greater angle than most Harley-Davidsons – 33 degrees to the right and 35 degrees to the left.

The 883 Sportster Hugger was clad in standard metal Sportster mudguards, which were quite appropriate for its no-frills persona, while clocks were mounted atop the buckhorn-type handlebars. The instruments consisted of electronic speedometer with odometer and trip meter. The Sportster came with rubber covered foot-pegs rather than foot-boards, and its equipment list was rounded off by mirrors and traffic indicators.

1996 XLH Sportster Hugger	
Engine model:	Evolution
Engine capacity:	54 cu. in. (883 cc)
Cases:	Harley-Davidson
Carburation:	1.5in (40mm) CV
Air filter:	Oval racetrack
Ignition:	Electronic
Pipes:	Staggered duals
Transmission:	Five-speed, belt drive
Frame:	Duplex tubular cradle
Suspension:	Front: telescopic forks
	Rear: swing-arm and coil-over dampers
Brakes:	Front: single disc
	Rear: disc
Wheels:	Front: 19in (483mm) wire-spoke
	Rear: 16in (406mm) wire-spoke
Mudguards (fenders):	Stock Sportster
Handlebars:	Buckhorn
Risers:	None
Headlight:	Stock Harley-Davidson sealed beam
Tail-light:	Stock Harley-Davidson

XL Sportster 1200 Custom

This XL Sportster Custom is equipped with an appropriately low-slung leather seat, with a backrest for the pillion, plus matching leather saddlebags and chromed rear luggage carrier.

One of the main upgrades to the Sportster specification that came in for 1996 was an increase in the size of the fuel tank, now with a 3.3-gallon (12.5-litre) capacity. Its proportions were thus much improved.

The bike rides on a 21in (533mm) laced wire-spoke wheel at the front, with a single ventilated disc brake, and a 16in (406mm) slotted aluminium-alloy wheel at the rear, enhancing the custom look.

New for 1996, the XL 1200 Sportster Custom was a deliberate move by Harley-Davidson to extend the marque's custom branding into Sportster territory. An ample evidence of chrome, such as the bullet headlight, bear witness to this.

Reverse view

This XL Sportster 1200 Custom is fitted with stock Harley-Davidson pressed steel fenders front and rear. The paint finish is two-tone platinum silver and black.

The power-unit is the 74 cu. in. (1200 cc) Evolution overhead-valve V-twin, featuring a typical ham-can air-filter cover and staggered shorty dual exhaust pipes with a horizontal cross-over pipe linking the two manifolds. To the left is the bike's oil tank, with rear master cylinder at the bottom.

As Harley-Davidson's longest-running line, it would be surprising if the Sportster engine had not passed through various guises and capacities over the years. During its four-decade life-span, it has always remained true to its original layout, however. In one sense, the Sportster 1200 Custom refers back to the XLCH Sportster of the late 1950s and early 1960s, a bare-boned bike intended for fast-moving riding on the ragged edge. The difference with the 1200 Custom version is that it provides a more practical slant to such pursuits, presented in a classic demeanour.

The nub of the XL Sportster 1200 Custom was its lowered suspension and re-designed 3.3-gallon (12.5-litre) fuel tank, which provided a better cruising range. A revised tank badge adorned the new item, and it was fitted with a new stepped dual saddle that came with a back-rest for the pillion. The period look was furthered by the fitting of a chrome-plated bullet-style headlight, with a single handlebar-mounted electronic speedo with odometer and trip meter. The bars themselves were low-rise affairs, making for an ideal uncontorted riding position. Also fitted were the pendant traffic indicators and mirrors; the moth screen was optional fitment. The advantage of screens of this size is that although they create more wind resistance, they do enable a higher cruising speed since the rider is not subjected to the same forces of nature as he would be on a screenless machine. The potential cruising speed is lifted – where legally permitted – by some 10 to 20mph (16-32km/h).

The 74 cu. in. (1200 cc) version of the alloy Evolution engine was introduced in 1988, and over the years it was subjected only to detail changes. Bore and stroke was 3.498in x 3.812in., with a compression ratio of 9.0:1.

Below: Both the 54 cu. in. (883 cc) and 74 cu. in. (1200 cc) versions of the Evo-Sportster V-twin engine are of unit-construction assembly, implying that the crankcase and gearbox casing are machined as a single unit, unlike the big-twins which have separate casings.

Left: Although the wind-shield is a useful extra on this XL 1200 Sportster Custom, the low-rise handlebars and solitary speedo are part of the custom package offered as standard fare.

it was the first road-going Harley-Davidson to feature adjustable sporting suspension. Other additions such as the 13-spoke wheels and twin-plug heads transformed it into one of Harley-Davidson's most adventurous models.

Many Sportster enthusiasts held the opinion that the original 1200 Custom provided an unbeatable combination of Sportster performance and Harley-Davidson looks. For 1999 the foot controls were shifted further forwards, taking the styling another notch into classicdom. Raked at 30.1 degrees, the front forks were now taller, with new high-rise drag bars on the Custom's chromed steering head. For those that veered towards the traditional look, the Sportster 1200 Custom was altogether a satisfying bike to look at. Apart from its period components, it was also equipped with smart leather saddlebags, minimal front mudguard and pert Sportster rear.

It developed 71lb/ft of torque at 4000 rpm, and would return 45 mpg (16 km/l) on an urban cycle and 52 mpg (18.5 km/l) out on the open road. On the Sportster 1200 Custom the Evo engine featured electronic ignition, five-speed transmission and belt final drive. Primary drive was by a triple-row chain. The exhaust pipes were in the staggered shorty dual format, and an oval 'racetrack' air-filter cover was present. The Custom was sold with a 21in (533mm) wire-spoke laced wheel at the front and a 16in (406mm) slotted cast-alloy wheel at the rear. It was retarded by a single disc brake at the front and another at the back. The braking distance from 60 mph (95 km/h) was 160ft (48.0m). The maximum angle of lean was 33 degrees to the right and 35 degrees to the left. The vital statistics of the XL Sportster 1200 Custom ranged from a length of 89.0in. (226.06cm) and a seat height of 27.56 in (70.0cm) to a ground clearance 6.25in. (15.87cm) and wheelbase measuring 60.0in (152.40 cm). The tyre size was MH90-21 at the front and MT 90 B16 at the back. The dry weight was 491lb (221.71 kg).

The Sportster Sport

One variant, the Sportster Sport, had uprated suspension and improved power output over the basic model to justify its S designation. In addition, the engine was fitted with twin-plug heads and had higher compression and revised camshafts in comparison with the base model. When the 1200 Sport was originally released in 1996,

1996 XL Sportster 1200 Custom	
Engine model:	Evolution
Engine capacity:	74 cu. in. (1200 cc)
Cases:	Harley-Davidson
Carburation:	Harley-Davidson
Air filter:	Racetrack oval
Ignition:	Electronic
Pipes:	Staggered shorty duals
Transmission:	Five-speed
Frame:	Tubular cradle
Suspension:	Front: telescopic forks
	Rear: swing-arm and dampers
Brakes:	Front: single disc
	Rear: disc
Wheels:	Front: 21in (533mm) spoked
	Rear: 16in (406mm) slotted alloy
Mudguards (fenders):	Sportster
Handlebars:	Low-rise
Risers:	Yes
Headlight:	Chrome bullet
Tail-light:	Stock Harley-Davidson

FXSTC Softail Custom

The king-and-queen dual saddle was suitably cushioned, placing the rider in a low-down position, matched by the bike's forward-mounted foot controls, and a padded backrest for the passenger perched above the rear wheel.

Chromed ancillaries on the FXSTC Softail Custom include the horseshoe oil tank, the gearbox inspection plate, rear fender bracket, instrument console and self-cancelling pendant indicators on the bars.

The FXSTC Softail Custom of 1996 was inspired by the chopper look, and targeted at riders who liked such imagery. Crucial to it were the widened and raked fork yokes, plus the chromed headlight and pull-back bars.

Reverse view

The fenders on the FXSTC are a mismatch of the lightweight XL Sportster type at the front with the bobbed Dyna Glide type at the back. The paint finish is patriot red pearl, with gold coachlines and an eagle silhouette tank badge.

This FXSTC Softail Custom plays off the tall, spindly 21in (533mm) laced wire-spoke wheel at the front against the brutish 16in (406mm) cast aluminium-alloy disc wheel at the rear.

The Evolution big-twin does duty as the power-unit, developing 58bhp at 7200rpm from its 80 cu. in. (1310 cc) two cylinders. The chrome air-filter cover shows the engine capacity, while the staggered shorty duals give a purposeful look – and sound.

Since the 1980s, Harley-Davidson has kept a weather eye on what custom builders get up to with their products and have made a point of offering their own factory-built interpretation of the style. Customizing is slightly constrained because a company like Harley-Davidson is legally bound by legislation that does not affect individual custom builders. Nevertheless, the company has offered a whole gamut of acceptably styled factory custom models, and the 1996 Softail Custom was exactly this type of bike. To the uninitiated, it looks like a neatly customized bike rather than an ordinary stock model.

Below: The Softail frame has the appearance of the old-fashioned hardtail chassis last seen on some of the Panhead models. The frame geometry cleverly incorporates the damper in the tubing. Note the belt-drive pulley and protective cover.

Key features of the FXSTC Softail Custom were its bobbed rear mudguard, stepped dual seat, Fatbob tank, minimal front mudguard and big pullback bars. Other visual hallmarks of the Softail Custom were the low stepped seat and raked profile created by the steeply raked – 32 degrees – chopper-style front forks. The attitude of the bike was set off by its 21in (533mm) interlaced wire spoked wheel, which contrasted with the 16in (406mm) cast alloy wheel at the rear. Tyre sizes were MH90-21 at the front, and MT90B16 at the back. Braking from 60 mph (95 km/h) required 177ft. (53.1m) of space to come to a standstill. Brakes were single discs front and rear, measuring 11.5 in. x 0.20in (29.21cm x 5.08mm) at the front and 11.5in. x 0.23in (29.21cm x 5.82mm) at the rear.

Classic Hardtail Imagery

The Softail Custom's classic hardtail imagery was based on the uncluttered Softail frame, invested with the distinctive lines of its chrome and wrinkle-black 80 cu. in. (1340 cc) Evolution V-twin engine. It was also fitted with forward-mounted foot controls, a buckhorn handlebar and an eagle-emblazoned sissy bar. In this way, Harley-Davidson assembled a host of custom parts around a big twin Evolution engine and five-speed transmission and, hey presto, a custom bike was available straight off the dealer's showroom floor. Prominent in the Softail Custom's arsenal of period features were the bobbed contours of the rear mudguard that revealed much of the rear cast alloy disc-wheel. The rear brake disc and the rear frame were also on show, demonstrating one of the Softail's trademarks. This was a hydraulic damper incorporated in the cleverly designed chassis swing-arm, meaning that although the frame looked as though it was a vintage hardtail, it was in reality a modern Softail with suspension. Suspension travel at the front forks measured 5.61in. (14.25cm), while the Softail rear dampers provided 4.06in. (10.31cm) of travel. The bike's maximum angle of lean was a somewhat restrained 28 degrees to the right and 29 degrees to the left. There were six other Softail models in the range in year 2001. They included the FXST Softail Standard, the FXSTB Night Train, the FXSTS Springer Softail, the FLSTF Fat Boy, the FLSTC Heritage Softail Classic, and the FLSTS Heritage Springer. Apart from the outlaw chopper, the historical point of visual reference for the Softail Custom chassis frame was the 1950s Hydra Glide. Overall length of the bike was 94.92in (241.1cm), with a seat height of 26.70in (67.82cm), while ground clearance was 5.94in (15.09cm), and wheelbase measured 66.5in (169.0cm). Its dry weight was 613lb (275.85kg).

1996 FXSTC Softail Custom

Engine model:	Evolution
Engine capacity:	80 cu. in. (1340 cc)
Cases:	Harley-Davidson
Carburation:	Stock Harley-Davidson
Air filter:	8in (203mm) circular
Ignition:	Electronic
Pipes:	Staggered shorty duals
Transmission:	Five-speed
Frame:	Tubular cradle
Suspension:	Front: telescopic forks Rear: Softail
Brakes:	Front: single disc Rear: disc
Wheels:	Front: 21in (533mm) wire-spoke Rear: 16in (406mm) cast-alloy disc
Mudguards (fenders):	Front: XL-type Rear: bobbed
Handlebars:	Pull-back
Risers:	Pull-back
Headlight:	Chromed sealed beam
Tail-light:	Stock Harley-Davidson

Power came from the 80 cu. in. (1340 cc) Evolution engine, the bore and stroke of which was 3.498in x 4.250in, with a fairly modest compression ratio of 8.5:1. It produced 76.0lb/ft of torque at 3500 rpm. The Evo motor was fed by a carburettor, and gave 43 mpg (15 km/l) around town and 55 mpg (19.5 km/l) when cruising. Primary drive was by double-row chain, and the belt final drive was concealed behind a guard and taken off the left-hand side of the gearbox to a pulley on the left of the cast alloy wheel. The fuel capacity of the trad Fatbob tank was 5.2 gallons (23 litres), which included a little more than half a gallon in reserve, while capacity of the chromium plated horseshoe oil tank was three quarts (2.8 litres). The exhaust system was the staggered shorty duals layout, with linking balance tube. The chopper-like ensemble was finished off with the polished fork yokes and a small chrome-plated sealed beam headlight and tank-mounted dash that contained an electronic speedo with odometer and trip meter.

FLHT Twin Cam 88

The FLHT is equipped with a nicely moulded fairing and wind-shield, protecting the handlebar controls and covering the headlight, spotlights and pendant indicators.

Either laced wire-spoke wheels or aluminium-alloy spoked wheels can be specified, in this case the latter, accompanied by twin ventilated disc brakes up front and a single disc at the rear.

The FLHT Twin Cam 88 earns its name from the so-called Twin Cam engine, the latest in the line of 45-degree V-twins. Its 88 cu. in. (1450 cc) engine produces 65bhp at 7250rpm.

While the majority of manufacturers use an overhead camshaft format, Harley-Davidson retains the time-served pushrod method of valve operation. Thus, the Twin Cam engine has a brace of cams, but not overhead ones.

The FLHT designation reveals this machine to be one of the Electra Glide family, a big beefy tourer that, curiously, omits the back rest, rear luggage rack and top box more normally associated with the model.

The big-twin's primary drive five-speed gearbox casing has endured with this appearance since 1984 when the Evolution engine came in. The final drive is by belt and pulley.

Above: The heart of the FLHT model is its 88 cu. in. (1450 cc) Twin Cam engine – so-called because the rocker covers resemble an overhead camshaft layout. The oval air cleaner cover hides the fuel injection system. Below are the crankcase cover, footboard and exhaust-pipe.

named the P22, the new engine was announced late in 1998 and had the authority of Willie G. Davidson stamped on it. The Twin Cam was not, in fact, a twin-cam design with a pair of cams lying side-by-side in the cylinder head, but a regular two-cam configuration in the grand old tradition of the company's 45-degree V-twin engine architecture. It was an advance on the previous Evolution engine that powered the earlier Tour Glide, in that cubic capacity rose from 80 cu. in. (1310 cc) to 88 cu. in. (1450 cc) and the engine was now managed by computerized fuel injection. While it still sounded the same, the Twin Cam-powered Harley was more powerful, more economical and with reduced emissions. Fans began calling it the Fat Head quite early on.

When the FLHT Electra Glide Twin Cam was introduced, the Harley-Davidson Motor Company's headquarters still lay at the end of Juneau Avenue in western Milwaukee, in the shadow of the vast Miller Brewing Company's main brewery. The original brick edifice that pre-dated World War I became an historic landmark and, at the year 2000, was the company's administration block. Manufacturing operations had been transferred long ago to the Capitol Drive and Pilgrim Road plants a few miles away, as well as York, Pennsylvania, and Kansas City. The aim was to produce 200,000 motorcycles by the company's one-hundredth anniversary in 2003. During the 1990s, output more than doubled to about 150,000 motorcycles a year. As of 2001, Harley-Davidsonís future rested with president and chief executive officer Jeff Bleustein, a bespectacled academic who had seen his company plunge to the brink more than once during the 1980s. Along with chairman Richard Teerlink, head of styling Willie G. Davidson and the retired Vaughn Beals, he had ensured that the company was on the up and up.

The Twin Cam engine was the powerhouse that propelled the companys range of big-twins into the new

The FLHT Electra Glide Standard of 2000 was powered by the Twin Cam 88 V-twin and was the motorcycle that, perhaps more than any other machine, embodied America's legendary love affair with the open road. The mainstay of Harley-Davidson's touring range, it had all the style of the original tourers that were to be seen on the highways in the late 1950s. There was more than a passing reference in the beefy fork tubes and massive chrome headlight to a 1960 Duo-Glide, while the cases and windscreen were in the best tradition of Harley-Davidson accessories.

The FLHT Electra Glide was built upon the well-tried tubular cradle frame, but what was really notable about this motorcycle was its Twin Cam 88 power plant. Code-

millennium. Harley-Davidson engineers kept faith with their traditional V-twin engine architecture, however, and ignored overhead camshafts and multi-valve cylinder heads when designing the new engine. They did fit sophisticated fuel-injection and electronic ignition systems, and sophisticated electronics provided the Twin Cam with data for the engine management system, which calculated optimum fuel-injection settings for a given speed and load. Beneath the cam cover could be seen the exposed chain-drive to the cams that replaced the gear-drive used on earlier engines and helped to reduce noise and manufacturing costs. However, the 1999 Twin Cam motor still relied on the trusty 45-degree overhead-valve layout. With a capacity of 88 cu. in. (1450 cc), the alloy crankcase unit was Harley-Davidson's biggest ever production engine. Although just 21 of the 450 components that constitute the Twin Cam engine were carried over from its predecessor, not many changes are obvious. The visual differences over the Evolution engine include polished pushrod tubes, two-piece alloy rocker

Above: Long-distance touring doesn't come much more effortless than on board this FLHT Electra Glide, sporting luggage cases, crash bars and thickly padded dual leather saddle.

covers and an oval air filter which hides the fuel injection mechanism. The Twin Cam 88 developed 79bhp and some 10 per cent more torque.

Vital Statistics

The FLHT Electra Glide Twin Cam measured 93.7in (237.8cm) in length, with a seat height of 27.3in (69.3cm), while ground clearance was 5.1in (13cm). Steering rake was 26 degrees and trail 6.2in (15.6cm). The bike's wheelbase measured 65.3in (161.2cm) and tyre sizes were MT90B16 71H at the front and MT90B16 74H at the rear. Fuel capacity was 5 gallons (18.95 litres), including just under one gallon (3.79 litres) in reserve. Its oil capacity was 4 quarts (3.8 litres) and the bike weighed 758lb (344.1kg . The brakes measured 11.5in x 0.20in (292.1mm x 5.08mm) at the front 11.5in x 0.23in (292.1mm x 5.82mm) at the rear. It could tolerate being leaned over to 33 degrees to the right and 31 degrees to the left. Primary drive was by double-row chain, with belt final drive. Wheels were nine-spoke cast aluminium alloy, with the laced wire-spoke variety an option. Its instrumentation comprised electric speedometer with odometer and re-settable trip meter, tachometer, fuel gauge, voltmeter, electrical power outlet, oil pressure indicator lamp, engine diagnostic light and an optional security system light.

2000 FLHT Electra Glide Twin Cam 88	
Engine model:	Twin Cam 88 overhead-valve V-twin
Engine capacity:	88 cu. in. (1450 cc)
Cases:	Harley-Davidson
Carburation:	Fuel injection
Air filter:	Oval Harley-Davidson
Ignition:	Electronic
Pipes:	Two-into-one
Transmission:	Five-speed, belt drive
Frame:	Tubular cradle
Suspension:	Front: telescopic forks Rear: swing-arm
Brakes:	Front: twin discs, four-piston calliper Rear: disc
Wheels:	Spoked aluminium alloy or wire-spoke (optional) front and rear
Mudguards (fenders):	Stock FLHT
Handlebars:	Flat
Risers:	Integral with bars
Headlight:	Chromed quartz-halogen
Tail-light:	Integral with mudguard (fender)

FXSTD Softail Deuce

The FXSTD Softail Deuce is powered by the
88 cu. in. (1449 cc) Twin Cam 88B big-twin,
pushrod-operated with two overhead-valves
per cylinder, with hydraulic self-adjusting
lifters. The bore and stroke measure 95.3mm
x 101.6mm – true to the Harley-Davidson
philosophy, the stroke is larger than the bore.

The custom look is enhanced by fitting
the traditional horseshoe oil tank,
over-and-under shotgun dual exhaust
pipes, plus the solitary speedo on the
tank-top instrument binnacle.

Controls on the FXSTD Softail Deuce include foot-pegs, forward-mounted brake pedal and gear shift lever, wide front brake and clutch levers, paired mirrors and pendant trafficators.

Reverse view

The owner can customize his or her Harley-Davidson to the hilt, using the company's own Screamin' Eagle range of kit, which encompasses virtually every aspect of the bike, from forks to exhaust pipes.

The Softail Deuce runs with a 21in (533mm) laced wire-spoke front wheel projected forward of the bike by its 34-degrees raked forks. The rear wheel is a 17in (432mm) deep-dish diamond-cut alloy disc, shod with Dunlop-made Harley-Davidson tyres.

The FXSTD uses the regular tubular cradle frame, made from mild steel with a rectangular section backbone and twin down-tubes. The forks are wide-set 41.3mm custom, with the swing-arm and Softail rear end incorporating horizontally mounted dampers.

Released along with a completely revised Softail range in 2000, the FXSTD Softail Deuce is an extension of the Super Glide family, combining looks, power and comfort. At nearly 88 cu. in. (1450 cc), the FXSTD's Twin Cam V-twin engine has greater cubic capacity than the average car engine. And it shows. Wind on the throttle as you exit a bend and it pulls so strongly and effortlessly that you are up to full cruising speed in no time. That it achieves this in supreme rider comfort is another factor in the Harley-Davidson attraction. There is none of the runaway sensation that is generated by a modern Supersports machine, except, perhaps, astride the street-fighter Buell X1 Lightning, where the power is there if you want it.

On any of the Sportsters and big Harley-Davidsons, the rider feels in command. The FLHRI Road King, for instance, which combines cool 1960s styling with a practical seating arrangement and adequate luggage capacity, is supremely comfortable. While the FXSTD Softail Deuce features forward foot controls, the Road

Above: The lean-and-mean look of the FXSTD Softail Deuce is created by such components as the unadorned flat-track style bars and the single speedo set in the tank-top instrument console.

King stays with footboards and the left-foot heel-and-toe gearshift. These big Harleys come with revised ignition switches in the centre console atop the 5-gallon (18.9-litre) fuel tank, where the fuel gauge is also situated. Standard equipment also includes electronic speedometer with odometer and resettable trip meter, oil pressure indicator lamp and engine diagnostic light. The oil tank is the traditional chrome horseshoe type, with chromed external oil lines. The exhaust pipes are the suitably extrovert over-and-under shotgun duals, while the Softail Deuce's chopperesque image is enhanced by the low-rise flat-track handlebars and low-slung custom seat.

Development at Lotus Engineering

Harley-Davidson engines have recently undergone development work at Lotus Engineering, the development consultancy arm of the celebrated sports car company based in Norfolk, England. In the case of the FXSTD Softail Deuce, the power unit is the 88 cu. in. (1450 cc) Twin Cam 88B, pushrod-operated with two overhead-valves per cylinder and hydraulic self-adjusting lifters. Bore and stroke are 3.75in x 4in (95.3 x 101.6mm). The big V-twin is fed by electronic sequential port fuel injection, with electronic breakerless ignition. Its five-speed transmission is via a double-row chain with mechanical tensioner and Gates aramid fibre-reinforced Poly Chain belt final drive.

The FXSTD uses the familiar cradle frame made from mild steel with a rectangular section backbone and twin down-tubes. Forks are wide 1.63in (41.3mm) custom, with swing-arm and Softail rear end with its horizontally

2001 FXSTD Softail Deuce	
Engine model:	Twin Cam 88B V-twin
Engine capacity:	88 cu. in. (1450 cc)
Cases:	Harley-Davidson
Carburation:	Fuel injection
Air filter:	Elliptical with spun aluminium insert
Ignition:	Electronic
Pipes:	Over-and-under shotgun duals
Transmission:	Five-speed, belt drive
Frame:	Tubular cradle
Suspension:	Front: chrome telescopic forks Rear: Softail
Brakes:	Front: single disc, four-piston calliper Rear: disc
Wheels:	Front: 21in (533mm) wire-spoke Rear: 17in (432mm) slotted alloy disc
Mudguards (fenders):	Front: lightweight Rear: straight-cut
Handlebars:	Flat-track
Risers:	Yes
Headlight:	Chromed quartz-halogen
Tail-light:	Integral with mudguard (fender)

mounted dampers. The custom image of the Softail Deuce means it looks best with a 21in (533mm) laced wire-spoke front wheel projecting forward of the bike in the 34-degree raked forks. The back end has a much more meaty look to it, featuring the 17in (432mm) deep-dish diamond-cut disc rear wheel. The wheels are shod with Dunlop-made Harley-Davidson Series II D402/K591s, MH90-21 54H at the front and 160/70B17 73H at the rear. The bike is slowed by two highly efficient discs, operated by four-piston callipers, front and rear.

There are several options with Harley-Davidson's custom bikes – it is all a matter of going with the particular 'look' which takes your fancy. For instance, the contemporary

Below: With masses of torque available from its 88 cu. in. (1449 cc) Twin Cam 88B V-twin engine, the Softail Deuce is capable of showing most vehicles a clean pair of heels. Although a screen would help aerodynamics, the rakish look would be compromised.

FLSTSF Fat Boy occupies similar territory, running the same 88 cu. in. (1450 cc) engine, but it is harder edged and has a heavier stance than the FXSTD Softail Deuce by virtue of its 16in (406mm) disc front wheel and traditional rear fender. The Fat Boy is also a slightly heavier bike, at 665lb (302kg) dry weight against 644lb (292kg) for the Softail Deuce. The latter can also be leaned over further in corners, at 36.7 degrees as opposed to 28.9 degrees.

You do not, however, have to be content with what the factory custom department dictates. You can customize your Harley-Davidson to the hilt, using the company's own Screamin' Eagle range of kit, which encompasses virtually every aspect of the bike, from forks to exhaust pipes. If you fit a windshield, a three-figure cruising speed becomes realistic. All these after-market products are available at Harley-Davidson dealerships, along with other Harley-branded goods, including practical biking gear.

Chapter 4

Special Editions, Customs and Small Capacities

Outside the recognizable mainstream Harley-Davidson models is a panoply of customized specials, often highly modified for speed or posing. Less well-known are the small-capacity bikes that Harley-Davidson built in the 1950s and 1960s through its Italian Aermacchi connection, and the modern-day Buells.

As well as its mainstream output, which today encompasses some 20 different models, Harley-Davidson Motors was responsible for the production of several ranges of small-capacity motor bikes as well as one or two decidedly oddball offerings. Among the latter ranks the Model GE ServiCar V-twin, a three-wheeled vehicle with cargo deck or luggage platform at the rear that remained in production from 1932 to the 1970s.

After the Second World War, Harley-Davidson

Left: Gatherings like the Rat's Hole Custom Show at Daytona, Florida, brought customized Harley-Davidsons closer to the mainstream fold. Still, just how extreme it's possible to be is exemplified by this stretched three-Knucklehead-powered machine.

Above: The three-wheel GE ServiCar enjoyed a long life as Harley-Davidson's utility model, running from 1932 to 1972. Powered by the archaic 45 cu. in. (738 cc) side-valve V-twin, the cargo box was mounted on a modified chassis sub-frame.

introduced a light-weight 7 cu. in. (125 cc) two-stroke machine with three-speed transmission that was a copy of the German pre-war DKW. The patents for the engine, which BSA in Britain was shortly also to build, were secured when they acquired German engineering products as part of Germany's war reparations. Harley-Davidson hoped to increase its options with this cheap motorcycle and acquired a factory in the Milwaukee suburb of Wauwatosa. In production throughout the 1950s, the cubic capacity was increased in 1953 to 10 cu. in. (165 cc) and hydraulic telescopic forks were fitted. It was re-designated the ST Hummer in 1955, but in 1959 it was finally dropped.

In the United States, the scooter craze was burgeoning in the affluent 1950s, mostly fuelled by Italian and German imports that rivalled native Simplex and Cushman brands, and in 1960, Harley-Davidson joined the fray with its own

offering, the 165 cc Topper. Although more aesthetically styled than the rudimentary Cushman products, it still managed to look like a mobile bread-bin and was nowhere near as chic as the Vespa. And in any case, the US scooter market had already begun to fall away.

It wasn't just the British 500 cc and 650 cc bikes that posed a threat to Harley-Davidson. From 1959, the arrival on the US scene of Honda and its Japanese compatriots brought a new attitude to motorcycling. Models like the 90 cc Super Cub C100 from 1958 made a huge impact economically and socially, bringing modest yet respectable mobility to thousands of people who had probably never ridden a motorbike. US sales skyrocketed as a new two-wheeled boom took off. Harley-Davidson responded with another small machine of its own. Alongside the Topper scooter, the air-cooled two-stroke 165 cc Model BT Super 10 came in to replace the Model ST single.

The following year Harley-Davidson bought 50 percent of the Italian motorcycle company Aermacchi when it was in financial difficulties, aided by the strength of the dollar and relatively low Italian production costs. The company

Aermacchi-Harley-Davidson S.A. was set up in Switzerland, with a ready-made range of models ranging from 3 cu. in. (50 cc) to 21 cu. in. (350 cc). The machines were introduced in the United States as the Shortster, the Baja and the Leggero. These were mostly off-roaders, and the range also included a scooter with plastic bodywork and centrifugal clutch. The first product of this American-Italian alliance to reach the United States was the Aermacchi Ala Verde in 1961. It had a 15 cu. in. (250 cc) four-stroke engine, and was renamed the Sprint for the American market, lasting until 1974.

Influence of Sporting Successes

During the 1960s, Harley-Davidson also made golf carts, and also bought the Tomahawk Boat Company and produced plastic parts there. By the time AMF took control of Harley-Davidson, it was clear that the Aermacchi division would have to go. It was a pre-condition for further investment that AMF sold off Aermacchi to the Italian Cagiva group in 1978. It was clear that the sporting successes of Aermacchi-Harley-Davidson riders like Italian Walter Villa – who was three-times 250 cc World Champion – did not have a positive effect on the sale of small two-stroke or boosted sales of the big four-stroke V-twins either.

In 1985 the Buell Motorcycle Company was founded by former Harley-Davidson employee Eric Buell. It manufactured expensive, high-quality sports bikes using Harley-Davidson engines fitted in multi-tubular chassis frames. The early models were encased in unusual bulbous bodywork, but in 1993 Harley-Davidson bought a significant stake in the company and a new model was introduced. Harley-Davidson was interested in producing sports machines, but not at the expense of alienating its traditional buyers. It helped Buell launch the Thunderbolt, which was intended for higher volume production at a lower cost than previous Buell machines. The bike was sold through Harley-Davidson dealers with a factory warranty, and was viewed as an alternative to the mainstream Sportster series.

But, undoubtedly, the most high-profile Harley-Davidson-based machines to be seen and ogled at motorcycle events are the extravagantly ostentatious custom bikes. These are built by skilled individuals or specialist customizing firms, and reveal some refreshing attitudes and innovative applications on the subject.

Below: The famous 'Wrecking Crew' racing team on a wood-block speedway. It is hard to convey what a terrifyingly slippery surface wood is to race on.

Peashooter Board Track Racer

The Peashooter was based on a tubular loop frame, incorporating a minimal saddle and bullet-shaped fuel tank with oil and petrol reservoirs. A diminutive rear mudguard was fitted, but none at the front.

The Peashooter Board Track Racer had external pushrods, with prominent carburettor and streamlined air filter. It got its name from the distinctive sound each beat of the engine emitted through the exhaust pipe – just like a child's peashooter.

The Model AA Peashooter had chain primary-drive and chain final-drive, with either a three-speed gearbox or single-speed with no clutch.

The Peashooter was the racing version of the Model A and B from 1926, powered by the 21 cu. in. (346 cc) single-cylinder side-valve engine. The cylinder-head design was done by Sir Harry Ricardo's engineering consultancy.

There was no suspension at the rear of the hardtail frame, and the bike had cantilevered leading-link type unsprung forks at the front. The saddle had a modicum of springing.

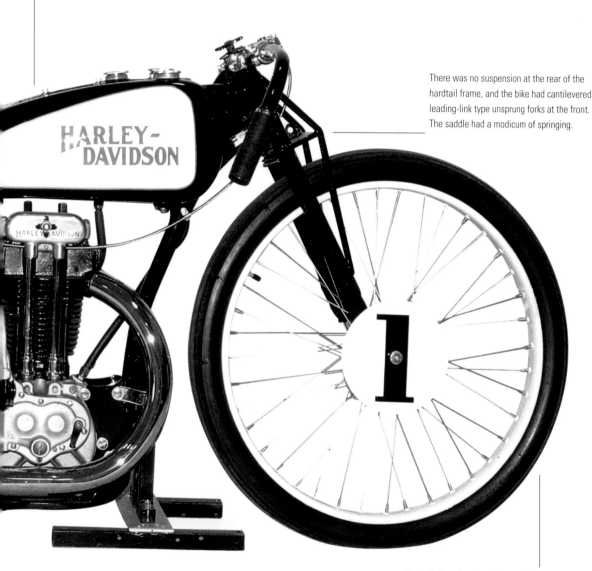

Typically for a board track racer, the Peashooter ran on 27in (68.5cm) laced wire-spoke racing wheels with clincher rims, shod with special grooved tyres.

Model-W Sport Twin was Harley-Davidson's first stab at the lightweight sector, but it failed to capture the imagination as an entry-level model. Three years later, the company tried again, this time with a four-bike range of single-cylinder machines designated the Model-A, Model-B, AA and BA. The BA was also known as the 21 OHV single. This range was powered by the vertically mounted 21 cu. in. (346 cc) Flathead single, which was basically half of the 43 cu. in. (700 cc) Flathead twin. The AA and BA models were available with overhead valves, a revelation in a road-going

Right: The favoured mount of the Harley-Davidson works team known as The Wrecking Crew was the Model-AA Peashooter, used to great effect at board track races. Drop-handlebars allow a lower riding position.

In 1925, the American Motorcycle Association sanctioned a new class for 21.35 cu. in. (350 cc) racing bikes and the inaugural event was staged at Milwaukee. Riders from The Wrecking Crew, Harley-Davidson's works team, included Joe Petrali, Jim Davis and Eddie Brinck, and they swept all before them with their 80mph (130km/h) Model-AA 21 Singles. The Peashooters had arrived. Their origins, however, were more prosaic than their achievements suggest.

From 1919 to 1923, the

single-cylinder bike, and, in 1927, these two models received Ricardo cylinder heads with hemispherical combustion chambers, and revised frame geometry. The Model A was phased out in 1930 and the Model-B was produced for export only from 1931 until its demise in 1934.

There was nothing especially remarkable about the design of these motorcycles and there were plenty of British machines that looked much the same. The main competitor for the Model-A was the Indian Prince. The frame was a simple tubular loop and there was ample space around the head and barrel. Mundane models can sometimes, however, provide a sound basis for competition machinery and the racing versions of the Model-AA and BA, with their overhead-valve layout and Ricardo heads, took Harley-Davidson to new levels in the competition arena. These no-nonsense bikes soon earned the nickname 'Peashooter' because of the pitch of the exhaust note, which on the race track was frequently emitted from an open pipe. It was not long before the entire range was identified by the Peashooter nomenclature.

Reliability and Economy

On the road, Model-A and B Peashooters did duty as transport for new riders, commuters and dispatch riders who wanted reliability and economy, and were not concerned with outright speed. Power was rated at 10hp, still enough to make 60mph (97km/h), while the OHV Models AA and BA put out 12hp and could top 70mph (113km/h). Transmission was via a three-speed gearbox with hand shift and chain drive. The clutch was operated by means of the left foot pedal.

The standard paint scheme for bikes in the Model-A and Model-B ranges was khaki green with maroon coachlines. While the Model-A was relatively spartan, the Model-B road bike was well-specified, with springer front forks – which were a brand new feature – and the patented telescopic sprung-seat mounting. A bike equipped with a battery could support a lighting system, while one with a magneto could not. A rear stand was normal fitment and a side stand was optional.

Racing bikes are inevitably austere, as weight reduction is paramount. The competition Peashooter 21 had a shortened loop frame and simple telescopic forks, triangulated for extra strength. The springer forks were discarded, as were the saddle spring and mudguards. Even the brakes and gearbox were dispensed with, and it ran a single gear with the clutch present just for starting. Peashooter 21s tended to run 27in (685mm) diameter treaded tyres on Clincher wheel rims, a larger diameter than the standard model's 26

x 3.5in (660 x 850mm) balloon tyres. They were built in small numbers and were raced successfully in Britain and Australia, as well as the United States. Only the advent of the British JAP-powered machines in the mid-1930s saw off the Peashooter.

Inevitably, the Wall Street Crash of 1929 had a profound effect not only on the US economy, but also impacted severely on Harley-Davidson and its competitors. Hardest hit of the four major US producers was Cleveland, which ceased trading in 1929. The Excelsior-Henderson company was forced to stop motorcycle production in 1931. Two years later, Harley-Davidson production had plummeted to less than 4,000 units, its lowest figure since 1910.

The road-going Peashooters were victims of a world recession; due to import tariffs being levied in certain markets, not enough machines were invoiced to make it worth continuing production. The side-valve Model-B remained in the catalogue until 1934, by which time stocks of parts had been used up. The Peashooter racing bike, on the other hand, went out on a high note, with the legendary Joe Petrali winning all 13 rounds of the US dirt-track championship on a works Peashooter in 1935.

1935 Model-AA Peashooter

Engine model:	Vertical single-cylinder
Engine capacity:	21 cu. in. (346 cc)
Cases:	Harley-Davidson
Carburation:	Harley-Davidson
Air filter:	None
Ignition:	Magneto
Pipes:	None
Transmission:	Three-speed, chain drive
Frame:	Tubular perimeter/loop
Suspension:	Front: leading link Rear: hardtail
Brakes:	None
Wheels:	26in (660mm) wire-spoke front and rear
Mudguards (fenders):	None
Handlebars:	Dropped
Risers:	None
Headlight:	None
Tail-light:	None

Model-GE ServiCar

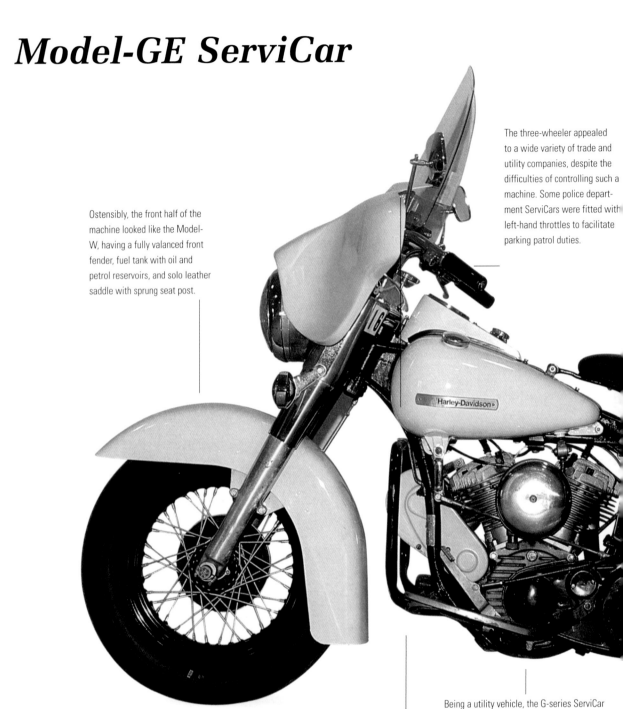

Ostensibly, the front half of the machine looked like the Model-W, having a fully valanced front fender, fuel tank with oil and petrol reservoirs, and solo leather saddle with sprung seat post.

The three-wheeler appealed to a wide variety of trade and utility companies, despite the difficulties of controlling such a machine. Some police department ServiCars were fitted with left-hand throttles to facilitate parking patrol duties.

Towards the end of its 42-year production run, the GE ServiCar was used as a guinea-pig for Harley-Davidson's incoming electric start set-up that graced the Electra Glide from 1965.

Being a utility vehicle, the G-series ServiCar was fitted with low-geared three-speed transmission and single-speed reverse. The power-unit was the cast-iron 45 cu. in. (738 cc) Flathead V-twin, with side-valves and carburettor air filter on the left-hand side.

The Model GE ServiCar came out in 1932
and was designed as a work-horse, having
a modified tubular cradle frame with a
rear sub-frame to support the cargo box.
Originally in sheet metal and wood, the
500lb (227kg) capacity box was made in
glass-fibre from 1967.

SUPPORTERS:

CANADIAN BIKER / SANDMAN INNS
MAGAZINE

DEELEY HARLEY-DAVIDSON

The 16in (406mm) laced wire-spoke
front wheel was standard Harley-
Davidson issue, but the back wheels
were similarly sized pressed steel discs,
adorned with chrome hubcaps.

When is a bike not a bike? When it's a tricycle. The Series G ServiCar was just that, a three-wheel Harley-Davidson motorcycle, launched in 1932 as a utility vehicle. The normal tubular cradle chassis frame incorporated a steel T-section rear subframe in its construction to support a platform between the back wheels, on which could be mounted a luggage box. This trunk was originally made up of a wooden frame and sheet steel side panels, but the ServiCar was such a long-running model, phased out only in 1973, that the construction of the luggage box went over to fibreglass in 1967.

The Model GE ServiCar was popular with all types of tradespeople, including grocery and hardware merchants, self-employed artisans and retailers, who found the trunk space ideal for carrying their wares, tools and materials. It also served as an emergency breakdown vehicle for garages. It was certainly capacious and could accommodate loads of up to 500lb (227kg). More particularly, however, the ServiCar enjoyed a lengthy relationship with numerous US police departments and, as well as normal custodial and emergency paraphernalia, the box contained a two-way radio. Being low-geared, they proved ideal for parking patrol duties, where the patrolling officer would cruise the parked cars and mark tyres with a piece of chalk on a stick.

If, on his or her return, the chalk mark still lay in the same position, a ticket was issued. The ServiCar could be fitted with left-hand throttle for the convenience of the patrol officer. In highway patrol format, the ServiCar displayed the police graphics on its windshield and there was a handlebar-mounted lever-operated siren. This device was situated on top of the front mudguard and, being dynamo driven, it could take as long as a minute for the sound to die away completely.

Dedicated Engine

From the saddle forwards, the GE ServiCar was more or less identical to the contemporary 45 cu. in. (740 cc) Flathead models typified by the W-series machines of the late 1930s and early 1940s. The 45 cu. in. (740 cc) side-valve Flathead motor was the ServiCar's dedicated engine throughout its 42-year production run. It received only modest updates and could be depended on to function indefinitely. Although easy to make and maintain, as there were no moving parts in the cylinder head that needed to be lubricated, with hindsight, the side-valve Flathead engine was not particularly efficient. The exhaust and inlet valves were situated adjacent to the cylinder, which gave the layout its name. Four cams were needed because the valve stems needed to be parallel. The inlet and exhaust ports were more or less L-shaped and it was this that rendered the side valve engine less than efficient. The inlet and exhaust tracts formed relatively complex curves, so gases were forced to take a long route in and out of the cylinders, resulting in poor performance and economy. However, during a period from the 1920s to the 1950s, simplicity prevailed over efficiency and the side-valve layout was ubiquitous in American cars and motorcycles. One advantage was that the

Left: In keeping with its pre-war origins, the GE ServiCar carries its speedo in the tank-top instrument console. A large windscreen makes it easier for tradesmen to operate in all weathers.

That said, a rider who was unfamiliar with conventional two-wheel motorcycling or bicycling might have experienced a tricycle as a child, and he or she would not have any difficulty with the GE ServiCar other than coping with the weight and engine mechanicals. With a 42-year production run the machine itself is a positive testament to the original 45 cu. in. (750 cc) side-valve engine – each valve with its own camshaft and straight valve angle – which was brought out in 1929 as a challenge to the Super X and Indian Scout. The ServiCar may seem like an oddity today, but, in a way, its survival could be seen as a microcosm of the company that built it.

Above: The hand-shift lever and gate for the ServiCar's three-speed-with-reverse transmission is mounted on the right of the fuel tank. Below it can be seen the case for the electric starter, which was introduced in 1964.

inlet ports met at the centre of the V, so that only a short carburettor manifold was necessary. In the side-valve era, continual engine lubrication was vital. The Flathead engine used the constant loss system in which oil was burned or blown out of the engine without being recirculated. It was linked to a three-speed gearbox, incorporating a reverse gear, which was a blessing for its hard-pressed users when parking or turning around.

After 1949, the GE ServiCar received the hydraulic front forks from the Hydra Glide big-twin, replacing the leading-link springer forks that were part of its original design. The single wire-spoked front wheel used a drum brake and balloon tyre, while the rear pair of wheels were 16in (406mm) pressed steel discs, adorned with chrome hubcaps. The front mudguard was a deeply valanced affair with chrome trim; the rear wheels were clad in normal cycle-type mudguards. When the trunk went over to fibreglass construction, the moulding incorporated the rear mudguards.

Tricycles are notoriously difficult to control for riders accustomed to two-wheeled machines. It was not a high-speed vehicle, however, and, in any case, many of those charged with its operation were novices who may not have experienced normal motorcycles.

1967 Model-GE ServiCar	
Engine model:	Side-valve V-twin
Engine capacity:	45 cu. in. (750 cc)
Cases:	Harley-Davidson
Carburation:	Harley-Davidson
Air filter:	Circular Harley-Davidson
Ignition:	Points
Pipes:	Two-into-one
Transmission:	Three-speed (forward), one (reverse)
Frame:	Tubular cradle with rear subframe
Suspension:	Front: telescopic forks
	Rear: swing-arm and coil-over dampers
Brakes:	Drum front and rear
Wheels:	Front: 16in (406mm) wire-spoke
	Rear: two, pressed steel
Mudguards (fenders):	Front: valanced pressed steel
	Rear: fibreglass, integral with box
Handlebars:	Wide-angle pull-back
Risers:	None
Headlight:	Chrome Harley-Davidson
Tail-light:	Integral with box

AH Topper Scooter

From 1912, a lever-operated rear hub clutch enabled the bike to be brought to a halt without having to stall the engine, although this was an optional extra.

The AH Topper was fitted with a 165 cc single cylinder two-stroke engine, located under a fibreglass cover beneath the dual seat and driving through an automatic three-speed gearbox.

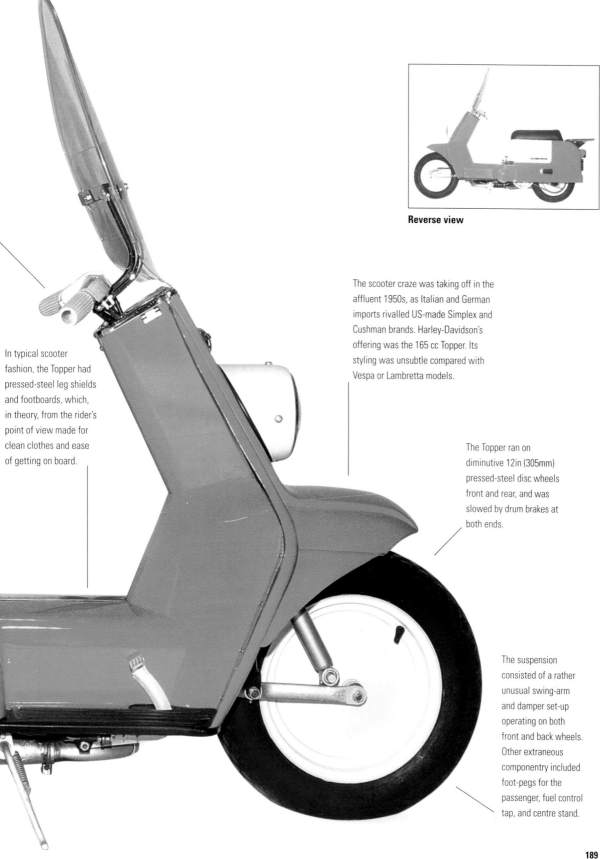

Reverse view

In typical scooter fashion, the Topper had pressed-steel leg shields and footboards, which, in theory, from the rider's point of view made for clean clothes and ease of getting on board.

The scooter craze was taking off in the affluent 1950s, as Italian and German imports rivalled US-made Simplex and Cushman brands. Harley-Davidson's offering was the 165 cc Topper. Its styling was unsubtle compared with Vespa or Lambretta models.

The Topper ran on diminutive 12in (305mm) pressed-steel disc wheels front and rear, and was slowed by drum brakes at both ends.

The suspension consisted of a rather unusual swing-arm and damper set-up operating on both front and back wheels. Other extraneous componentry included foot-pegs for the passenger, fuel control tap, and centre stand.

The AH Topper was Harley-Davidson's contribution to the flourishing US scooter market of the 1950s. The problem was that it was a late arrival and, by then, the craze had to an extent subsided, although it continued in Europe into the mid-1960s. The A-series Topper was powered by the 10 cu. in. (165 cc) single-cylinder air-cooled two-stroke engine from the ST model, launched in 1954, which gave 7hp and was allied to a centrifugal clutch and automatic three-speed gearbox with belt drive. It was started by means of a hand-pull recoil device, akin to a lawn mower or outboard boat engine. The Topper could top 55mph (88km/h). It was built on a steel frame, with swing-arm and damper suspension back and front. The forward-hinged seat lifted up to provide a storage locker andm while the engine cover was in fibreglass, the leg shields were in steel. The passenger was provided with foot pegs, while the rider had the traditional platform.

The history of scooter development goes back to the 1920s, when a scooter boom occurred in Great Britain and the United States. One of the leading manufacturers was Reynolds, whose Runabout model used a 16 cu. in. (269 cc) two-stroke engine hidden under the seat, with oil and fuel tanks located behind the leg shields. The German DKW firm made the Lomos from 1922. The earliest US make was the 21 cu. in. (350 cc) Ner-A-Car from the 1920s, designed by Carl A. Neracher, which had enormous mudguards and leg shields that prevented riders getting dirty. Another manufacturer was Salisbury, which came out with its first scooter in 1935; although its pos-war designs were more sophisticated, they still looked remarkably like ride-on vacuum cleaners. Salisbury ceased production in

Below: All the elements for a scooter are in place – the pressed-steel leg shields, the rubber-covered foot-boards, faired-in fender, dual saddle, and back brake pedal – but sadly, the Topper was an aesthetic disaster.

1949, but it had inspired Cushman of Lincoln, Nebraska, which made the Auto-Glide models that were supplied to the military and used in action by paratroops during the Second World War.

Proto-scooters

Cushman's early offerings from the late 1930s were bizarrely comical and even austere in appearance. Production of these proto-scooters started in 1937. The basic Auto-Glide frame was made of channel-section steel, while the engine was a simple industrial side-valve Husky power unit; it lacked the benefits of either suspension or a gearbox. The Cushman 30 series came out in 1942, followed by the 32 in 1945. This model had a sprung front fork and was fitted with 'Floating Drive', which consisted of an automatic clutch and transmission system. Although it was still an extremely rudimentary machine, its restyled bodywork incorporated a luggage compartment and front and rear lighting equipment was standard. The 32 Auto-Glide's 15 cu. in. (244 cc) engine was concealed behind a louvered panel and capacity was subsequently upped by 2cc, which gave a commensurately

Above: The Topper's controls are very simple, with the speedo mounted in the steering yoke panelling. Further protection from the elements is provided by what was somewhat disparagingly known as an elephant screen, which was viewed as uncool.

1964 AH Topper	
Engine model:	Single-cylinder two-stroke
Engine capacity:	10 cu. in. (165 cc)
Cases:	Harley-Davidson
Carburation:	Harley-Davidson
Air filter:	Harley-Davidson
Ignition:	Coil
Pipes:	Single with expansion chamber
Transmission:	Automatic three-speed
Frame:	Steel
Suspension:	Swing-arm and damper front and rear
Brakes:	Drum front and rear
Wheels:	12in (305mm) pressed steel
Mudguards (fenders):	Pressed steel
Handlebars:	Flat
Risers:	n/a
Headlight:	Integral with panelling
Tail-light:	Integral with bodywork

higher performance. The Cushman Highlander was based on the regular Auto-Glide, but without the bodywork, and the seat and fuel tank were mounted on a simple tubular structure. From 1949, it was known as the Highlander and was subsequently fitted with a rather unusual leading-link front-fork layout. Other US makes included the Indian Papoose, which was a 6 cu. in. (98 cc) Villiers-powered version of the Brockhouse Corgi available between 1948 and 1954. The Simplex, which was totally rudimentary, was manufactured between 1956 and 1960.

The quintessential scooter was the Italian Vespa, closely followed by the Lambretta. Both marques started life in 1946 and the Lambretta's horizontal engine mounting gave it slightly better stability than the Vespa's side-mounted engine. The prettier of the two, the Vespa was made by Italian aircraft makers Piaggio, which first came out with the 6 cu. in. (98 cc) model. Designed by an aircraft designer with no preconceptions of the motorcycle industry, its pressed steel frame was attractively styled from the outset. Other examples of scooters contemporary with the Harley-Davidson Topper included the Zundapp Bella 201 from 1953 to 1964, the 11 cu. in. (174 cc) and 15 cu. in. (249 cc) Triumph Tigress that lasted from 1959 to 1965, and the Heinkel Tourist that was made between 1953 and 1965. The AH Topper was dropped from the Harley-Davidson line-up after the 1965 season.

M-50 Moped

While the Sport version was fitted with an appropriately sporty dual seat, the M-50 Moped had separate saddles for rider and pillion, which had the benefit of reasonably generous padding.

The moped had very little in the way of fairings, with a simple cycle-type front mudguard in pressed steel, and a rear fender also in steel with attached rear-light housing.

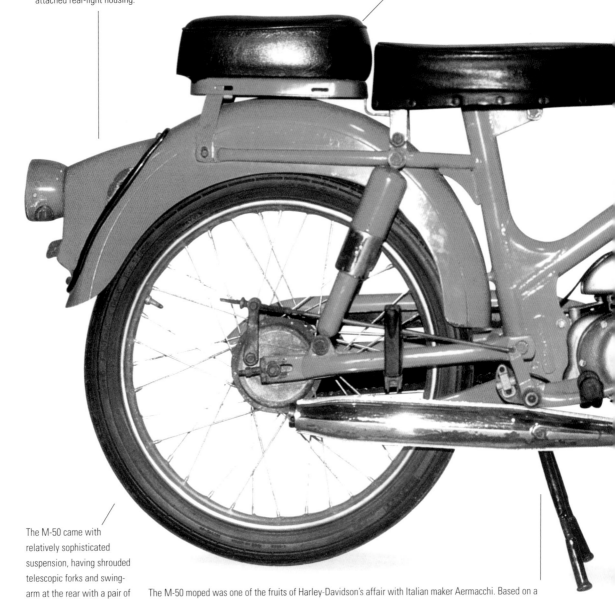

The M-50 came with relatively sophisticated suspension, having shrouded telescopic forks and swing-arm at the rear with a pair of telescopic dampers.

The M-50 moped was one of the fruits of Harley-Davidson's affair with Italian maker Aermacchi. Based on a tubular spine frame, the machine was sold in large numbers in Europe, but never caught on in the United States.

Reverse view

The interchangeable laced wire-spoke wheels and tyres were 17 x 2in (43 x 5cm) in diameter, with small hub-centre drum brakes front and rear.

The engine of the moped was a 49 cc single-cylinder two-stroke fed by an Italian Dell'Orto carburettor and driving through a three-speed gearbox and chain final-drive. An expansion chamber type exhaust was fitted.

Although Harley-Davidson traditionalists may balk at the idea of their favourite company being associated with the production of lightweight bikes, let alone mopeds and scooters, for the best part of 30 years, that is just what it did. Little Italian-style hornets followed in the wake of the H-D ST, a German-sourced DKW copy, followed by the Pacer 10 cu. in. (165 cc) and Bobcat 11 cu. in. (175 cc) two-strokes. In actual fact, not many of these minnows made the voyage across the Atlantic to the United States, so native Harley buffs would seldom

have been confronted with the issue. However, it wasn't just the European machines that posed a threat to Harley-Davidson. From 1959, the arrival on the US scene of Honda and its Japanese compatriots brought a whole new attitude to motorcycling. Models like the Honda 90 cc Super Cub C100 from 1958 made a huge impact economically and socially, bringing modest yet respectable mobility to thousands of people who had probably never ridden a motorbike. Indeed, Honda's promotional material deliberately targeted non-riders, and US sales skyrocketed as a new two-wheeled boom took off.

Small-capacity machines and mopeds always sold in volume in Europe and the Far East, but were less well suited to US cities and particularly to the vast hinterland of wide open spaces where the culture of long-haul biking held sway. Paradoxically, Harley-Davidson chose to import the Aermacchi M-50 moped in 1965. This was the year that the company dropped its 10 cu. in. (165 cc) Topper scooter, so in a sense the M-50 was a replacement of sorts for the commuter machine. At least it actually looked like a motorcycle rather than a mobile bread bin, which was how the scooter had once famously been described.

Designated the Model-M, the M-50 was propelled by a single-cylinder air-cooled 3 cu. in. (49 cc) two-stroke motor, with an integral mounting point on the finning of the alloy cylinder head for attaching it underneath the tubular spine-frame of the step-through moped. It used a three-speed gearbox operated via a twist-grip on the left-hand side of the bars, themselves relatively high-rise. The throttle grip was on the right-hand side. A pillion passenger could be accommodated on a squab on top of the rear mudguard. Being of Italian extraction, the tiny carburettor was by Dell'Orto.

A Sport Model

The following year, the M-50 was available as a sport model, which was based on the moped driveline and chassis, but with the addition of a conventional lozenge-shaped 2.5-gallon (9.5-litre) motorcycle fuel tank, a racing-style seat and a streamlined rear-light housing. In many ways it was quite sophisticated and a match for contemporary Japanese mopeds. The telescopic forks were neatly shrouded and the rear suspension was by swing-arm and twin telescopic dampers. The brakes were small drums front and rear, mounted in chromed wire-spoke wheels shod with 17 x 2in (432 x 50mm) tyres. The ignition coil was mounted on the spine and hidden away under the fuel tank, and the banana-like exhaust pipe culminated in a long ovoid combustion chamber. A chain guard and a centre-stand were also fitted.

In 1970, the Model-M moped also sired the M-65 Leggero, the 6 cu. in. (100 cc) MSR Baja off-roader (featuring huge, knobbly tyres, plastic mudguards and high-level exhaust) and the 7.5 cu. in. (125 cc) MLS Rapido versions, but these had a relatively short life span of just two years.

Unsurprisingly, the M-50 was the smallest-capacity bike ever to wear the Harley-Davidson badge. Although Aermacchi built 10,500 units of the M-50 Sports in 1966, only a few were imported into the United States. Potential

1965 M-50	
Engine model:	Single-cylinder
Engine capacity:	3 cu. in. (49 cc)
Cases:	Aermacchi-Harley-Davidson
Carburation:	Dell'Orto
Air filter:	Dell'Orto
Ignition:	Coil
Pipes:	Expansion chamber
Transmission:	Three-speed
Frame:	Tubular spine
Suspension:	Front: telescopic forks Rear: swing-arm, hydraulic dampers
Brakes:	Drum front and rear
Wheels:	Chrome wire-spoke front and rear
Mudguards (fenders):	Pressed steel
Handlebars:	Flat, chromed
Risers:	Integral with bars
Headlight:	Aermacchi-Harley-Davidson
Tail-light:	Circular, streamlined mounting

buyers could not be tempted even by a list price of $225, so any that did find their way into the US market tended to hang around in the showrooms. In a bid to spice things up a bit, Aermacchi boosted cubic capacity by 1 cu. in. (15 cc) in 1967 and the resulting M-65 Sport was, incredibly, reckoned to have 62 per cent more power than the model it superseded. Despite being promoted as a fun machine for Americans of any age, the inevitable demise came in 1972, when poor sales obliged Harley-Davidson to drop the moped line.

The reality was that they could not compete with the Japanese manufacturers in terms of volume, and therefore price, not even taking into account issues such as equipment levels, reliability and build quality – Japanese bikes had electric starters and did not leak. More fundamentally, the North American market was not especially receptive to small motorcycles and mopeds – the distances regularly travelled there were far too great and there was absolutely no tradition of small-scale transportation. Having had its fingers rather badly burned this time, Harley-Davidson decided never to venture into that particular sector again.

CRTT Ala d'Oro Racer

The suspension was provided by top-quality Ceriani telescopic forks, with double-sided swing-arm at the rear, controlled by coil spring-over-damper units on either side.

The CRTT Ala d'Oro (Golden Wing) was designed by Alfredo Bianchi and featured a tubular spine frame that harboured the engine and had a pared-down look befitting its race-bike status.

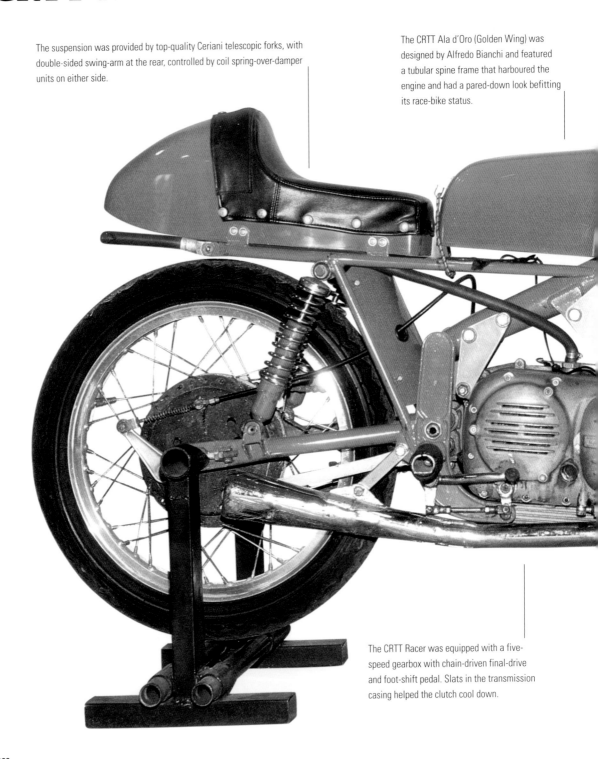

The CRTT Racer was equipped with a five-speed gearbox with chain-driven final-drive and foot-shift pedal. Slats in the transmission casing helped the clutch cool down.

The long low fuel tank was made of glass-fibre, and extended back over much of the chassis, leaving the rider's posterior crouched over the back wheel on the austere race seat. This was moulded into an aerodynamic tail-piece.

The CRTT Ala d'Oro used laced wire-spoke wheels with flanged aluminium-alloy rims and a rear tyre of bigger section than the front. It was slowed by Ceriani twin-leading shoe drum brakes front and rear.

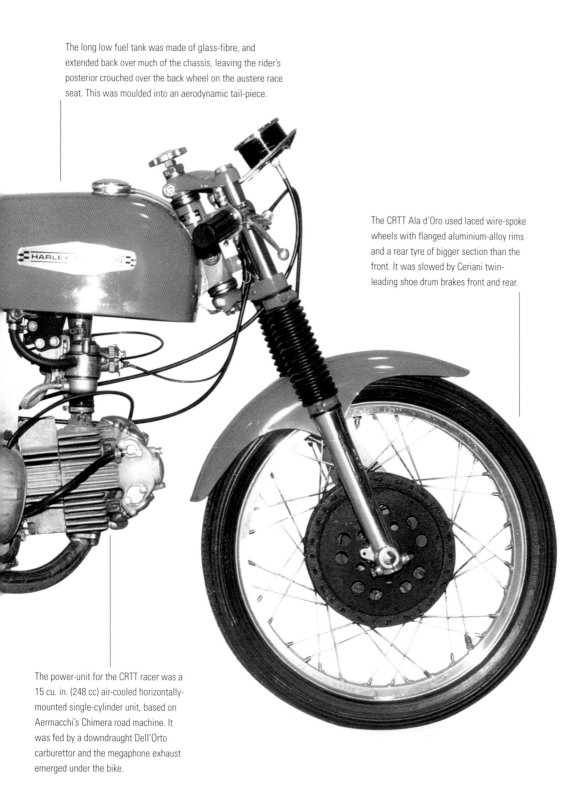

The power-unit for the CRTT racer was a 15 cu. in. (248 cc) air-cooled horizontally-mounted single-cylinder unit, based on Aermacchi's Chimera road machine. It was fed by a downdraught Dell'Orto carburettor and the megaphone exhaust emerged under the bike.

Above: Like all race bikes, the CRTT Ala d'Oro has no extraneous componentry. Bars are lightweight clip-ons, attached to the forks above the fork yoke, and the only instrumentation is the rev counter.

It seems strange to consider a motorcycle with a Harley-Davidson badge having its origins in Varese, Italy, but that is the case with the CRTT Ala d'Oro (Golden Wing) racing bike. Harley-Davidson's amalgamation with (and subsequent acquisition of) Aermacchi in 1960, of course, provided the connection. The two firms were almost polar opposites in terms of product and operations. Originally known as Aeronautica Macchi, Aermacchi began in 1912 as the builder of seaplanes. It came on the scene as a motorcycle manufacturer after the Second World War, when it was easier to rebuild by making transport for the masses than building aircraft.

Aermacchi's prototype two-wheeler was electrically powered, but the more conventional 7.5 cu. in. (125 cc) 125N went into production in 1950. It was a cross between a motorcycle and a scooter, based on a step-through frame with a dummy fuel tank. In the mid-1950s, Aermacchi launched the 10.5 cu. in. (172 cc) single-cylinder Chimera, which featured a distinctive full fairing. Its failure in the marketplace was redeemed by its achievements on the racetrack, including new 3 cu. in. (50 cc) and 4.5 cu. in. (75 cc) speed records. In 1957, Aermacchi released unfaired versions of its 11 cu. in. (175 cc) and 15 cu. in. (250 cc) four-stroke singles. Now their characteristic horizontal cylinders were on display for all to see. Sales began to improve and this attracted the attention of Harley-Davidson, at the time actively seeking a manufacturing partner with a range of small-capacity motorcycles in order to lift its market share in the United States. In 1960, Harley-Davidson bought 50 per cent of Aermacchi and the joint company Aermacchi-Harley-Davidson SA was established in Switzerland. The symbiosis seemed to work. In 1964, 75 per cent of the Varese plant's output was exported to the United States; a decade later, Harley-Davidson took complete control.

A small quantity of racing bikes was built from 1961 onwards, including 15 cu. in. (250 cc), 21 cu. in. (350 cc) and 24 cu. in. (402 cc) versions, but the CRTT racer was only produced for one year, 1967, with just 35 units in total. Its 15 cu. in. (250 cc) overhead-valve single-cylinder engine put out 35bhp at 10,000rpm, via a five-speed transmission with chain drive. The engine was originally designed by Alfredo Bianchi and was based on the 11 cu. in. (175 cc) unit that powered Aermacchi's distinctive Chimera road bike in the 1950s. Not surprisingly, the CRTT race bikes differed from the road-going machines in several respects. The machine was based on a stout spine frame, with the horizontally mounted engine attached to the frame by massive triangular plates. Engine cases were sand-cast in magnesium alloy and provision was made for a dry clutch and crankshaft-driven magneto ignition. The engine was air cooled, with overhead valves, and was fed by a Dell'Orto carburettor. It had a megaphone exhaust pipe and there were vents in the crankcase to cool the dry-plate clutch. The CRTT was slowed by huge, state-of-the-art Ceriani twin-leading shoe drum brakes front and rear, and it ran on wire-spoke alloy wheels. Suspension was by Ceriani telescopic forks and coil-over dampers at the rear. There was a steering damper on the yoke, and clip-on bars and an elongated fibreglass fuel tank and an aerodynamic seat completed the specification.

Competition Success

The Aermacchi-built 11 cu. in. (175 cc) and 15 cu. in. (250 cc) lightweight singles were as good as anything available at the time, certainly in Europe. Capitalizing on successes in competition, it remained in the catalogue up to the early 1970s. Black Bart Markel was US Champion on a CRTT in 1962, 1965 and 1966. Aermacchi's new two-stroke range based on the M125 Rapido came out in 1967 and this formed the basis for a new generation of two-strokes that included 5.5 cu. in. (90 cc), 6 cu. in. (100 cc) and 7.5 cu. in. (125 cc) trail bikes. At a more specialized level, Aermacchi-Harley-Davidson also fielded the RR250 and RR350 two-stroke racers, which were very successful at world-class level in the mid-1970s. In a bid to keep up with the competition, the Sprint four-stroke single was

1966 CRTT Racer	
Engine model:	Four-stroke single
Engine capacity:	15 cu. in. (250 cc)
Cases:	Harley-Davidson/Aermacchi
Carburation:	Dell'Orto
Air filter:	n/a
Ignition:	Magneto
Pipes:	Megaphone
Transmission:	Five-speed, chain drive
Frame:	Tubular spine
Suspension:	Front: Ceriani telescopic forks
	Rear: swing-arm, coil-over-dampers
Brakes:	Front: Ceriani twin leading shoe drum
	Rear: twin leading shoe drum
Wheels:	Wire-spoke alloy front and rear
Mudguards (fenders):	Front: racing
	Rear: none
Handlebars:	Racing clip-ons
Risers:	None
Headlight:	None
Tail-light:	None

lifted to 21 cu. in. (350 cc) and the two-stroke bikes were subsequently built as 11 cu. in. (175 cc), 15 cu. in. (250 cc) and 21 cu. in. (350 cc) singles in both road-going and trail bike format.

Although they looked the part, the SX and SST ranges could not compete on specification and price with the Japanese competition. Meanwhile, large quantities of unsold machines were piling up in warehouses in the United States and, in 1978, Harley-Davidson's AMF management decided to pull the plug on its Italian connection. Aermacchi was bought by the Castiglioni brothers, who owned the fledgling Cagiva concern. Their first offerings were 7.5 cu. in. (125 cc) bikes based on the previous Harley-Davidson models. They made a huge success out of Aermacchi, going on to buy Ducati in 1985 and Husqvarna, Morini and CZ in the following couple of years, confirming perhaps that a transatlantic partnership between two completely dissimilar manufacturers was never going to work. Aside from economic circumstances, US riders never had an appetite for small motorbikes.

Model-BTH Scat

Introduced in 1962 and having only a three-year production run, the BTH Scat was presented as a trail bike, featuring a number of off-road components such as the high-rise exhaust system and scramble type mudguards.

The power unit for the BTH Scat was the 175 cc air-cooled single-cylinder two-stroke unit, with alloy-construction in-unit three-speed gearbox and chain final-drive, with pressed-steel protective cover.

The BTH Scat was equipped with a regular Harley-Davidson shaped fuel tank, albeit with only 2-gallon (7.5-litre) capacity. A solo sprung saddle was fitted.

Like all serious off-road machines, the Scat's front fender or mudguard was mounted with substantial supporting stays well clear of the wheel, so as not to trap mud.

The Model-BTH Scat was built on a tubular cradle frame, and had its origins in the post-war Harley-Davidson Model-S, which grew from the German DKW RT125 bike that Harley-Davidson inherited the rights to produce after the Second World War.

The front suspension on the Scat was via telescopic forks, in which the fork sliders were adjacent to the wheel hub and telescoped into the upper leg sections. Rear suspension was by pressed-steel swing-arm and horizontal springs located under the frame.

Prior to the acquisition of the Italian Aermacchi concern in 1960, Harley-Davidson had addressed the small-capacity market with the Model-S. This model came on the scene in 1947, when Harley-Davidson acquired the rights to produce the single-cylinder two-stroke DKW RT125 as part of the reparations that Germany was required to make in the wake of the Second World War. The British BSA firm also took up the option to copy the DKW bike.

The German machine was gradually restyled by Harley-Davidson along the lines of its larger models. Major parts that impacted visually on the bike's image, such as the headlight, fuel tank, mudguards, saddle and other detailing, were modelled on those items fitted to bigger machines in the Harley-Davidson range – the headlight was similar to that of the 1951 Hydra-Glide. The resulting bike was designated the Model-S.

The 7.5 cu. in. (125 cc) Model-S was based on a regular tubular cradle frame, fitted with the characteristic Peanut tank shape that was carried over into the Sportster range. Other distinctive hallmarks were the bullet-shape rear light and shapely mudguards with flip-up bottom edges. An upward-facing ammeter was mounted on top of the

battery box. In 1953, capacity was lifted by 40 cc to 165 cc to create the Model-ST, which was sold alongside the Model-S, marketed as the Hummer from 1954. The bigger engine resulted in a power output of 7bhp. It was allied to a three-speed gearbox and chain drive, which was taken off the right-hand side of the gearbox. The carburettor was encased in a finned cast-alloy cover that matched the cylinder barrel of the engine. One of the characteristics inherited from DKW was the running of the foot-operated gearshift and the kick-start on the same axis. Drum brakes were fitted front and rear, and, from 1951, the Model-S was fitted with Tele Glide forks. Predictably, there was no suspension at the rear. The small Harleys would not attain that degree of sophistication until 1963.

New Lines

The 7.5 cu. in. (125 cc) Model-S was in production for 11 years to 1959 and the Model-ST lasted seven years. The 10 cu. in. (165 cc) BT Super 10, which only lasted until 1962, superseded both versions. Two new lines were ushered in at this point, based on the 10 cu. in. (165 cc) engine and an 11 cu. in. (175 cc) version. In smaller-capacity format, they were known as the BTU Pacer and BTF Ranger; with the slightly larger unit, they were the BT Pacer and BTH Scat. That line-up was rationalized the following year when the 10 cu. in. (165 cc) versions were dropped, leaving just the Pacer and Scat. They were last produced in the 1965 model year and were replaced by the Model-BTH Bobcat. That, however, was a one-year wonder and was axed in 1966.

Production and marketing of the Model-B singles and their derivatives was set against the incoming tide of small-

Left: True to its off-roading aspirations, the Model-BTH Scat was fitted with a high-level megaphone-style exhaust pipe, which had a heat shield for the rider's leg as it looped past the cylinder head. The rear suspension springs are visible under the frame.

fuel tank, a centre section surmounted by the saddle – which could be single or dual – plus rear mudguard and tail-light. This slightly bizarre, somewhat ungainly image was offset by an attempt to turn the bike into an off-roader by giving it the Scat's high-rise bars and a high-level exhaust pipe, which also incorporated a heat shield for the rider's calf.

As the company's Italian subsidiary Aermacchi was busy making small-capacity machines, it was deemed pointless fighting against the overwhelming competition from the Japanese manufacturers, so production of the Model-BTH ended in 1966.

Above: The basic cycle parts of the Scat include interchangeable 49- or 84-tooth rear sprocket, rear brake pulley and chain drive, which is protected by a pressed-steel cover.

capacity Japanese machines. The Japanese machines were generally well-made, reliable, well-specified and supported by a worldwide service network. To riders wanting basic transport, they made perfect sense. That made it hard to sell even traditional small-capacity machines such as the Model-B singles.

In 1963, the old Model-S based bike was revamped as the BT Pacer and, with a 10 cc capacity hike, the BTH Scat. The 11 cu. in. (175 cc) single-cylinder two-stroke now gave 10bhp and continued to use the three-speed gearbox with chain-drive from the right-hand side. The rear sprocket was generally a 49-tooth item, which could be swapped for an 84-tooth version for off-road riding. There was a new tubular cradle frame with a single down-tube, with rear suspension provided by a pressed steel swing-arm and horizontal springs. Up front, the fork slider telescoped up into the forks. The Scat was presented in off-road guise with high-level exhaust and high-rise bars, bobbed rear mudguard, high-mounted front mudguard and knobbly tyres.

In its final form, the BTH Scat metamorphosed into the BTH Bobcat. What marked this out as something really rather special was its elongated, one-piece fibreglass bodywork, which incorporated the 2-gallon (7.5-litre)

1965 Model-BTH Scat

Engine model:	Two-stroke single-cylinder
Engine capacity:	11 cu. in. (175 cc)
Cases:	Harley-Davidson
Carburation:	Harley-Davidson
Air filter:	Harley-Davidson
Ignition:	Points
Pipes:	Single expansion-chamber type
Transmission:	Three-speed, chain drive
Frame:	Tubular cradle
Suspension:	Front: telescopic
	Rear: swing-arm
Brakes:	Front: drum
	Rear: hub
Wheels:	18in (457mm) wire-spoke front and rear
Mudguards (fenders):	Pressed steel, bobbed (rear)
Handlebars:	Chrome, flat
Risers:	Integral with bars
Headlight:	Single
Tail-light:	Single

RR250 Racer

The bike's aerodynamics are immeasurably improved by the all-enveloping full-fairing and windshield, mounted on the frame via brackets and emblazoned with race numbers and sponsor decals.

The RR250 ran on Borrani aluminium-alloy laced wheels front and rear, shod with Dunlop racing tyres and hauled up by twin discs and Scarab callipers at the front and cable-operated twin-leading shoe drum at the back.

The machine's two-stroke engine gulped fuel and was equipped accordingly with a large-capacity gas tank, sculpted to accommodate the rider's knee, with the frame-mounted ignition coil located just below.

While Harley-Davidsons are more readily associated with flat-track racing, the marque actually won three straight World Road Racing Championships with the RR250, ridden by Walter Villa, in 1975, 1976, and 1977. The aerodynamic tail fairing is just one of its competition components.

The racing suspension was by Ceriani telescopic forks up front and box-section swing-arm allied to coil-over-damper shock absorbers at the rear.

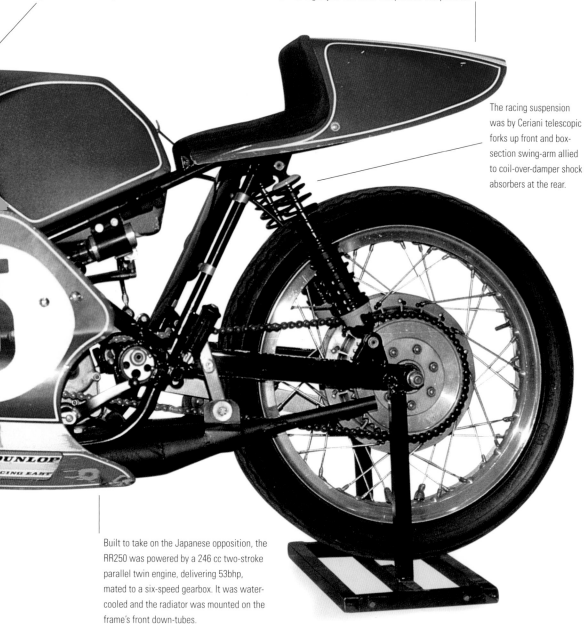

Built to take on the Japanese opposition, the RR250 was powered by a 246 cc two-stroke parallel twin engine, delivering 53bhp, mated to a six-speed gearbox. It was water-cooled and the radiator was mounted on the frame's front down-tubes.

Harley-Davidson was not a make readily associated with World Championship racing and not since the days of the Peashooter did it have the kind of success enjoyed in the mid-1970s. The machine that took three straight wins in the 250cc category in 1974, 1975 and 1976 was the RR250, ridden by the Italian star Walter Villa. Like the CRTT Ala D'Oro racer from a decade earlier, the RR250 was only in production in a very limited way; it only appeared in the Harley-Davidson catalogue for one year, 1976, so consequently is extremely rare.

The RR250 was in a sense the culmination of a swathe of Varese-built Harley-Davidson-badged sports machines that went back to 1961, starting with the overhead-valve single-cylinder 15 cu. in. (250 cc) Sprint. This used the same horizontally mounted four-stroke that powered the Aermacchi Chimera in the 1950s, suspended from the concave-curved spine frame, with pushrod-operated valves and a four-speed gearbox and chain drive. With telescopic

Below: The World Champion's eye view of the instrument panel on board the RR250, with rev counter prominent. The bars are pulled in and set extremely low so the rider can crouch behind the cross-braced fairing.

forks, rear swing-arm and coil-over dampers, the Sprint was a competent enough bike, and variants included the Sprint H trail bike with high-level exhaust and the Sprint C that came with conventional exhaust and mudguards. For the US market, high-rise bars were fitted, while European versions had low-set bars.

Long Production Life

The Sprint had a long production life, which says much for its capability, and was phased out in 1974. Its direct replacement was the 250SS, a 15 cu. in. (250 cc) two-stroke, air-cooled single with a five-speed gearbox, based on a more conventional tubular cradle frame. It contrived to look much more up to date by virtue of minimal fibreglass front and rear mudguards and contemporary AMF and Harley-Davidson graphics on the fuel tank. The battery box was prominent and filled the triangle in the frame beneath the dual saddle. Long Betor telescopic forks were fitted, along with rear swing-arm and coil-over dampers. Drum brakes gave way to a disc at the front, and the rear wheel featured a conical hub and snail cam-chain adjuster.

The two-stroke singles were available in either SS road-going format or SX off-road guise, and with 7.5 cu. in. (125 cc) and 11 cu. in. (175 cc) engines from 1974, and the 15 cu. in. (250 cc) unit from 1975. The SX trail bike found more buyers and stayed in the line-up until 1978. By contrast, the SS version was less popular and it lasted just one year, with only 1417 units invoiced. After 1978, when Aermacchi was sold off to Cagiva, the two-stroke singles provided the bedrock that got the new Italian owners off to such a flying start. By the early 1980s, Cagiva was selling 40,000 units a year.

The RR250 that preceded the Aermacchi sell-off by a couple of years had much more in common with Italian racing machinery than the traditional Milwaukee-built V-twin. Its two-stroke twin-cylinder engine put out 53bhp, which, combined with its light weight – just 240lb

1972 RR250

Engine model:	Two-stroke twin-cylinder
Engine capacity:	15 cu. in. (250 cc)
Cases:	Aermacchi-Harley-Davidson
Carburation:	Dell'Orto
Air filter:	None
Ignition:	Points
Pipes:	Two expansion-chamber type
Transmission:	Six-speed, chain drive
Frame:	Tubular cradle
Suspension:	Front: Ceriani telescopic
	Rear: swing-arm and coil-over-dampers
Brakes:	Front: twin discs, Scarab callipers
	Rear: twin leading shoe drum
Wheels:	Borrani wire-spoke front and rear
Mudguards (fenders):	Front: competition
	Rear: none
Handlebars:	Clip-on
Risers:	None
Headlight:	None
Tail-light:	None

(109kg) – gave it a top speed of 140mph (225km/h). The idea was to take the fight to Yamaha, which held the 15 cu. in. (250 cc) world road-racing title in the early 1970s, and Walter Villa succeeded in doing this three years running. The RR250's winning run was cut short by Kawasaki's disc-valve machines, which were dominant at the end of the decade under riders Kork Ballington and Toni Mang.

Naturally, the specification of the RR250 was race-orientated. Its parallel twin engine was water cooled, so it had a jacket around the cylinder barrels and a water pump, and the radiator was mounted ahead of the cradle frame. Transmission was by six-speed gearbox and chain drive, with foot-operated gear lever on the right-hand side. The dry-plate clutch was open to the elements, while the bulbous expansion chambers of the twin exhausts ran under the engine. Ceriani telescopic forks were fitted,

Right: The RR250's radiator serving its liquid-cooled two-cylinder engine is visible behind the bike's fairing. Ceriani forks and twin disc brakes are fitted but mudguards are absent.

with box-section swing-arm and coil-over dampers at the rear. Inboard eccentric swing-arm mounts provided chain adjustment. Progress was retarded by a twin-leading shoe drum at the rear and twin discs with Scarab callipers at the front. The bikes were shod with 18in (460mm) Dunlop racing tyres on wire-spoke Borrani alloy wheels with flanged rims. There was a moulded racing seat with aerodynamic seat hump, so minimal that the bike was rather dominated by its enormous fuel tank. A fairing that shrouded the whole of the frontal area was fitted for racing. Instrumentation was down to the bare minimum – just a water temperature gauge and rev counter.

Present-day road racing is more diverse than it was in the days of the RR250. There are categories for Grand Prix, which includes GP500, GP250 and GP125, then there's WSB, the World SuperBike Series, SuperSport and SuperStock categories. Included in this are special endurance races like the Bol d'Or classic lasting 24 hours. At a national level, there are race series like the British SuperBike championship, with assorted drag and sprint events, as well as a host of club meetings at national and local level. Historic and vintage events would feature machines along the lines of the RR250.

KRTT Grand National Racer

Dirt-track racing manifest in the Grand National Series grew in popularity during the 1950s and 1960s to become the premier form of motorcycle racing in the United States, and the stripped-for-action KRTT was the machine to have. Organized by the American Motorcycle Association (AMA), Grand National racing celebrated its 46th anniversary in 2000.

The KRTT of 1961 was powered by the 45 cu. in. (750 cc) side-valve V-twin, even though the road-going K-series had been phased out in 1957. A circular competition air-filter was fitted, with magneto ahead of the leading cylinder.

The AMA Grand National series combined four dirt-track variations – mile, half-mile, short-track and TT steeplechase racing – combined with road-racing to crown the best all-round rider. Hence, the KRTT ran without brakes and suspension in dirt-track and with them fitted for road-racing.

The KRTT was equipped with a large-capacity oil tank, located within the frame beneath the solo saddle, while the fuel tank held a modest 2.5 gallons (9.5 litres), sufficient for one race.

The KRTT ran on aluminium-alloy wheel rims front and rear, shod with appropriate racing tyres, and slowed by ventilated drum brakes. The telescopic forks were derived from the Sportster model, with double-sided swing-arm and coil-over dampers at the rear.

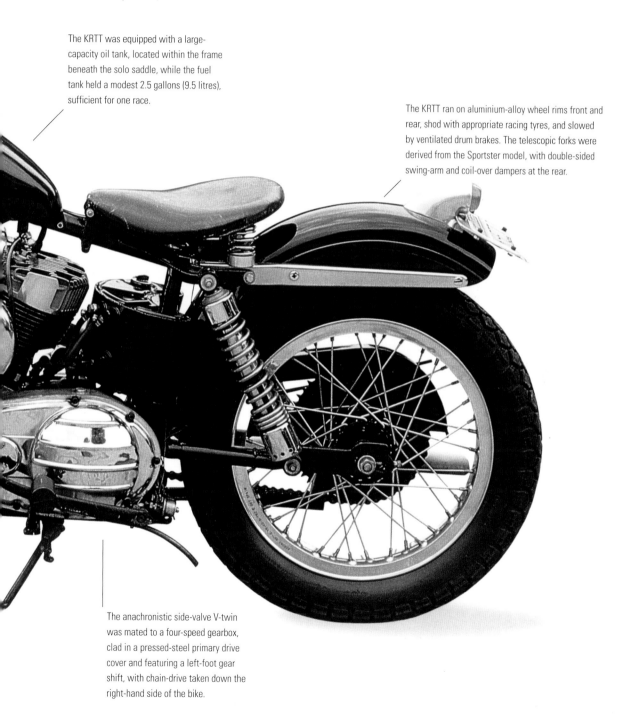

The anachronistic side-valve V-twin was mated to a four-speed gearbox, clad in a pressed-steel primary drive cover and featuring a left-foot gear shift, with chain-drive taken down the right-hand side of the bike.

There have been successive threats to Harley-Davidson sales over the years, ranging from economic downturns to invasions of foreign products. In the decade after the Second World War, high-performance British motorcycles with good handling posed the greatest threat. Harley-Davidson's response in 1952 was to come up with the Model-K, which was also its first important new machine since the 61 cu. in. (1000 cc) Knucklehead V-twin of 1936.

The Model-K was powered by the 45 cu. in. (740 cc) side-valve V-twin fitted in a tubular cradle frame, which was built in-unit with the four-speed gearbox. It developed 30bhp and was capable of 85mph (136km/h), which was improved when the 54 cu. in. (880 cc) KH appeared in 1954. Other innovations included the adoption of the typical British left-hand clutch and right-hand foot gearshift, to swing-arm rear suspension and telescopic forks.

In 1957, the 54 cu. in. (880 cc) V-twin was given overhead valves and introduced in the XL Sportster model. The formula was spot on and the Sportster remains one of the most enduring of all motorcycles. A larger bore and shorter stroke of the cast-iron cylinders gave more horsepower; with a top speed of more than 90mph (145km/h), the XL Sportster was able to match the performance of most

Above: This shot gives a good idea of the relative width of the KRTT's side-valve V-twin and its cylinders' slatted cooling fins. The air-filter cover is prominent, with magneto ahead of the engine, crankcase cover below, and oil tank to the rear.

of the British imports. While some owners preferred the stripped-for-action look of a dirt-track bike, the Sportster could also be customized. The accessories were ideal for touring and personalizing, although they were probably not what was envisaged as the real concept of the Sportster. The smaller 2.25-gallon (8.5-litre) Peanut fuel tank, with half the capacity of the regular tank, was fitted on the XLC in 1958, diminishing its touring potential, but defining the Sportster look still further. The XLC also came with pared-down mudguards and an absence of lights.

The Model-KR

Meanwhile, in 1952, Harley-Davidson also came out with a racing version of the Model-K, which, quite logically, was known as the KR. It was constructed on the tubular cradle frame as a dirt-track racer, in which format the brakes and suspension were omitted. For road racing, of course,

on the new banked oval circuit at Daytona in 1961 in the hands of Roger Reiman. Others to star on the KRTT included Brad Andres, Joe Leonard, Carroll Resweber and George Roeder.

Despite the standard Model-K road bike being dropped in 1958, the racing KR machines remained in action in the same format until the late 1960s. However, changes in the rules for 1969 meant a switch to overhead valves in the 45 cu. in. (750 cc) category. Successor to the KR was the 90bhp XR-750, which could top 115mph (185 km/h). Like the Sportster road bike, it originally came with cast-iron cylinders; however, by 1972, it ran with alloy barrels and cylinder heads, fed by twin Mikuni carburettors. The XR-750 was good enough to take the American Motorcycling Association championship that year and was still active in US dirt-track competition in the 1990s. A road-race version called the XRTT CR was also on the scene in the early 1970s, ridden successfully by Cal Rayborn among others. Although the power output was similar, it could reach 130mph (210km/h) because it was fully faired.

Above: The small-capacity Peanut fuel tank is perched on the KRTT's frame top tube, while its staggered exhaust pipes emerge from the 45 cu. in. (750 cc) Flathead V-twin to exit down the right-hand side of the motorbike.

these attributes were vital and were therefore included in the specification. A cursory glance revealed the KR's side-valve 45 cu. in. (750 cc) V-twin to be similar to that of the basic Model-K: however, it contained a number of race modifications, including bigger valves and cams, modified cylinder-head porting and new bearings. A racing air filter was used and the oil tank replaced the battery box, while a magneto was mounted on the front of the engine. It had a pressed-steel crankcase cover and many cycle parts were made as light as possible. There was just a small aluminium rear guard and a simple sprung saddle. Suspension was by telescopic forks at the front, with bare coil-over dampers and swing-arm at the rear. A ventilated brake drum was fitted at the front and, for safety reasons, the block-tread tyres were attached to the rims of the wire-spoke alloy wheels with four screws on either side.

Although the KR was principally a dirt-track racer, as the KRTT it won the first 200-mile (322-km) race held

1961 KRTT	
Engine model:	Side-valve V-twin
Engine capacity:	45 cu. in. (750 cc)
Cases:	Harley-Davidson/competition
Carburation:	Harley-Davidson
Air filter:	Competiton
Ignition:	Magneto
Pipes:	Two-into-one straight-through
Transmission:	Four-speed, chain drive
Frame:	Tubular cradle
Suspension:	Front: Sportster telescopic forks
	Rear: swing-arm, coil-over dampers
Brakes:	Front: ventilated drum
	Rear: drum
Wheels:	Aluminium alloy wire-spoke front and rear
Mudguards (fenders):	Front: none
	Rear: competition alloy
Handlebars:	Clip-on (road racing), wide (dirt-track)
Risers:	Integral with bars (dirt-track)
Headlight:	None
Tail-light:	None

FXRSS Custom Lowrider

The bodywork on the Custom Lowrider is minimal, but includes the side panel framing the oil tank, fuel tank and mini fairing, all painted metallic British Racing green and yellow, like the Lotus F1 Grand Prix cars from the 1960s.

The styling cues hail from the world of the race track and drag strip, featuring head fairing and ventilated rear hugger. The specially made fuel tank is banana shaped to follow the curvature of the re-worked frame tubes.

Customizing began in earnest in the late 1940s and was allied to flat-track racing and drag racing, in which narrow front wheels and oversize back tyres were the norm, which is where the Lowrider is coming from.

The power plant for this extravagant custom machine is the 80 cu. in. (1310 cc) Evolution V-twin, put together by specialists Battistini's Custom Cycles of Bournemouth, England.

A tinted screen protects the pull-back drag-style handlebars, while the fairing houses the sealed-beam headlight. The rider makes do with a thinly padded solo seat, which tapers away into the tail fairing.

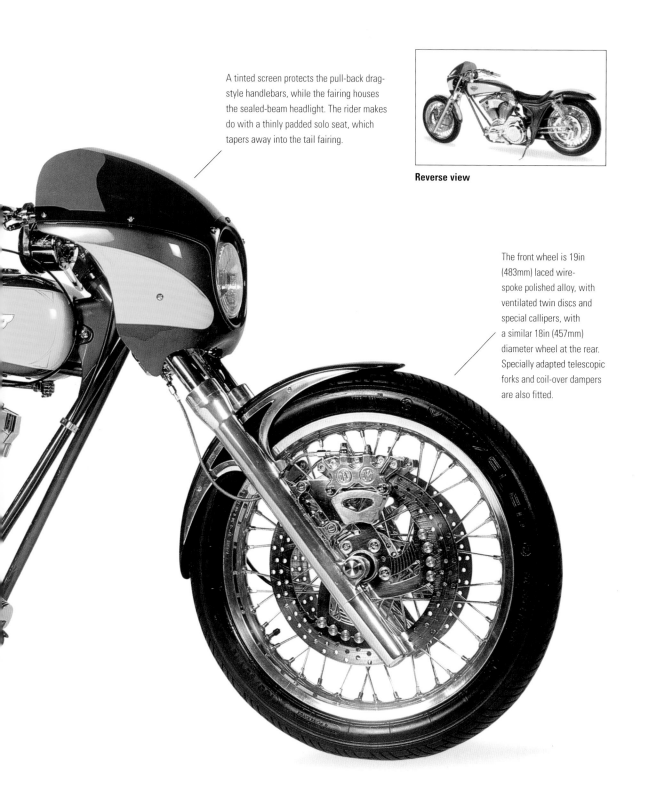

Reverse view

The front wheel is 19in (483mm) laced wire-spoke polished alloy, with ventilated twin discs and special callipers, with a similar 18in (457mm) diameter wheel at the rear. Specially adapted telescopic forks and coil-over dampers are also fitted.

The trend for customizing motorcycles, and Harley-Davidsons in particular, grew out of the practice of bobbing and chopping, exercises in personalising one's own bike back in the late 1940s. Bobbing the rear mudguard meant cutting a section off the front of it – effectively underneath the frame ahead of the back wheel, and moving the whole item round so the tail end of the original mudguard bobbed up in the air. Added to this was the practice of unbolting or, in some cases, hacking or chopping off extraneous pieces of kit that would not only alter the appearance of the bike but quite possibly make it a bit lighter and thus handle better.

Customizing grew out of these activities, and was allied to flat-track racing where again, bikes like the XR750 were pared down to the bare minimum, and also drag racing, where lightweight missiles hurtled a quarter of a mile at rocket-ship speeds. Often, dragsters – the four-wheeled variety – had improbably narrow front wheels and colossal back tyres for minimal wind resistance and maximum traction, and in a sense the Lowrider mimics this.

Customized Harley-Davidsons such as this are referred to as Lowriders because their styling is designed to be long and low, like a drag bike. Although customizing was carried out on an individual basis, specialists soon came to the fore who could do it that much better, operating from private workshops. Before long these small-time customisers developed their own specialities, idiosyncratic styling themes and paint schemes and as reputations soared, so did their output and business premises. Machines such as the ones featured display top-class workmanship.

Low-slung Attributes

To arrive at the Lowrider chassis, the standard Harley-Davidson frame is modified to give it these low-slung attributes, and this is achieved in one or two different ways. The frame can made to ride lower by reducing the

1995 FXRSS Custom Lowrider	
Engine model:	Evolution
Engine capacity:	80 cu. in. (1340 cc)
Cases:	Harley-Davidson
Carburation:	S&S
Air filter:	None
Ignition:	Electronic
Pipes:	Custom dual
Transmission:	Five-speed
Frame:	Modified tubular cradle
Suspension:	Front: telescopic forks
	Rear: custom swing-arm and coil-over-dampers
Brakes:	Front: twin discs
	Rear: disc
Wheels:	Front: 19in (483mm) wire-spoke
	Rear: 18in (457mm) wire-spoke
Mudguards (fenders):	Arlen Ness custom
Handlebars:	Pull-back drag
Risers:	Integral with bars
Headlight:	Fairing-mounted sealed beam
Tail-light:	Cat's eye

length of the rear shock absorber and altering the rake of the forks, which both lengthens and lowers the machine. More fundamentally, the triangulations of the cradle frame can be cut and shut to produce a compressed version, but since it will still need to accommodate a Harley-Davidson V-twin engine the possibilities are somewhat limited.

Once the frame modifications have been carried, out the lowered look is enhanced through the use of modified fuel tanks and mudguards, and by fitting appropriate parts such as the custom seat. Many early Harley-Davidson Lowriders were powered by Sportster engines and transmissions because the compact size of that combined unit meant that it was possible to build a machine that long, low and elegant. However, it was impossible for some customizers to resist the temptation to use the big twin 80 cu. in. (1340 cc) Evolution engine and gearbox. In the case of the FXRSS Custom Lowrider, so many custom parts were used in its construction by the British custom bike shop Battistini's Custom Cycles of Bournemouth, Hampshire, that in fact very little of its componentry actually came from the Harley-Davidson factory. Many of the parts used were sourced from specialist after-market manufacturers, such as the legendary Californian customizer Arlen Ness.

Starting with a specially built tubular cradle frame, at the heart of the bike was the 80 cu. in. (1340 cc) Evolution engine, which used an S & S carburettor, electronic ignition, and serpentine custom short dual exhaust pipes. The engine and transmission of the Lowrider were rebuilt incorporating a number of specialist-made parts fashioned from aluminium alloy billet in items such as the primary drive cover and the ignition coil cover. The machine had a pair of two-piston calliper disc brakes at the front and a single one at the rear. Up front was a 19in (48cm) wire-spoked wheel with an 18in (457mm) wire-spoked wheel at the back. The suspension was by extended front forks and swing-arm and adjustable coil-over gas dampers at the rear.

The elongated fuel tank displayed the Battistini logo, and along with the triangular side panel that framed the oil tank and the mini fairing, was finished in metallic British Racing green and yellow reminiscent of Grand Prix Lotuses from the 1960s. The tinted windscreen protected the pull-back drag-style bars and the fairing housed the sealed-beam headlight. A thinly padded solo seat was the final touch in this ground-hugging projectile's chassis.

Below: Seldom has a Harley-Davidson V-twin and its transmission casing been so lavishly buffed as in the case of this 80 cu. in. (1310 cc) Evolution engine, featuring S & S carb and serpentine pipe-work.

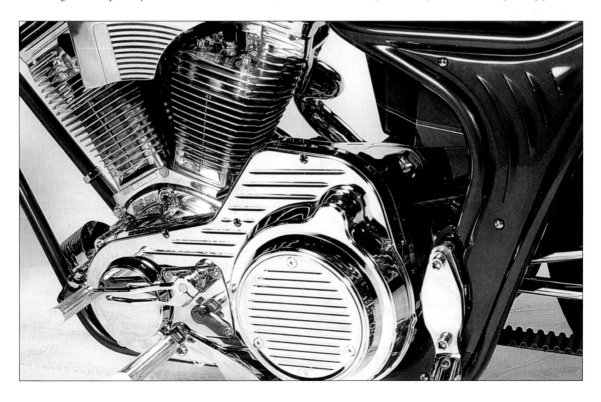

Knucklehead Chopper

True to type, the Knucklehead chopper is provided with an upholstered leather king-and-queen seat, which places the rider in a low-slung position above the oil tank, and the pillion above the rear wheel, with the benefit of a small backrest.

Chrome-plated accessories and ancillaries play a major role in the customizing process, exemplified by the horseshoe oil tank, air-filter cover, footboards, headlight and dragster-type exhaust pipes.

Being a privately made custom, rather than a factory job, this chopper gets away with no front mudguard, while a basic fender enclosed the rear wheel to protect the passenger and saddlebags from road dirt.

The origins of this Knucklehead chopper in the 1960s make it a contemporary of the counter-culture portrayed in the cult 1969 movie Easy Rider, although it was restored in the 1990s. The key elements in the design are the extended leading-link springer forks.

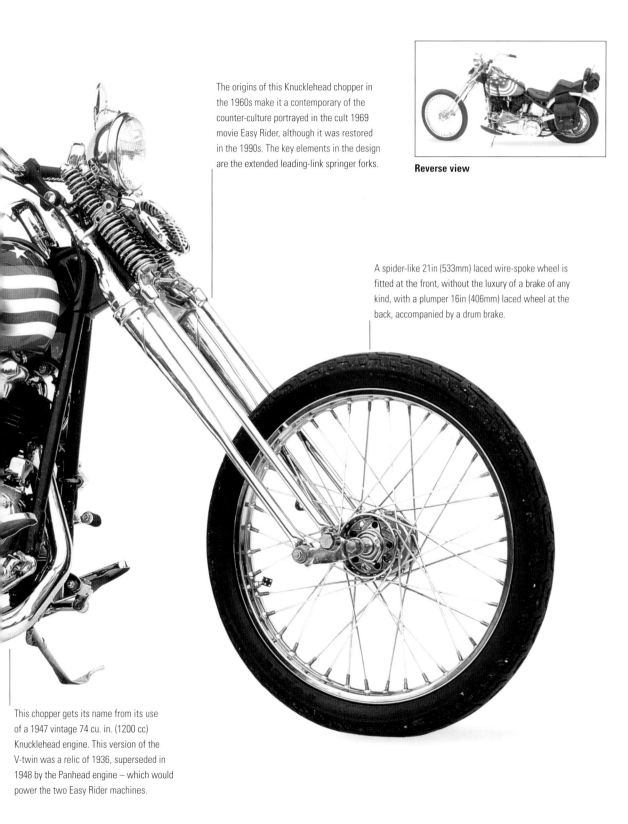

Reverse view

A spider-like 21in (533mm) laced wire-spoke wheel is fitted at the front, without the luxury of a brake of any kind, with a plumper 16in (406mm) laced wheel at the back, accompanied by a drum brake.

This chopper gets its name from its use of a 1947 vintage 74 cu. in. (1200 cc) Knucklehead engine. This version of the V-twin was a relic of 1936, superseded in 1948 by the Panhead engine – which would power the two Easy Rider machines.

The Knucklehead Chopper was calculated to conjure up images of the two machines that starred in the 1969 Easy Rider movie, as well as the Captain America bike. The Easy Rider choppers were powered by Panhead engines, while the Captain America machine was also a Panhead. This particular machine was built in the 1960s, and then restored in the 1990s, and was one of the original trend-setting machines from the era of extravagant and outrageous customizing.

The hallmark of the chopper was its radically angled head-stock, modified to accommodate the extended leading-link springer forks. By the time this bike was built, they were an anachronism, replaced on the production line in 1949 by hydraulically damped forks. The point was, such components as the springer forks and the equally outdated 74 cu. in. (1200 cc) Knucklehead engine were readily available in the form of a secondhand bike or as scrap or spares. They could then be reconstituted and rehabilitated by the specialist builder or customizer as something completely different such as a chopper. They would be a fraction of the price of new parts, naturally, but the downside was that the archaic Knucklehead motor relied on six-volt electrics and an electrical system governed

Above: The Knucklehead Chopper featured steeply raked leading-link springer-type forks, minuscule Bates headlight and air-horn, while the Fatbob tank was decorated with a 'trompe l'oeil' Stars and Stripes colour scheme.

by contact breaker points. The alternator replaced the generator from 1970.

Although the factory continued to deliberately distance itself from the outlaw fringe, that overt one percent of the biking population in the United States during the mid-1960s, interest was nevertheless widespread in the customized bobbers and choppers, most of which were still Harley-Davidsons. Dedicated shows and special events were staged, and there was even a magazine called Street Chopper to cater for owners of this kind of bike. While most official dealers refused to serve custom riders with the type of aftermarket parts they needed, the small-time back-street operators made a living supplying these spares. Some developed into entrepreneurs who had the expensive Harley-Davidson spares copied in large quantities in the far East and offered them at cheap rates. At this stage, Harley-Davidson would still not acknowledge that the groundswell of popular support for its products, the customizing fraternity with their custom machines, were responsible for a substantial element of the Harley-Davidson image. The movement was reflected in a series of Hollywood films with famous stars, in which bikers, most of them genuine ones, played subordinate roles or appeared as extras. When Easy Rider, starring Peter Fonda, Dennis Hopper and Jack Nicholson became a cult film post 1969, the notion of a biker movement spread around the world. Unwittingly, Harley-Davidson thus found itself to be an indispensable part of the biker image.

Stars and Stripes

Returning to the Knucklehead Chopper, with its modified rigid 'straight-leg' frame, the familiar design cues were present in the shape of the Fatbob tank was bedecked with a 'trompe l'oeil' Stars and Stripes, the chromed horseshoe oil tank and circular chrome air filter. Most of the engine parts were chromed, including the Knucklehead rocker covers, and the 6in (150mm) extended springer forks. The front wheel was a 21in (533mm) chrome-rimmed interlaced wire-spoke item with stock star hub, with a 16in (406mm) version at the rear. In the interests of style, the front brake was absent, a curious omission when it is that particular device that provides any motorcycle with the

Below: This highly polished 1947 Knucklehead engine was one of the last to be produced, prior to its replacement by the Panhead V-twin. The pedal-type kick-start is retained, while the air-filter cover bears the Harley-Davidson logo.

1947 Knucklehead Chopper	
Engine model:	Knucklehead overhead-valve V-twin
Capacity:	74 cu. in. (1200 cc)
Cases:	Harley-Davidson
Carburation:	Stock Harley-Davidson
Air filter:	Circular chrome
Ignition:	Points
Pipes:	Drag
Transmission:	Four-speed
Frame:	Tubular cradle
Suspension:	Front: extended springer forks Rear: hardtail
Brakes:	Front: none Rear: drum
Wheels:	Front: 21in (533mm) wire-spoke Rear: 16in (406mm) wire-spoke
Mudguards (fenders):	Front: none Rear: bobbed flat
Handlebars:	Dresser
Risers:	Dogbone
Headlight:	Bates
Tail-light:	Cat's eye

majority of its stopping power. The Knucklehead Chopper relied on a single drum brake at the back to bring it to a halt. It was steered by dresser type bars and dog-bone risers, and illumination was provided by a Bates headlamp and cat's eye tail light. There was a speedo located in the tank-top console. Rider and pillion were accommodated on the frame and mudguard hugging king-and-queen saddle, with petite saddlebags and footboards and pegs for the feet. The kick-start was fashioned from an antique pedal, with straight-through drag pipes blasting away to herald its arrival.

Shovel Trouble Two

Part of the custom imagery comes from exaggerating certain components and making them smaller or more prominent than normal. Hence, the use here of the small-capacity peanut-type Sportster fuel tank.

Built in 1980, this chopper's purposeful attitude is rather compromised by the absurdly meagre seating arrangement. Without the benefit of saddle springs and riding on a hardtail chassis, it's not going to be a comfortable ride.

Forward-mounted foot-controls include the back brake-pedal on the right-hand side of the bike, preceding the specially made, discreetly fastened shotgun-barrels that constitute the twin exhaust pipes.

Attention to detail includes the cylindrical oil tank suspended beneath the frame, with braided hoses. The Evolution engine has an electronic ignition system with twin-plug heads for improved efficiency.

Reverse view

The Shovel Trouble Two's frame was based on a rigid 1950s type Harley-Davidson chassis, with wide-yoked, steeply raked telescopic forks, supporting risers and pull-back handlebars.

Created by Phil Piper, this custom chopper uses a bored-out Evolution V-twin, measuring 88 cu. in. (1442 cc), fed by a single side-draught Dell'Orto carb and K & N air filter. Such is the extravagant frame geometry that the engine appears small within the tubing.

Built in 1980, this Custom Chopper is another example of the customizer's art. Such machines were assembled in such an extravagant way that they went beyond being mere pastiches of the Harley-Davidsons on which they were based, and took on an identity of their own.

In this case, that machine was Shovel Trouble Two, a chopper built by Phil Piper of Leicester in the UK, and centred not on a regular old-time Harley-Davidson hard-tail chassis, but one which had been custom-made to accommodate a special yoke, plus the characteristic raked and extended forks. It was also modified in such a way as to allow the use of a solid rear wheel that appeared to have more in common with a road roller than a motorcycle. Many specially made computer-numerically-controlled machined parts were obtained for Shovel Trouble Two, including the fork yokes and the rear wheel. The bike's Shovelhead motor was opened out to 88 cu. in. (1442 cc). The original Shovelhead started life in 1966 as a 74 cu. in. engine, increasing in capacity to 80 cu. in. in 1970, when the generator was replaced by an alternator. The later engine

Above: The front wheel of this custom chopper, known as the Shovel Trouble Two, is a 21in (533mm) diameter 80-spoke laced wire wheel, with a single ventilated disc brake.

got ten cooling fins on the cylinders and a smaller cone-shaped timing gear case instead of the finned casing. The beauty of the Shovelhead V-twin as the basis for a custom bike or chopper is the interchangeability of parts and readily available aftermarket componentry for uprating its specification and tuning for greater performance. Shovel Trouble Two's 88 cu. in. engine utilized an Italian twin-choke Dell'Orto carburettor allied to a K & N sports-type air filter. The shotgun barrel exhaust pipes were one-offs made for the bike. It also featured twin plug heads and a specially designed 12-volt Accel ignition system. The four-speed transmission's primary belt drive was exposed, and the final drive was by chain, with kick starter retained. As is often the case with choppers, a Sportster fuel tank was used because of its smaller size, which helps deconstruct the accepted Harley-Davidson silhouette. A custom-made

1980 Custom chopper 'Shovel Trouble Two'

Engine model:	Modified Shovelhead
Engine capacity:	88 cu. in. (1450 cc)
Cases:	Harley-Davidson
Carburation:	Dell'Orto
Air filter:	K&N
Ignition:	Accel
Pipes:	Shotgun-style
Transmission:	Four-speed
Frame:	Modified tubular cradle
Suspension:	Front: telescopic forks Rear: hardtail
Brakes:	Front: single disc Rear: disc
Wheels:	Front: 21in (533mm) wire-spoke Rear: 15in (381mm) cast-alloy disc
Mudguards (fenders):	Custom
Handlebars:	Pull-back
Risers:	Integral with handlebars
Headlight:	Bates
Tail-light:	Cat's eye

Above: Shovel Trouble Two is equipped with electronic ignition and two plugs per cylinder, and, curiously, the speedo is located alongside the frame just ahead of the seat.

like back wheel was served by a twin calliper disc set up. The rider was provided with minimal cushioning on the solo seat, and steered the bike by means of pull-back bars, while foot controls were forward mounted. A Bates headlight mounted on the fork yokes lit the way, while the speedo was mounted on the frame, just inside the rider's left thigh.

spherical oil tank was located beneath the frame ahead of the rear wheel. The bike's front and rear mudguards were also made specifically for it, and the 21in (533mm) front wheel corresponded with the modern trend for more than the normal 40 spokes, having double that number and interlaced in a much finer pattern. A single disc brake was the neat solution for the front, while the dragster-

Right: Shovel Trouble Two tank graphics recall those of Second World War bomber aircraft. The tank itself is a small 2.25-gallon (8.3-litre) Sportster model, while fork yokes are of the Wide Glide variety.

Twin Supercharged Harman

A double horseshoe oil tank arrangement
marks out the bike's midriff, with
handmade staggered dual exhaust
pipes exiting down the right-hand side.
Transmission is via a four-speed gearbox
with chain-driven final-drive.

The Twin Supercharged Harman carries relatively
large quantities of bodywork, including the specially
made fuel tank, seat and fenders, all the work of
Dave Batchelor at P & D in Sussex, England. The deep
cherry-red custom paint job is by Matt-the-Painter.

The wheels are equally distinctive, consisting of a 19in
(483mm) laced wire-spoke at the front, accompanied
by twin discs and gothic-style Billet 6 callipers, and an
18in (457mm) diameter laced wheel at the back.

The Twin Supercharged Harman has specially made pull-back handlebars with unusual grips, emerging from billet risers and fronted by a handmade headlight. The tail-lights are merged into the rear fender.

Reverse view

The modified frame of the Twin Supercharged Harman incorporates braced swing-arm rear suspension and chrome-cased gas dampers, with telescopic front forks sourced from a Suzuki GSX-R1100 and modified accordingly.

At the heart of this machine beats a specially modified 120 cu. in. (2000 cc) Shovelhead-Harman engine, fed by a pair of superchargers and a couple of twin-choke 2in (45mm) Dell'Orto carburettors and K & N air filters.

They really didn't come much more extreme than this. A mélange of chopper and drag-bike, it was powered by a very special 1988 Harley-Davidson-based Harman engine. Not only was the cubic capacity of the Shovelhead-based engine stretched to a colossal 120 cu. in. (2000 cc), it employed forced induction in the shape of a pair of superchargers. These required a vast amount of specialist machining to manufacture and install. The system incorporated a pair of twin-choke 1.8in (45mm) Dell'Orto carburettors capped with K & N sports air filters, which were fitted to the superchargers that were bolted to the engine with specially machined manifolds. The supercharger drive was built from scratch, while manifolds and drive pulleys were fabricated and geared to enable the superchargers to run at the engine-to-blower ratio of 1:1.

The complex engine assembly has been fitted into a heavily modified Harley-Davidson cradle frame, built by P & D in Sussex, England. The frame incorporated swing-arm rear suspension, supplemented by chrome-cased gas dampers. The telescopic front forks on the Twin

Right: What looks like a Shovelhead V-twin is actually a Harman unit, bored out to 120 cu. in. (2000 cc) and fitted with twin superchargers fed by twin 1.8in (45mm) Dell'Orto carbs. The supercharger drive is at the lower left.

Supercharged Harman are not Harley-Davidson items, but were sourced from a Suzuki GSX-R1100, and had to be modified. The brakes were exceedingly high-tech and incorporated no less than four Harrison-Billet 6 six-piston callipers on the front pair of discs. The rear brake featured a pair of similar callipers.

The bike belonged to Richard Taylor of Kent, Great Britain, and much of the componentry including the customized one-off fuel tank, seat and mudguards were made by Dave Batchelor at P & D's workshops in Sussex, England. The seat followed the contours of the frame and rear mudguard that clad the low-profile Metzeler rubber. The front wheel was a 19in (483mm) interlaced wire spoke job, with an 18in (457mm) wire spoked wheel at the back. The distinctive mudguards in particular were reminiscent

1995 Twin Supercharged Harman	
Engine model:	Harman
Engine capacity:	120 cu. in. (2000 cc)
Cases:	Harman
Carburation:	Twin 1.8in (45mm) Dell'Orto
Air filter:	Twin K&N
Ignition:	Crane HI-4
Pipes:	Straight singles
Transmission:	Four-speed
Frame:	P&D modified tubular cradle
Suspension:	Front: telescopic forks
	Rear: swing arm and dampers
Brakes:	Front: twin discs, four Billet 6 callipers
	Rear: disc, Billet 6 calliper
Wheels:	Front: 19in (483mm) wire-spoke
	Rear: 18in (457mm) wire-spoke
Mudguards (fenders):	P&D handmade
Handlebars:	Pull-back
Risers:	Billet
Headlight:	P&D handmade
Tail-light:	Twin cat's eyes

Below: The distinctive fenders were reminiscent of the streamlined bodywork seen on sports racing cars from the 1930s, such as the Alfa Romeo 6C 2300B Mille Miglia, styled by Touring Superleggera of Milan. Here, joke paintwork indicates light sources.

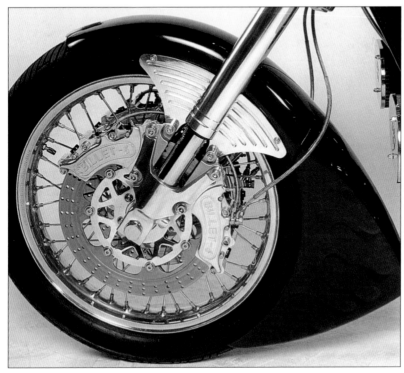

of the kind of streamlined bodywork employed on sports racing cars from the 1930s. Incorporating styling cues such as these and making it look right was sophistication indeed. Paintwork and chroming were also carried out to an exquisite standard, lavished on many of the cycle parts as well as the handmade horseshoe oil tank. The headlight was also specially crafted, while a cat's eye tail light was fitted. Clocks were custom-built miniatures, and the handlebars and foot-pegs were also made-to-measure items.

Left: The front fender matched that of the rear, as did the high-tech braking arrangement, relying on no fewer than four Harrison-Billet six-piston callipers on the front pair of discs. The forks were from a Suzuki GSX-R1100.

Boothill Panhead

The Boothill Panhead uses a regular in-period front fender while the rear one has been bobbed so that its trailing edge sticks up like a duck's tail. The rear light is thus on the underside of the fender for better visibility.

Other original equipment on the bike included the chromed horseshoe oil tank, tank-top instrument console, fish-tail exhaust pipe, kick-starter, and plastic luggage case with flying wing symbol.

Based on a 1956 frame, the Boothill Panhead is, unsurprisingly, powered by a Panhead V-twin motor but, perversely, it is fed by an S & S Super B carb with knucklebone air filter. The difference is its stroke has been increased to 86 cu. in. (1409 cc).

Reverse view

The front forks were anachronisms, belonging to a more modern bike, but the lack of shrouds made them acceptable. The only other suspension was the 'Ful-Floteing' seat post, since the frame was a hardtail.

Based on a 1956 frame, the Boothill Panhead is, unsurprisingly, powered by a Panhead V-twin motor but, perversely, it is fed by an S & S Super B carb with knucklebone air filter. The difference is its stroke has been increased to 86 cu. in. (1409 cc).

The Boothill Panhead ran on 16in (406mm) laced wire-spoke wheels front and rear, with drum brakes at either end. The appearance of the front drum brake was refined by an aluminium trim, said to assist cooling.

Above: Bizarre, some may say, but what price individualism? A skull-topped hand-shift plus a fires-of-hell rendition by Arthur Slade's Boothill Motorcycles on the Fatbob fuel tank help to create the machine's unique identity.

Below: The Panhead V-twin is normally a 74 cu. in. (1213 cc) capacity engine, but in this particular case, the piston stroke has been increased to give 86 cu. in. (1410 cc). It has four-speed transmission and chain final drive.

Retrospective customizing is great fun and leads to all kinds of imaginative solutions. The Boothill Panhead is just such a machine, its wild colour scheme depicting overt symbols of mortality. In modern times when most aspects of Western day-to-day life are pretty secure and risk-free, escapism is rife, and individuals who don't care to be glued to a computer screen in their spare time indulge in high-risk thrill activities like rock-climbing or sky-diving. The more down to earth version of this adventurous spirit is motorcycling.

The Panhead in this customized bobber is a fine example of the Harley-Davidson heritage. The Milwaukee-built V-twin qualifies as a piece of benchmark engineering in the history of technology, simply because it has been in continuous production longer than any other internal-combustion engine. Since its introduction in 1909, the principle of operation, number and arrangement of cylinders, cooling system and number of valves have not changed. It was always an air-cooled four-stroke two-cylinder narrow-angle V-twin, with two valves per cylinder. The only alteration during its first 20 years' service was the method of valve operation. However, since 1936 the engine has also remained unchanged in this respect and only small details have been refined.

Valve Layout

The 61 cu. in. (1000 cc) engine was first modified in 1936, when the side valves were bypassed and it was fitted with overhead valves, or ohv. With this system, both valves hung in the cylinder head and were operated by the camshaft, which was still positioned underneath, via lifters, push rods and rocker arms. This valve mechanism naturally necessitated a larger cylinder head because it needed to house the valves as well and, generally, one or more cylinder head covers provided access to the internals. As engine technology advanced, other configurations of valve layout and operation followed the ohv unit, including the overhead camshaft (ohc) or double overhead camshafts (dohc), with four, five or eight valves per cylinder. However, Harley-Davidson kept faith with the ohv two-valve engine up to the present day, and devotees differentiate between the various generations of engine according to the shape of the cylinder head or the rocker cover. The head of the big twin that was introduced in 1936 reminded people of the knuckles of a fist, and became known as the Knucklehead. In 1948, a generation of engines known as Panheads followed in the big twins. Eighteen years later, they were replaced by the Shovelhead.

The Boothill Panhead featured here is a modern version of the customized bobber from the 1950s, when, in the early days of customizing, bikes' mudguards were cut down and the rear end of the back mudguard bobbed up in the air. In many cases, smaller fuel tanks were fitted, such as those from the Sportster or even the Mustang moped. Bobbers that retained the stock two-piece Harley tanks, such as this Boothill Panhead, were referred to as Fatbobs and, like many colloquial expressions, the term was widely used and became generally accepted and used by the factory as a description of its own product.

This Panhead engine was referred to as a stroker because its displacement was enlarged by increasing the stroke of the pistons. Engine capacity was stroked to 86 cu. in. (1409 cc) through use of big-twin Flathead flywheels, but retained the standard bore and 1963 cylinder heads and engine casings. It was fed by an S & S Super B carburettor with a knuckle air filter. The electrical system was upgraded to 12-volts, and the exhaust system was a period two-into-one ending in a fishtail silencer. There was a four speed transmission, and chain final drive. Sixteen-inch (406mm) wire-spoked wheels were fitted front and rear, with drum brakes at either end. The front drum brake was enhanced by the fitment of an aluminium trim ring, which assisted in cooling the brake drum and eliminating brake fade. The front forks were sourced from a later model. The manual gear shift knob took the form of a miniature skull, in deference to the Boothill graveyard theme, but pool balls and door knobs were also sometimes used. The bike was otherwise not drastically altered from the regular FL Panhead, and the fibreglass panniers were another authentic period touch.

1956 Boothill Panhead	
Engine model:	Overhead-valve Panhead V-twin
Engine capacity:	86 cu. in. (1410 cc)
Cases:	Harley-Davidson
Carburation:	S&S Super B
Air filter:	Knuckle
Ignition:	Points
Pipes:	Two-into-one fishtail silencer
Transmission:	Four-speed
Frame:	Tubular cradle
Suspension:	Front: telescopic forks Rear: hardtail
Brakes:	Drum front and rear
Wheels:	16in (406mm) wire-spoke front and rear
Mudguards (fenders):	Front: Modified FL Rear: bobbed
Handlebars:	Flat
Risers:	Yes
Headlight:	9in (229mm) chromed FL-type
Tail-light:	Cat's eye

Indian Fendered Evo

The heavily tooled leather saddle conveys
Western iconography, enhanced with fringes
on its lower edge. The parallel exhaust pipes
could be construed as shotgun barrels.

The Indian Fendered Custom is kept in Genk, Belgium, and is built
up on a stock 1991 Harley-Davidson Softail frame, which, although
modified in the customizing process, helps convey a classic stance.

The specially made fuel tank follows the general curvature of the Indian-like fenders, and its shape is echoed by the teardrop-shaped air-filter cover. It is perhaps eccentric to use a Harley-Davidson to re-create a rival make.

The concept behind this custom machine is an exploration of what an Indian Chief from the early 1950s might look like in a modern incarnation. Crucial styling cues are the fenders, which exaggerate the original Indian styling.

The Evo in the bike's title not only suggests an evolved Indian, but also implies that its power-unit is the 80 cu. in. (1310 cc) Evolution V-twin, mated to a five -speed transmission with belt drive.

The Indian Chief was among the most stylish motorcycles ever made, and this rendition is a good reappraisal of the marque. The wheels are 16in (406mm) cast aluminium-alloy discs front and rear, with single disc brakes.

Indian Motorcycles of Springfield Massachusetts were Harley-Davidson's last great rival on the US domestic scene, but closed down in 1953. One of Indian's best known motorcycles was the Chief, which featured mudguards so large that they were almost a caricature. Some modern-day custom builders have taken the concept of the Indian mudguard and applied it to the Harley-Davidson frame. Apart from being a work of art in its own right, this 1991 model shows what a customized Indian Chief might have looked like if the company had survived.

For much of its life, the fortunes of Indian ran parallel with Harley-Davidson. Founded in 1901 by race promoter George Hendee and Oscar Hedstrom, production of Indian machines began in Springfield, Massachusetts. They built high-quality, single-cylinder machines with all-chain transmission and twist-grip controls, and these were followed by V-twins in 1907. Notice the parallel with Harley-Davidson here, when the founders also came out with a V-twin. However, Indian quickly established itself as the largest motorcycle company in the world, and by 1914 had come up with the first motorcycle with an

Above: The graceful curvature and ample proportions of the rear fender on this Harley-Davidson-based pastiche of a 1953 Indian Chief, last of the breed, are complemented by a heavily tooled leather saddlebag.

1991 Indian Fendered Harley	
Engine model:	Evolution
Engine capacity:	80 cu. in. (1310 cc)
Cases:	Harley-Davidson
Carburation:	Stock Harley-Davidson
Air filter:	Custom teardrop
Ignition:	Electronic
Pipes:	Shotgun-type
Transmission:	Five-speed
Frame:	Tubular cradle
Suspension:	Front: telescopic forks
	Rear: hardtail
Brakes:	Front: single disc
	Rear: disc
Wheels:	16in (406mm) cast-alloy disc
Mudguards (fenders):	Indian Chief-style
Handlebars:	Flat
Risers:	None
Headlight:	Custom sealed beam
Tail-light:	In saddlebag

electric starter. In 1916, side-valve singles and V-twins designed by Charles Gustafson replaced the earlier inlet-over-exhaust designs, and indeed, side-valve engines would feature on Indian bikes until their demise in 1953. Back in 1917, a short-lived lightweight flat-twin was introduced, and then in 1920 the Indian Scout came out, followed in 1922 by the Chief. These two models formed the bulk of Indian production until the Second World War. They also made the side-valve and overhead-valve single-cylinder Prince model from 1925 to 1928, but in general terms, a lack of development placed Indian at a disadvantage to Harley-Davidson.

The Four-cylinder Ace

In 1927, Indian bought the rights to produce the four-cylinder Ace, and built in-line fours until 1942. From 1945, Ralph B. Rogers took control of Indian, and a range of new Torque designed single-cylinder and parallel-twins was built, but they were unsuccessful. The last Indian Chiefs were built in 1953, and afterwards the name changed several times and badged a variety of unworthy imports including side-valve 15 cu. in. (250 cc) Brockhouse singles,

Royal Enfields, Italian-framed Velocette hybrids, and assorted small-capacity two-strokes. In the late 1990s there were rumours of a revival of the Indian marque, but at that point there was only the Indian-Fendered Evolution to contemplate.

Owned by Danny Fransen of Genk, Belgium, the bike was based on a modified Harley-Davidson Softail frame, in which the rear suspension was completely absent, just like a late 1940s hardtail. It was powered by the Harley-Davidson 80 cu. in. (1310 cc) Evolution engine with electronic ignition. The custom ancillaries included a special tear-drop air filter and shotgun barrel exhaust pipes. It used a stock five speed transmission, with front telescopic forks and ran a pair of 16in (406mm) cast alloy Fat Boy disc wheels, retarded by single disc brakes both front and rear. The bike used flat black-painted bars with no risers, and the instrument panel was in its normal place on the tank-top. One personalized item was the whisky-bottle label that was incorporated in the speedo face. The Fatbob tank was lengthened in order to curve down to the hand-tooled cowboy-style saddle. A single

matching saddlebag that was also hand tooled and had been cut to match the shape of the rear mudguard was mounted on the left of the bike. The traditional horseshoe oil tank, so often chromed, was discreetly painted black to match the overall colour scheme and lines of the bike. Its duo-tone paint finish with pin-striping was tastefully executed, complementing the curvature of the Indian-style mudguards.

The anticipated revival of the Indian marque came about in 1998, with the merger of three companies to create the Indian Motorcycle Company. In 1999, they released the Indian Chief, a big cruiser powered by a four-stroke S&S Super Stock 45 Degree 88 cu. in. (1442 cc) V-Twin. This was followed in 2000 by the Scout, which looked uncannily like an H-D Sportster, and in 2001 by the Spirit model. All three Indians used the same running gear and drive-lines.

Below: The standard Harley-Davidson Fatbob fuel tank has been lengthened so that it curves down to amalgamate with the leather saddle. Tooled leather-craft forms a tank-guard and surrounds the instrument console.

Custom Shovelhead

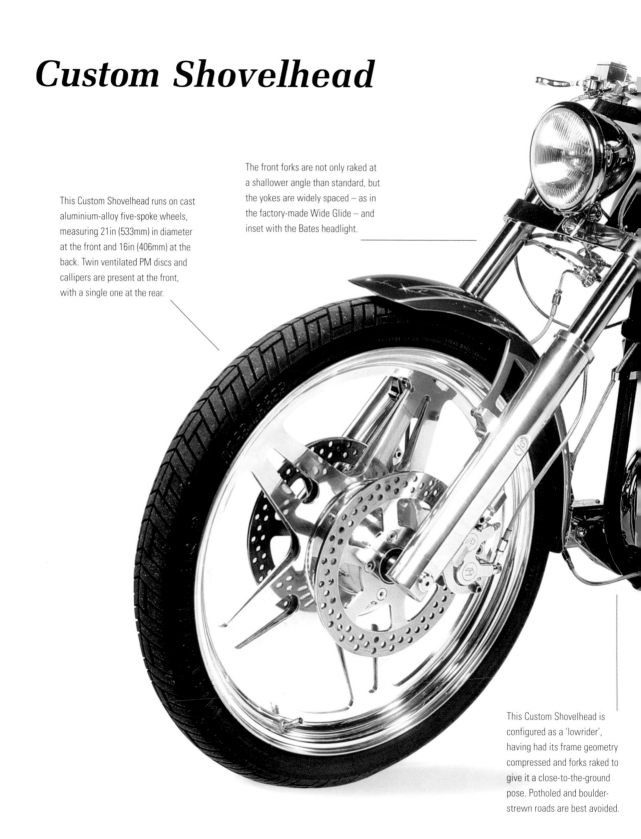

This Custom Shovelhead runs on cast aluminium-alloy five-spoke wheels, measuring 21in (533mm) in diameter at the front and 16in (406mm) at the back. Twin ventilated PM discs and callipers are present at the front, with a single one at the rear.

The front forks are not only raked at a shallower angle than standard, but the yokes are widely spaced – as in the factory-made Wide Glide – and inset with the Bates headlight.

This Custom Shovelhead is configured as a 'lowrider', having had its frame geometry compressed and forks raked to give it a close-to-the-ground pose. Potholed and boulder-strewn roads are best avoided.

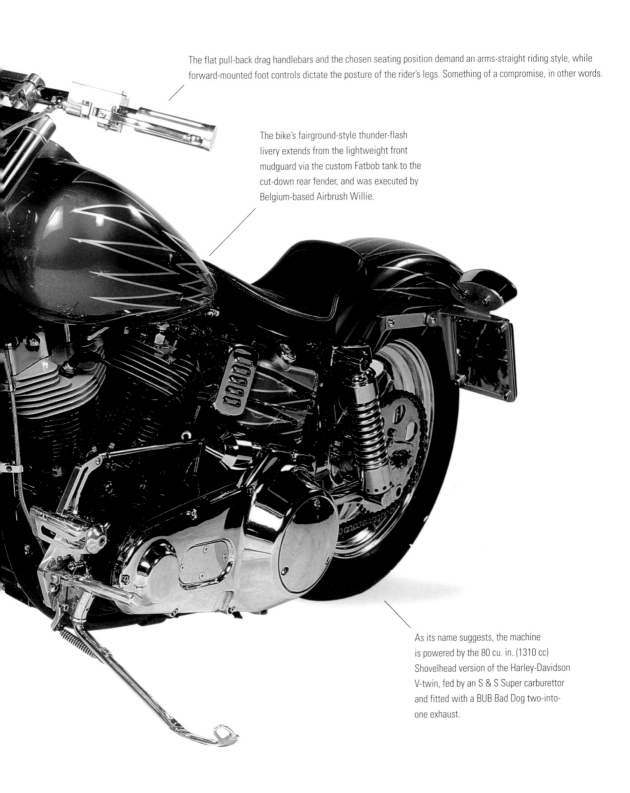

The flat pull-back drag handlebars and the chosen seating position demand an arms-straight riding style, while forward-mounted foot controls dictate the posture of the rider's legs. Something of a compromise, in other words.

The bike's fairground-style thunder-flash livery extends from the lightweight front mudguard via the custom Fatbob tank to the cut-down rear fender, and was executed by Belgium-based Airbrush Willie.

As its name suggests, the machine is powered by the 80 cu. in. (1310 cc) Shovelhead version of the Harley-Davidson V-twin, fed by an S & S Super carburettor and fitted with a BUB Bad Dog two-into-one exhaust.

When a Harley-Davidson is customized in such a way as to give it a long, low and lean stance, it is described, quite logically, as a Low Rider. The reason for taking this route is that a low-slung machine is immediately endowed with a more purposeful racing stance; it can also project a sense of menace, like an animal about to pounce. There is always the association with the outlaw fringe and the Easy Rider fraternity. To achieve this particular look and attitude, the standard Harley-Davidson frame can be modified through a variety of techniques. Without cutting into the frame tubes to alter the triangulations, the simplest method is to reduce the length both of the rear shock absorbers and the front forks, which has the effect of dropping the whole bike nearer to the road. Altering the rake of the forks at the yoke both lengthens and lowers the machine.

Once these modifications have been carried out to the forks and suspension, it is possible to enhance the long, low look through the use of modified fuel tanks and mudguards, as well as careful choice of after-market components such as the seat. All these techniques have

Below: The Custom Shovelhead's 80 cu. in. (1310 cc) V-twin is fitted with an S & S Super carburettor, with a chromed S & S teardrop air filter, and a set of BUB Bad Dog exhaust headers.

been used in the construction of this custom Shovelhead. Its suspension is by swing-arm and coil-over dampers at the rear, with telescopic upside-down forks at the front. Although it sounds conventional enough, it is where they are acquired and how they are fitted that counts.

Creating a Custom Machine

After the bike is built, the cosmetics are completed by fitting numerous custom parts sourced from specialists such as Performance Machine. Much emphasis is placed on use of chrome and stainless steel. One of the secrets of creating a good-looking custom machine is to minimize the number of extraneous brackets, so that the lines of the bike remain uncluttered. In this case, the numberplate bracket also carries the cat's-eye tail-light and is fixed to the rear mudguard mounting strut on the left-hand side of the bike. Finally, the painter – Airbrush Willie in this case – works on the multi-hued geometric paint job, carrying the design through front and rear mudguards and the custom Fatbob fuel tank.

This machine was created in 1995 and the power-unit is the 80 cu. in. (1310 cc) version of the Shovelhead V-twin that started life in 1966. This is the motor at the heart of

many a classic chopper and its engine's main characteristic was the new cast-alloy rocker boxes atop revised cylinder heads. These distinctive Shovelhead covers replaced the one-piece lids used on the Panhead. Initially, the bottom end of the Shovelhead unit was closely related to the Knucklehead, while the cylinder heads were based on the Sportster's. Post-1970, Shovelheads received alternators instead of generators for their electrical systems. There was thus no further need for the external timing case and forward mounting point for the generator. The timing gear case on the later engine was a small, cone-shaped item instead of the horizontally finned version. Ten cooling fins on the cylinder heads indicate that this is indeed a 80 cu. in. (1310 cc) engine: earlier 74 cu. in. (1200 cc) models only had nine. For the most part, Shovelhead componentry is interchangeable, which enables customizers and classic buffs to update and upgrade early versions. The Shovelhead was in production for 18 years and was phased out in 1984 and replaced by the Evolution engine. The Shovelhead

Above: The rear shock-absorber and Performance Machine brakes are prominent, but the fender's uncluttered lines are achieved by locating the licence plate and tail-light on a bracket attached to the fender strut on the left-hand side of the bike.

1995 Custom Shovelhead	
Engine model:	Shovelhead
Engine capacity:	80 cu. in. (1310 cc)
Cases:	Harley-Davidson
Carburation:	S&S Super
Air filter:	S&S Teardrop
Ignition:	Points
Pipes:	BUB Bad Dog
Transmission:	Four-speed
Frame:	Tubular cradle
Suspension:	Front: telescopic forks
	Rear: swing-arm, coil-over dampers
Brakes:	Front: twin Performance Machine discs
	Rear: Performance Machine disc and calliper
Wheels:	Front: 21in (533mm) custom five-spoke
	Rear: 16in (406mm) custom five-spoke
Mudguards (fenders):	Front: custom
	Rear: modified Harley-Davidson
Handlebars:	Pull-back drags
Risers:	Integral with triple tree
Headlight:	Bates
Tail-light:	Cat's eye

motor also featured what was called a ham-can air filter on the right-hand side, in this case a Smith and Smith (S&S) Teardrop version. S&S is a renowned American after-market performance equipment manufacturer of long standing, specializing in items such as these S&S Super carburettors and distinctive air-cleaner covers. Each component on this custom Harley has been carefully selected and polished or painted.

On this motorbike, the foot controls and pegs have been mounted as far forward as possible. A deliberately aggressive set of stumpy BUB Bad Dog exhaust pipes has been selected, while the rear brake disc and calliper are from Californian specialists Performance Machine and have been installed on a custom-made 16in (406mm) alloy rear wheel. At 21in (533mm) diameter, the five-spoke alloy front wheel is deliberately large to accentuate the Lowrider image. Exactly how low it is reasonably practicable to go depends on the type of roads you ride. Bottoming out is no fun.

Twin Dell'Orto

The bike's 'raison d'être' is its dragster-
inspired nitrous-oxide injection, achieved via
canisters fastened to the rear fender struts
that supply the two Dell'Orto carburettors
through siphon tubes.

Built in 1993, the machine's 80 cu. in. (1310 cc)
Evolution V-twin was specially adapted to suit the
high-performance modifications. Breathing was aided
by fitting individual straight-through Porker pipes.

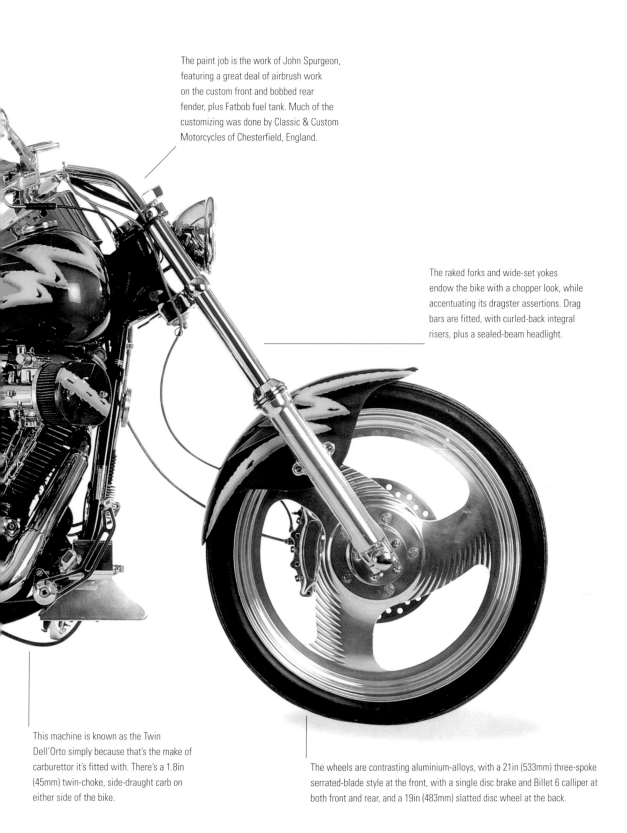

The paint job is the work of John Spurgeon, featuring a great deal of airbrush work on the custom front and bobbed rear fender, plus Fatbob fuel tank. Much of the customizing was done by Classic & Custom Motorcycles of Chesterfield, England.

The raked forks and wide-set yokes endow the bike with a chopper look, while accentuating its dragster assertions. Drag bars are fitted, with curled-back integral risers, plus a sealed-beam headlight.

This machine is known as the Twin Dell'Orto simply because that's the make of carburettor it's fitted with. There's a 1.8in (45mm) twin-choke, side-draught carb on either side of the bike.

The wheels are contrasting aluminium-alloys, with a 21in (533mm) three-spoke serrated-blade style at the front, with a single disc brake and Billet 6 calliper at both front and rear, and a 19in (483mm) slatted disc wheel at the back.

Standard engines can be coaxed to perform more efficiently and deliver more power in various ways. Bolt-on forced induction systems such as turbos and superchargers, which work without resorting to internal modifications such as high-lift cams, re-jetting carburettors or re-chipping engine management systems, are just one example of this. This so-called Twin Dell'Orto chopper takes a more subtle approach. It employs chemistry, blending a heady mix of nitrous oxide with its fuel to obtain more horsepower.

Greater efficiency and power are delivered by fixing a couple

Above: The Twin Dell'Orto is based on a Softail frame with concealed dampers. The stock brake discs at both front and rear have a 'Billet-6' calliper fitted, while the exhaust pipes are individual straight-through Porker style.

Below: The nitrous oxide canisters are attached to the rear fender brackets and feed the two Dell'Orto carbs through siphon tubes. The tail-light is a cat's eye with a blue dot. The licence plate could be considered offensive by some people.

of nitrous oxide cylinders to the bike's rear mudguard stays; the supply is linked via siphon tubes to the Dell'Orto carburettors, one on either side of the bike. The carburettors are standard and do not need re-jetting. When the nitrous oxide is heated on the compression stroke, it breaks down and releases extra oxygen, which burns more fuel. The resulting higher cylinder pressures liberate more power. As pressurized nitrous oxide is injected into the intake manifold, it changes from a liquid to a gas, which reduces the temperature and helps create additional power in the process.

Nitrous oxide kits are readily available and are designed for use on demand and only when the throttle is wide open. Gains in performance using nitrous injection depend on factors such as engine size, carburettor jetting and gearing, but improvements of three seconds and 15mph (24km/h) over a quarter of a mile (400m) are typical. The bottles can last for up to ten quarter-mile (400m) passes, but it does depend on how long the button is depressed. When used up, the canisters can generally be refilled at designated performance centres. Nitrous injection can be safely applied above 2500rpm and works just fine with normal pump fuel. For racing, where higher compression ratios are used, a higher fuel octane is desirable, as well as more retarded ignition. There are two types of nitrous system: plate injection and direct port. The advantages of a plate system are ease of installation and removal, while direct port systems provide ultimate distribution and power.

Nitrous Injection Kits

A nitrous injection kit can be installed in just a few hours, using regular hand tools and referring to the makers' installation drawings, wiring diagrams and bottle-mounting procedures. If you are seeking even more power, nitrous injection also works efficiently in conjunction with a turbocharger, in that turbo lag is completely eliminated with the addition of a nitrous system. The other advantage with nitrous injection is that it is a cost-effective means of increasing power, if only for a limited period. It provides big gains in torque without having to rev the engine drastically. High revs and big twins are not natural bedfellows.

The owner of the Twin Dell'Orto, Chris Butler, began the project with an almost standard 1993 Harley-Davidson Softail FXSTC. Specialist companies such as Classic and Custom Motorcycles of Chesterfield, England, carried out much of the customizing. Before the nitrous injection was fitted, the 80 cu. in. (1310 cc) Evolution big

1993 FXSTC Softail 'Twin Dell'Orto'	
Engine model:	Evolution
Engine capacity:	80 cu. in. (1310 cc)
Cases:	Harley-Davidson
Carburation:	Twin Dell'Orto
Air filter:	Twin K&N
Ignition:	Electronic
Pipes:	Porker
Transmission:	Five-speed
Frame:	Tubular cradle
Suspension:	Front: telescopic forks Rear: Softail
Brakes:	Front: single disc Rear: Billet six-calliper and disc
Wheels:	Front: 21in (533mm) alloy Rear: 19in (483mm) alloy
Mudguards (fenders):	Front: Arlen Ness Rear: Fatbob
Handlebars:	Drag bars
Risers:	Integral with bars
Headlight:	Custom sealed beam
Tail-light:	Cat's eye with blue dot

twin was rebuilt and, along with the Milanese Dell'Orto carburettors and K&N air filters, a pair of straight Porker performance exhaust pipes was fitted. The purposeful look of the bike was achieved by tilting the steeply raked forks and fitting a minimal Arlen Ness mudguard and 21in (533mm) serrated three-spoke alloy wheel at the front. The triangular Softail portion of the frame was chromed and the Harley-Davidson Fatbob tank retained. The rider sat astride a Le Pera custom solo seat. At the rear, the Fatbob mudguard covered a 19in (483mm) Revtech custom alloy disc wheel, with a Billet brake calliper acting on the stock Harley-Davidson brake disc bolted to the wheel. Performance Machine forward-control pedals were used and the rear light was a cat's eye with a blue-dot faceted lens. The zigzag paint job was carried out by John Spurgeon and the custom look was completed by pull-back handlebars and custom oval rear-view mirrors. Altogether, it was quite a machine, with performance to match the looks.

Buell S3 Thunderbolt

When stationary, the bike leans on a side-stand that's less substantial than a Harley's, while the foot-operated gear-shift can prove difficult to get the toe under. Despite rubber engine mounts, the machine is dogged by vibrations, especially at a standstill.

The power-unit for the S3 is the 73 cu. in. (1203 cc) version of the Harley-Davidson Sportster V-twin motor, fed by electronic fuel injection and featuring a serpentine two-into-one exhaust system.

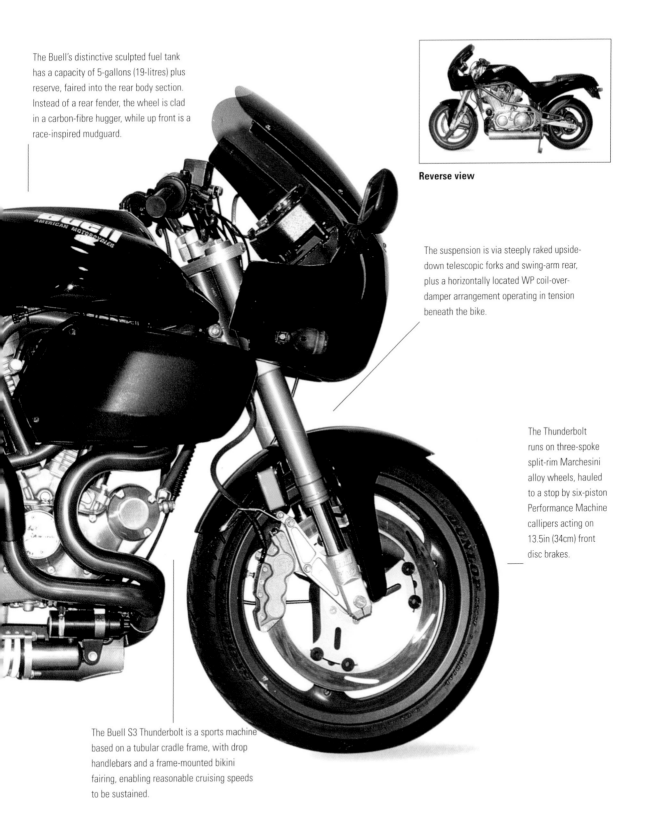

The Buell's distinctive sculpted fuel tank has a capacity of 5-gallons (19-litres) plus reserve, faired into the rear body section. Instead of a rear fender, the wheel is clad in a carbon-fibre hugger, while up front is a race-inspired mudguard.

Reverse view

The suspension is via steeply raked upside-down telescopic forks and swing-arm rear, plus a horizontally located WP coil-over-damper arrangement operating in tension beneath the bike.

The Thunderbolt runs on three-spoke split-rim Marchesini alloy wheels, hauled to a stop by six-piston Performance Machine callipers acting on 13.5in (34cm) front disc brakes.

The Buell S3 Thunderbolt is a sports machine based on a tubular cradle frame, with drop handlebars and a frame-mounted bikini fairing, enabling reasonable cruising speeds to be sustained.

Above: With speedo and rev-counter prominent, the instrument binnacle on board the Buell S3 Thunderbolt is shrouded by the screen fronting the bikini fairing. Also visible are the chromed handlebars and fuel-tank breather pipe.

come out of the new association and it first appeared in 1994. A production run of 700 units was envisaged, even though this was an enormous increase on Buell's previous output of around 100 bikes. Then, as now, distribution was via Harley-Davidson dealerships, with normal warranty and service back-up. This arrangement gave Buell licence to develop sports-orientated bikes with the benefit of the financial backing and security of the parent company.

Using the Uniplanar powertrain vibration isolation system, or rubber installation mounts, the S2's engine was fitted in a chrome-molybdenum cradle frame composed of triangulations and tube runs different from the regular Harley chassis, and a rear subframe that supported the dual seat and rear bodywork. The Thunderbolt was designed to match that elusive marriage of performance allied to rider comfort, with handling to match.

There is nothing on the market quite like a Buell and one of the most visually striking aspects was the two-into-one exhaust, which took the two stainless-steel pipes in a forward direction and then exited to the left of the bike via a car-type silencer. Improvements to the 74 cu. in. (1200 cc) V-twin's intake and exhaust systems meant that the S2 immediately benefited from a 20 per cent increase in power, rated at 76bhp. For the 2001 model year, the S3 Thunderbolt ran with the fuel-injected 101bhp 74 cu. in. (1200 cc) Thunderstorm V-twin engine.

The Buell marque gets its name from its founder Eric Buell, who worked for Harley-Davidson before he established his own operation in the early 1980s. His first project was the RR1000, a sports bike powered by the 61 cu. in. (1000 cc) XR-derived overhead-valve V-twin, commissioned by the Vetter Fairing company. The bike was dwarfed by acres of plastic, exaggerated by its small-diameter 16in (406mm) wheels.

From the outset, Buell produced sports bikes with Harley-Davidson Sportster engines. They were based on multi-tubular frames built with premium-quality chassis components, suspension, wheels and brakes. Bikes were hand-built in low volume and came with high price tags.

By 1993, it was clear that there was some demand for the Buell and Harley-Davidson, keen to attract buyers from outside its normal catchment, acquired a 49 per cent stake in Buell. The S2 Thunderbolt was the first bike to

Performance Machine Callipers

The Thunderbolt's five-speed transmission retained Harley-Davidson's belt-drive system, but huge six-piston Performance Machine callipers acted on 13.5in (340mm) front disc brakes to reduce speed. The wheels were three-spoke Marchesini items and suspension was by WP upside-down telescopic forks and a horizontally mounted adjustable coil-over damper, located beneath the bike and operating in tension. This location meant that the bike could only have a side-stand. The Buell S2 contained some fine engineering and the chassis was actually capable of supporting more performance than the 74 cu. in. (1200 cc) Sportster engine could muster.

Other characteristics of the S2 were the frame-mounted bikini fairing with an aerodynamic windscreen, inset rectangular headlight and air intakes, plus instrument binnacle inside. A brief racing-style front mudguard was fitted, slightly at variance with its chrome-plated handlebars, and the bike had a 5-gallon (19-litre) fuel tank that included a 0.6-gallon (2.2-litre) reserve. The front air vents were matched by another set beside the rear light.

For touring purposes, Buell released the Thunderbolt S3T in 2000, complete with colour-coordinated saddlebags with fitted inner luggage to stow road gear and a full-face helmet. Further storage was available under the seat, while fairing lowers protected the legs. An upright riding position was provided by the high-rise handlebars.

Above: The Buell S3 Thunderbolt features an unusual suspension arrangement, with a WP coil-over-damper mounted horizontally beneath the frame, operating in tension on the swing-arm.

1996 Buell S3 Thunderbolt

Engine model:	Thunderstorm
Engine capacity:	74 cu. in. (1200 cc)
Cases:	Harley-Davidson/Buell
Carburation:	Dynamic Digital fuel injection
Air filter:	K&N
Ignition:	Electronic
Pipes:	Buell two-into-one
Transmission:	Five-speed, belt drive
Frame:	Buell tubular perimeter chrome-molybdenum
Suspension:	Front: Showa telescopic forks Rear: swing-arm, plus Showa extension-type damper
Brakes:	Front: twin disc, six-port Performance Machine callipers Rear: disc, single-piston calliper
Wheels:	17in (432mm) cast-alloy front and rear
Mudguards (fenders):	Front: Buell Rear: carbon-fibre hugger
Handlebars:	Flat, chromed
Risers:	Integral with bars
Headlight:	Integral with fairing
Tail-light:	Integral with tail section

For 1999, Buell announced the more refined Lightning model, still using the 74 cu. in. (1200 cc) Evolution engine in 101bhp trim, now allied to a sophisticated Dynamic Digital fuel injection and engine management system. The big V-twin was set in a complex tubular cradle frame, to which were added smaller subframes for the rear pegs and a big alloy support that held the dual seat. The Lightning's aggressive styling cues included a carbon-fibre hugger and belt guard, belly pan and black nylon airbox. Minimal front mudguard and moth screen completed the plastic parts. A smaller 4.6-gallon (17.4-litre) tank was used and the Lightning ran on three-spoke cast-alloy wheels shod with Dunlop Sportmax tyres. Suspension was by Showa upside-down forks and the horizontal WP shock absorber underneath the bike, plus a single gas damper at the rear. In theory, a Lightning was capable of 140mph (225km/h); however, without a full fairing, such speeds are unrealistic.

As well as the X1 Lightning, Buell also offered the fuel-injected M2 Cyclone in its line-up. This machine was fitted with stainless steel headers in 2001, replacing black-finish items that tended to peel. The exhaust porting was in stainless steel. A heat deflector shield, added in mid-1999, remained in place. New cargo loops, similar to those found on the X1, were added to the tail section, allowing bungee cords and other cargo equipment to be utilized more efficiently. The helmet lock, while not a cosmetic change, was redesigned to improve security.

Buell X1 Lightning

The X1 features an arrowhead-shaped alloy subframe acting as a seat support, matched by a similar shape fibreglass belly pan. The belt-drive cover and rear hugger are in lightweight carbon-fibre.

The Buell's ohv 73 cu. in. (1203 cc) Sportster-derived V-twin is enclosed within the multi-tubular cradle frame, and develops 101bhp at 6000rpm, driving through the five-speed gearbox with belt drive.

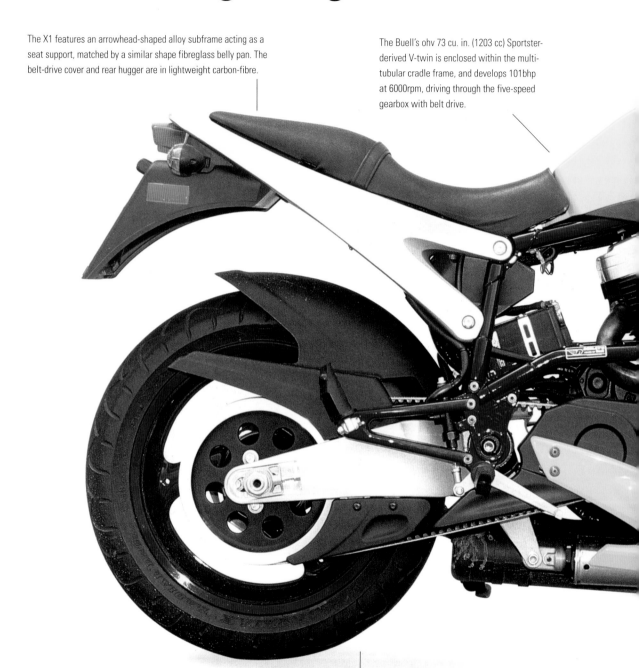

Suspension on the Lightning consists of steeply raked upside-down Showa adjustable forks, with alloy swing-arm incorporating tension adjuster, and under-frame mounted shock-absorber.

The Lightning comes across as much more of a hard-edged street-fighter than the Cyclone or Thunderbolt models, by virtue of its flat bars and lack of a full fairing.

Reverse view

The X1 rides on 17in (432mm) diameter three-spoke Marchesini cast-alloy wheels, shod ex-factory with Dunlop Sportmax tyres. Disc brakes with Buell callipers are fitted and Dot 4 brake fluid is used.

The X1 comes with a radically sculpted 4.5-gallon (17.4-litre) fuel tank, flanked by a vast nylon airbox that feeds the bike's Dynamic Digital electronic fuel injection and engine management system.

After gaining an engineering degree, Erik Buell worked for Harley-Davidson as a test engineer. At the time, he rode big Japanese bikes. An amateur racer in his spare time, Buell designed and built his own competition machine, the Buell RW750, which was raced by the American Machinists Union. In 1983, he left Harley-Davidson to concentrate on building the RW750; however, when the American Motorcycle Association (AMA) announced that Formula One was being replaced by World Superbikes, the RW750 was instantly rendered obsolete. Buell's career was saved when an ex-colleague at Harley-Davidson asked him to create an American sports bike for a dealer conference. The result was the RR1000, which incorporated Buell's patented Uniplanar chassis design, with which all Buells are fitted. The Harley-Davidson V-twin engine was incorporated as an integral stressed chassis member, which was quite avant garde in the mid-1980s, especially when the engine was a Harley-Davidson. The Buell set-up was different in that it virtually eliminated vibration, achieved by suspending the

Above: The front end of the Buell X1 Lightning features a three-spoke cast-alloy Marchesini wheel plus ventilated disc and Buell calliper, race-type mudguard and upside-down adjustable Showa forks. The steep rake makes turn-in pin-sharp.

1999 Buell X1 Lightning

Engine model:	Overhead-valve V-twin Thunderstorm
Engine capacity:	74 cu. in. (1200 cc)
Cases:	Harley-Davidson/Buell
Carburation:	Dynamic Digital fuel injection
Air filter:	K&N
Ignition:	Electronic
Pipes:	Stainless-steel two-into-one
Transmission:	Five-speed, belt drive
Frame:	Buell tubular perimeter chrome-molybdenum
Suspension:	Front: Showa telescopic forks Rear: swing-arm, plus Showa extension-type damper
Brakes:	disc front and rear
Wheels:	17in (432mm) three-spoke cast-alloy front and rear
Mudguards (fenders):	Front: Buell sport Rear: carbon-fibre hugger
Handlebars:	Flat
Risers:	None
Headlight:	Chrome rim
Tail-light:	Integral with tail section

engine from three rubber mounts, while four adjustable rods allowed it to move in the vertical plane, but not laterally. Another Buell hallmark was the under-slung rear damper, which worked in tension rather than compression, and this was retained as a feature of modern Buells. The aerodynamic fairings of the RR1000 completely enveloped the bike, including the front wheel, so that any relationship to a Harley-Davidson was highly doubtful. Fifty units were produced between 1987 and 1988, until the supply of XR1000 engines dried up.

It was clear that an untapped market existed for a sporting Harley-Davidson as, by this time, the Sportster was lagging behind in the performance stakes. The Buell's excellent handling promised to bridge the gap once again, and a batch of 74 cu. in. (1200 cc) Sportster engines was acquired to power a new range of Buells. The RR1200 was bereft of most of the bulbous bodywork of the RR1000, apart from a half-fairing, and it marked Buell's transition from racers to pure road bikes. A dual seat with a hinged rear backrest was fitted on that model, while the similar RSS was a single seater. Only top-class components were used, with WP forks and rear damper, plus Performance Machine six-piston front-brake callipers. Its Sportster V-twin was standard and not as quick as many Japanese machines, but it did open up a market for sports roadsters.

As Buell's sales grew, the company became attractive to Harley-Davidson, which had made a full recovery from the early 1980s. Recognizing that it needed to broaden its market into sports and sports-touring bikes, Harley-Davidson bought a 49 per cent stake in Buell in 1993. Erik Buell remained in control and the company relocated to a bigger factory at East Troy, where it was able to increase production and lower prices. From 100 units a year, Buell was soon making 800 machines annually. The S2 Thunderbolt was released in 1994, using the same Buell chassis allied to a 74 cu. in. (1200 cc) Harley-Davidson Sportster engine. It had now adopted all-new naked street-fighter styling and volumes were sufficiently high that tuning the V-twin engine could be justified. The Thunderbolt had 20 per cent more power, largely due to improved breathing via the substantial and somewhat ungainly air filter on the right-hand side of the engine.

The following year, the S1 Lightning was introduced. This machine featured radically abbreviated styling,

Below: The X1's 73 cu. in. (1203 cc) Sportster-derived V-twin engine features a huge nylon airbox and cross-over exhaust headers that exit down the bike's left-hand side. The dart-shaped belly pan is its only fairing.

although it was mechanically identical to the Thunderbolt. The solo-seat stripped-down look of the Lightning typified the street-fighter fashion that was becoming popular as a reaction against the ubiquitous fully faired sports bikes. In 1996, Buell launched a sports-touring version of the Thunderbolt, which justified the touring designation by virtue of panniers and leg shields. Even with panniers, the Thunderbolt was still a raw sportster, lacking some of the sophistication and attention to detail of the Japanese and European touring machines. A cheaper model known as the Cyclone was introduced the same year, fitted with conventional Showa forks, instead of the upside-down WP units with which the rest of the range was equipped. The S1 White Lightning was released in late 1997, with new cylinder heads, camshaft and flywheels fitted, lifting power output to 93bhp. By this time, Buell's output was in excess of 4000, with more than 6000 bikes built in 1998.

Fuel-injected X1

The fuel-injected X1 Lightning was unveiled in 1998 for the 1999 model year. It was still based on the Buell chassis and the Sportster V-twin, but its image was now more polished and refined than earlier models, even if it did retain the oddball styling for which Buells were famed. It featured a carbon-fibre hugger over the rear wheel, chin fairing, racing-type front mudguard, an alloy seat subframe and an enormous swing-arm incorporating the chain adjuster. The ride was also improved with Showa upside-down forks and rear dampers. New Dynamic Digital electronic fuel injection was added to the 74 cu. in. (1200 cc) Sportster version of the Evolution V-twin, which increased outright power to 101bhp to give a top speed of 140mph (225km/h) and made for a smoother power delivery.

It was at this point that Harley-Davidson took the logical step of taking over Buell altogether. Erik Buell remained chairman and chief technical officer, and the stage was set for great things in the new millennium.

Index